DESIGN PROCESS
A Primer for Architectural and Interior Design

Sam F. Miller, AIA

VAN NOSTRAND REINHOLD
I(T)P™ A Division of International Thomson Publishing, Inc.

New York • Albany • Bonn • Boston • Detroit • London • Madrid • Melbourne
Mexico City • Paris • San Francisco • Singapore • Tokyo • Toronto

Copyright © 1995 by Van Nostrand Reinhold

I(T)P ™ A division of International Thomson Publishing, Inc.
The ITP logo is a trademark under license

Printed in the United States of America

For more information, contact:

Van Nostrand Reinhold
115 Fifth Avenue
New York, NY 10003

International Thomson Publishing GmbH
Königswinterer Strasse 418
53227 Bonn
Germany

International Thomson Publishing Europe
Berkshire House 168-173
High Holborn
London WCIV 7AA
England

International Thomson Publishing Asia
221 Henderson Road #05-10
Henderson Building
Singapore 0315

Thomas Nelson Australia
102 Dodds Street
South Melbourne, 3205
Victoria, Australia

International Thomson Publishing Japan
Hirakawacho Kyowa Building, 3F
2-2-1 Hirakawacho
Chiyoda-ku, 102 Tokyo
Japan

Nelson Canada
1120 Birchmount Road
Scarborough, Ontario
Canada M1K 5G4

International Thomson Editores
Campos Eliseos 385, Piso 7
Col. Polanco
11560 Mexico D.F. Mexico

1 2 3 4 5 6 7 8 9 10   QEB-KP   01 00 99 98 97 96 95

Library of Congress Cataloging-in-Publication Data

Miller, Sam F.
    Design process: a primer for architectural and interior design/Sam F. Miller.
        p.   cm.
    Includes bibliographical references and index.
    ISBN 0-442-01394-9
    1. Architectural design—Methodology.   2. Design—Methodology.
3. Architects—Interviews.   I. Title.
NA2750.M536   1995   94-38803
747'.01—dc20   CIP

CONTENTS

PREFACE

This book is about the fusion of two worlds: the intersection of practicality and art, the essence of architectural and interior design. The practical side of this dichotomy embodies physical materials and functional needs; all known and concrete "things." Conversely, the artistic component embraces the creative, intangible aspect of the designer's work; the unknown, the personal, the subjective.

The structure of my approach is straightforward. The design process is followed through in a sequence of three parts. Based on my experience and research, there appears to be a fundamental cycle of information gathering by the designer, followed by creative synthesis on a continuing basis, then a return to the "facts" for checking, communication, and feedback: a cycle from substantive reality to the creative realms of mind and then back again. The book is structured to reflect this cycle of learning followed by creativity. The first part introduces objective components and elaborates basic building materials, systems, and environmental concepts. Research and programming are presented as tools to construct a mental platform for the assembly of ideas into building forms. The second part studies the subjective aspects of the design process. This portion of the book reflects on sketching, modeling, and creativity placing emphasis on how these tools work in the context of practice. The final part returns to the known, and looks at how we test the success of our work, where presentations are made, and finally comments on issues germane to the practice of design and its importance to our culture and the environment.

Day by day, a designer is judged by the quality of his or her work. It may be argued that quality design is a direct result of a quality design process: excellent work cannot be brought to fruition through a haphazard approach. Therefore, it is critically important that the designer uses a process yielding the best possible chance for doing quality work. I have made a concerted effort to use this three part strategy to elucidate the skills and issues supporting a path to quality design. I would posit that there is tremendous value in this approach. First, for the student, a continuous thread of ideas guides the apprentice along a path where essential skills are elucidated, but all options left open. We may take the text in pieces or beginning to end in its entirety: the guiding principle of quality design is left intact. For the practitioner, the book may be used as a reference providing the opportunity for reflection, study, and renewal. We are given the opportunity to reconsider our paradigms and the chance to set them in a critical light as we continue our journey of self-discovery.

If we try to define what the design process is, and ask a variety of practitioners, the resulting definitions seem to correspond to the number of people answering the question. However, the underlying structure does not appear to waver along with awareness of its embedment in the political complexities imposed by reality. Interestingly, each individual designer spins his or her own particular style over this conceptual structure and the result is often nothing short of magical. The interviews herein bear this hypothesis out. As you read about each designer, it will be clear that their long term goal is consistent from case to case: quality design. How they get to their solutions varies dramatically. Within the interviews we can see hints of background, influences, and attitude.

I believe that design is inclusive of each activity we undertake in the creation of space; from the first time we open a book on structures to the moment we walk inside our finished work. Design is a state of mind, a process of becoming and doing: a continuing evolution of the individual who receives, translates, and mirrors his environment while simultaneously having the opportunity to guide and enrich the aspirations of our clients and culture.

ACKNOWLEDGMENTS

Many people have contributed time, expertise, and knowledge to this project. Kathy Charley stands out in my mind for her patient effort in translating my original outline through a number of generations to completion. She also transcribed a majority of the interviews from tape. This book would not exist in its present form without her skills. I also wish to thank Paul Laseau for his insight into design and for a critical appraisal of the work when it was in its infancy. He graciously spent an entire morning with me talking at length about writing, publishing, and design. He helped me in many ways, all valuable now and in the future. My wife, Cindy, has provided continuing moral support and patience beyond reason. Her tolerance as I stared at the CRT has been superhuman. I also want to thank my editor, Wendy Lochner, for her unfailing belief in the value of this project. She was always available to answer my sometimes absurd questions and spent many hours studying the text, providing insight, well crafted questions, and correcting my sometimes less than adequate grammar.

Kirby Miller introduced me to desktop publishing. His graphic expertise is largely responsible for the design of the book proper. We spent many hours hunched over the computer breathing life into a project with a design process all its own. He is a remarkable talent and I am proud to call him my friend and brother. Renee Guilmette and Geraldine Albert at VNR provided close scrutiny of the evolving graphic design and kept me honest as we developed each section of the book. They both were supportive, enthusiastic, and flexible throughout the duration of this project. I would also like to express my gratitude to Mike Conly for voluminous comments on my outline and insight into the real world practice of architecture.

To the design professionals who contributed interviews and, in several cases, additional assistance in the form of criticism, illustrations, and moral support, I offer my sincere thanks for efforts above and beyond the call of duty.

Lastly, I want to thank Rob Fields for the offhand comment that challenged me to take a few pages of notes and transform them into what you see here. It has truly been a remarkable trip.

PART ONE

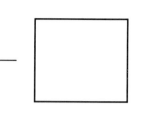

The Known

From the first moment when we question how buildings and spaces are created, we begin the continuing process of assimilating, modifying, and reinventing our base of practical knowledge. Each beginner stands in front of a symbolic mountain, preparing to climb. Old hands have ascended a good part of the way on a trip that often encompasses the better part of a lifetime.

The experience takes many forms: we all take varied routes with divergent goals. The base of design knowledge resides in an understanding of how to build, coupled to a method of understanding how buildings are used. Our techniques for gathering information and turning it into knowledge are critically important to design quality and effective design process.

What follows is a brief study of four areas that are fundamental to design. Well-honed knowledge of each exponentially increases the effective skill of the practitioner seeking to fashion quality work.

CHAPTER 1

Basics

Enclosure summarizes the result of any design effort. The creation of shelter embraces the complete range of elements making up any building in three dimensions. Architecture and design are complex; however, the idea of enclosure, in and of itself, is simple and therefore a good place to begin. By creating a structure separating outside from inside, the designer has exercised his or her craft. When we look to identify root concepts, we see that all buildings invariably consist of floor(s), walls, and roof (Thiis-Evenson 1987). The materials vary widely, but the concept of enclosure remains constant.

Structure

Every building incorporates structure in one form or another. Skeleton or bearing-wall systems are the two overriding types (1-1). The previous paragraph mentioned floors, walls, and roof, which, at first glance, are straightforward. But when we move from the pristine concepts of theory into the real world with all its attendant contexts, matters become quite a bit more complicated. Generally, four major types of structural materials are easily procured: wood, steel, masonry, and concrete. Each has advantages and disadvantages, strengths and weaknesses. A designer needs a minimum of knowledge about each option to be able to consider the pros and cons of each choice. For example, wood is easy to fabricate and generally inexpensive. However, the strength of wood varies significantly depending on the species, age of tree, and where the wood is cut from the trunk. Steel is the single strongest material used in construction. Its combination of tensile and compressive strength is unsurpassed by any other

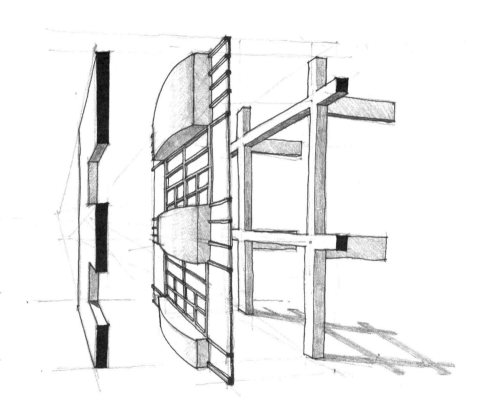

1-1: Skeleton, curtain, and bearing wall construction

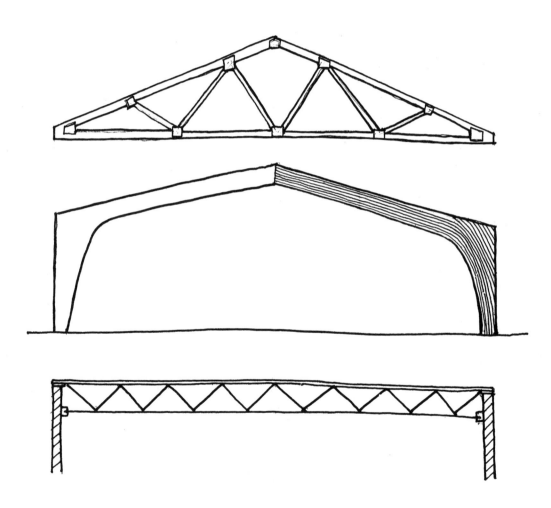

1-2: Examples of building material systems

material commonly used in buildings. However, steel is difficult to fabricate without expensive tools and requires specialized knowledge for its structural design. Masonry's prime strengths are its nearly unlimited variety as a material and enormous compressive strength. But masonry is poor in tension. Lastly, concrete is an incredible invention and like masonry, possesses great compressive strength coupled to the ability to be formed into nearly any shape. Its compressive strength varies depending on the composition of the mix and weather conditions during placement. Also, reinforced concrete combines steel bars and plastic concrete to harness steel's tensile strength with concrete's compressive character. This combination has created magnificent structures and provides unparalleled fire resistance. The design of reinforced concrete is a complex discipline requiring extensive study. In addition, not only is the design of the concrete challenging, but the formwork to support concrete as it dries and cures can be as difficult, if not more so, than the initial engineering and design.

Basic materials are often combined into systems such as wood trusses or glue laminated beams, columns, and bents (1-2). Material systems accomplish greater spans, improve economy, shorten construction time, and improve quality control. The designer is charged with the task of acquiring a minimum knowledge, not only about basic materials, but the various material systems we may consider as the design process begins.

Certain materials and material systems predominate in specific building types. Economics typically is the driver for this trend: we find wood framing and trusses in houses, steel or concrete in office buildings, concrete in parking structures, and so on. Real clients with hard currency affect basic choices about the components used in a building. The predominant scenario for considering costs √ most often focuses on first cost, followed by life cycle costs, and occasionally environmental costs. These three types of cost are manifestations of √ energy expended (labor and material = money = energy) over time. In the case of first cost and life cycle cost, each is associated with a distinct phase in a structure's life. First cost, as the name implies, is money spent directly for construction. Life cycle costs are monies expended over the life of a building in upkeep and maintenance. Environmental costing extends the reach of cost analysis beyond a building's lifetime. It includes the time prior to construction and after demolition plus what happens during a building's useful life. The analysis considers energy expended and the volume of waste created at each stage of a material's life including initial mining or extraction, transport, refining, subsequent transport, installation, use, and demolition or salvage for reuse. Some practitioners have begun to analyze the effect of materials extraction on the biome of its origin (1-3). One of the prime goals of environmental cost analysis is to lay the groundwork for sustainable building practices. Environmental cost research on any large scale is a relatively new line of inquiry. Good sources on the "state of the art" may be found through the Environmental Protection Agency (EPA) and publications like the American Institute of Architects' *Environmental Resource Guide.*

Rain Forest Biome:
- 90% plus nutrients in life from top of soil to limit of tree canopy

- Stripping the forest kills it: no regeneration

- Staggering diversity in a compact space

First Stage Environmental Cost Impacts
- Species destruction
- Releases greenhouse gases
- Destroys "carbon sink"
- Forest regeneration difficult or impossible
- Mining uses energy, releases greenhouse gases
- Lowers rate of CO_2 absorption

Advancing mining or development

1-3: Impact of biome destruction in a rainforest

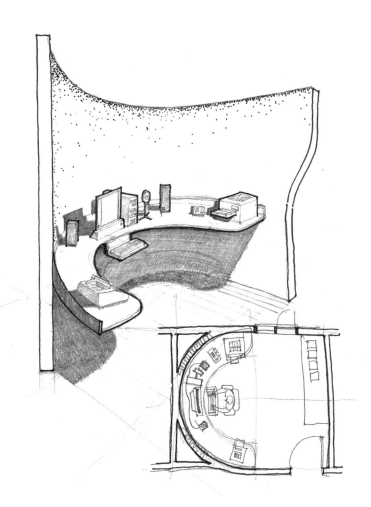

1-4: The electronic office

To summarize, the designer has the basic requirement to understand the nature of materials, how each material may be used in a material assembly, the material assembly's characteristics, and the cost implications for each. This is not learned overnight: internalizing the full range of available options generally takes years. In school, cost will seldom be an issue. Academia tends to focus on creativity. In practice, cost will often be the overriding issue in the client's mind. The worst case scenario is a client whose only concern is first cost. The best case is a client willing to take all three types of cost into account. A building's structure/enclosure is often the most expensive single component of a completed project. Therefore, a departure from a structural system known to be appropriate, with widespread use, should be researched, verified, and developed before it sees the light of day.

Systems

Another important, largely unseen, part of any building are its systems. These devices serve the occupants' basic physical needs, maintain a baseline environmental quality, and support activity in a space. Plumbing systems, in the form of drinking water and toilet facilities, serve basic human physical needs. Draining water off a roof keeps water out of a building, extends the life of a roof system, and controls the structural load imposed by snow or standing water. Heating, cooling, and humidity control (HVAC) maintain a baseline range for human comfort and affect the quality of the indoor air. Electrical power and lighting support the activity in a space. The business of electricity and electronics leads to a new building system subset: that of communication and information systems (1-4).

> *Because so much of business now depends on getting and sending information, companies around the world have been rushing to link their employees through electronic networks. These networks form the key infrastructure of the 21st century...Some of these are "local area networks" or LANs, which merely hook up computers in a single building or complex. Others are globe-girdling nets that connect Citibank people the world over or help Hilton reserve its hotel rooms and Hertz its cars (Toffler 1990).*

These devices are ubiquitous now. Fax, telephone, computers, modems, local area networks, television, the global communications network, audio systems, and more are indications of society and culture in transition. As we design new structures, the needs of the human user and our communications systems are dual concerns for the designer to contend with.

In an anatomical sense, if structure is the skeleton or skin, systems like heating and air conditioning are the organs of a building, contributing to its life and the inhabiting life forms. Building systems typically are sandwiched between ceiling/floor cavities. Duct sizes, slopes for drain piping, and lighting, combined with structural depths and ceiling height, work in concert to determine floor to

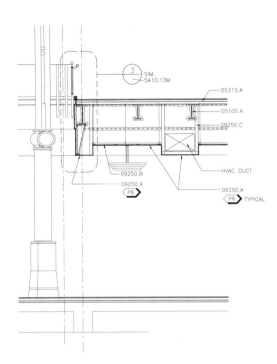

1-5: Section detail illustrating systems and structure—Centre Venture Architects, copyright City of Indianapolis, 1993

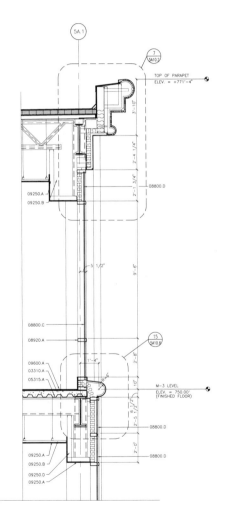

1-6: Curtainwall section—Centre Venture Architects, copyright City of Indianapolis, 1993

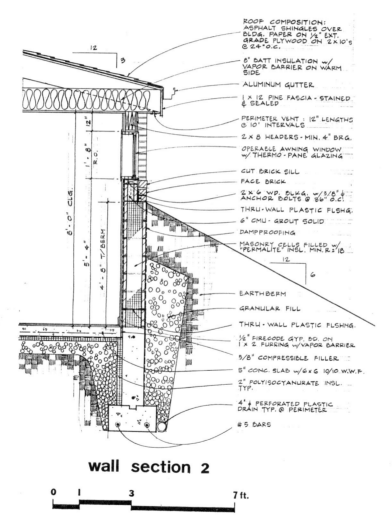

ROOF COMPOSITION:
ASPHALT SHINGLES OVER
BLDG. PAPER ON ½" EXT.
GRADE PLYWOOD ON 2 x 10's
@ 24" O.C.

8" BATT INSULATION w/
VAPOR BARRIER ON WARM
SIDE

ALUMINUM GUTTER

1 x 12 PINE FASCIA - STAINED
& SEALED

PERIMETER VENT : 12" LENGTHS
@ 10' INTERVALS

2 x 8 HEADERS - MIN. 4" BRG.

OPERABLE AWNING WINDOW
w/ THERMO - PANE GLAZING

CUT BRICK SILL

FACE BRICK

2 x 6 WD. BLKG. w/3/8" ⌀
ANCHOR BOLTS @ 86" O.C.

THRU-WALL PLASTIC FLSHG.

6" CMU - GROUT SOLID

DAMPPROOFING

MASONRY CELLS FILLED w/
"PERMALITE" INSL. MIN. R = 18

EARTHBERM

GRANULAR FILL

THRU - WALL PLASTIC FLSHNG.

½" FIRECODE GYP. BD. ON
1 x 2 FURRING w/VAPOR BARRIER

5/8" COMPRESSIBLE FILLER

5" CONC. SLAB w/6 x 6 10/10 W.W.F.

2" POLYISOCYANURATE INSL.
TYP.

4' ⌀ PERFORATED PLASTIC
DRAIN TYP. @ PERIMETER

5 BARS

wall section 2

0   1   3   7 ft.

1-7: Residential wall section

floor heights (1-5). Ceiling height and shape may be directly affected by building systems like lighting and ductwork. Some floor assemblies are specifically designed to allow for distribution of electrical power, information system cabling, and air supply. They are modular with easy access to provide for changes in the layout of a space. We begin to see that not only do building mechanical, electrical, plumbing, and communication systems support space activities and environment, but also directly affect clearances, envelopes, and physical characteristics of a design.

Building Skin

In temperate and cold climates, a building's skin provides a watertight separation between inside and outside. A successful skin keeps water at bay and provides transparency, solidity, access, and insulation. There are a variety of available skin systems. For example, curtainwalls are modular stick built assemblies forming uninterrupted surfaces connected to a backing structure (1-6). A building's supporting structure can also double as skin. Masonry bearing walls and precast concrete are often used examples. In one widely used approach, the skin enclosure is adapted for use as part of a system like wood stud framing with sheathing at interior and exterior, insulation, and a vapor barrier. The completed assembly serves multiple functions. The previous examples are generally thought of as wall systems (1-7). A consideration of roofing options and criteria is also required. The requirements for roofing typically become more stringent as the roof approaches horizontal. Flat roofs are carefully crafted membranes whose entire area, in theory, is a gently sloping monolithic plane. Penetrations of any kind are thoughtfully detailed and built to keep water out of the interior. As slope increases to 3 inches in 12 or above, shingles may be used in place of full membranes. Some curtain wall systems have performance characteristics allowing them to be used as roofs. Many companies manufacture sophisticated skylights in a variety of geometries and sizes. One skylight company even makes huge operable units!

Circulation

We have briefly highlighted a series of basic building components which are universal to any environmentally conditioned structure. We may now, in concept, place people inside and consider the varietal characteristics contributing to the experience of interior space proper. One immediately identifiable, almost unconscious feature of an interior is the process of moving through the space: the circulation (1-8). The act of moving through space is the dynamic experience of each volume and its articulation. How spaces are arranged plays a subtle melody to our physical senses. A deftly handled design may actually cause an emotional reaction in the people who experience the spaces. The unexpected, movements like ascending and descending, have psychological and embedded cultural meaning. Circulation moves us through these possibilities and establishes a hierarchy of spaces that represents functional choices made by the designer side by side with the cultural intent, conscious or unconscious, inherent in the resulting design.

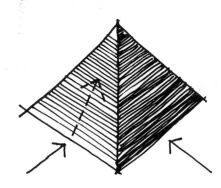

Egyptian Pyramid

• Implied circulation: visual, spiritual.
In symbolic form only.

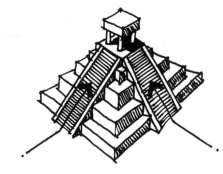

Mayan Temple

• Actual circulation: physical ascension.
Ceremony at the pinnacle, the physical presence of the participants.

1-8: Circulation, both actual and implied (visual)

1-9: Looking down a corridor—photo by Mark Platt

1-10: Looking behind our view in Figure 1-9—photo by Mark Platt

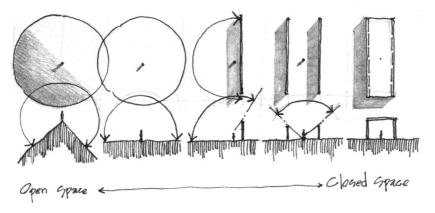

1-11: Enclosure diagrams

√The circulation path can be conceived as the perceptual thread that links the spaces of a building or any series of interior or exterior spaces, together.

Since we move in TIME
through SEQUENCE
of SPACES,

we experience a space in relation to where we've been, and where we anticipate going (Ching 1979).

We begin to see a functional, objective aspect to circulation which then weaves in psychological, emotional, cultural, and even ritual considerations. These subjective concerns are not merely layered over the functional aspects of circulation in design; they are commingled in the sum of ideas and experience each designer brings to a project. This fusion of ideas is yet another example that illustrates the delicate balance of both subjective and objective concerns in design.

Regardless of the pattern or options available during circulation, the cyclical nature of the process is close to invariable: we almost always begin and end exactly where we started. When we return, the experience is new (and why does it always seem to take less time?). Have you ever driven or walked somewhere new, not looked back, and been nearly lost when you tried to return? I have. I look back now to get an idea of the future experience awaiting when I come back through (1-9,10). It appears that we should add two more basic notions to Mr. Ching's original slate. Circulation is fundamentally linked to the following:

—TIME
—SEQUENCE
—SPACE
—CYCLICAL EXPERIENCE
—ORIENTATION

The circulation experience is inherently linked to our perception of space. There are an infinite number of spatial experiences; the most natural of which is standing out in the open under a blue sky (1-11). From a complete lack of enclosure we may identify a range of variations. Partial enclosure places a mass, a wall, or walls in relation to our view. Consider the difference between a wall above eye level or at knee height. An eight foot high wall may serve the security and privacy needs of those beyond it. The knee high wall may help keep my toddler out of someone's flowers. The purposes are different, the spatial experience is different, but the circulation path may be the same. These examples describe typical exterior possibilities.

As we pass from exterior to interior, the subtle embrace of full enclosure surrounds us. Once inside, we move through or within an introductory space and then from space to space as function or opportunity dictates. The "how" of circulation is strongly linked to the type of building under consideration. A museum may contain large central spaces with galleries attached or a clearly defined, almost prescribed linear path if a single subject's history is chosen and the designer determines that the historic

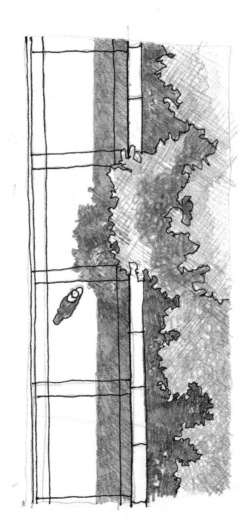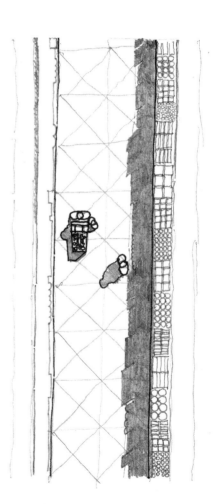

1-12: Circulation defined by differing architectural features

1-13: Directing attention by the use of light

timeline must be followed by all patrons. A grocery store is radically different. Multiple parallel aisles are arrayed with innumerable options for the user to browse, identify goods, and purchase items. As we imagine our museum and grocery store, another feature of circulation becomes apparent. Scale in proportion to number of people and spatial activity clearly determines the width, height, and shape of each space. We also may identity multiple treatments of the same device, reinterpreted to fit the context while still directing circulation. If we return to the example of the high privacy wall, we also notice that the shelves defining aisles in a supermarket create the same effect (1-12). A wall of paintings in the center of a museum gallery creates essentially the same separation as well. Two things occur: first, a device is created to channel circulation and control views; and second, depending on context, use, and articulation, this same device may become many things.

In our treatment of circulation so far, we have conjured various simple examples for consideration. Each evokes internal visions based on previous experience. As we review our privacy wall, museum, and supermarket, we may be struck by another feature which directly and indirectly affects circulation and design. The finishes and materials employed in any space are generally nonstructural, but their importance to the quality of the experience is essential and cannot be underestimated.

Material choices are affected by a variety of issues. The fundamental point for consideration is typically functional: the flooring in a house is radically different from the flooring in a hospital's operating suite. Successfully handling functional requirements may allow the use of several materials in all but the most specialized environments. With many options open, we have available a broad range of creative choices. Materials may be chosen with respect to a desired psychological impact. There is a distinct difference in the "feeling" of a room finished in rusticated stone, varnished wood, or porcelain enamel panels. How finishes are used affects the perceived size of a space. Color is particularly important in this area. Lighter colors make spaces appear larger; darker colors have the opposite effect. The arrangement of materials and the creation of contrasts can successfully direct our attention in a given space (1-13). Materials may be used to guide, direct, or inhibit circulation by use of contrasts in texture, type of material, color, or combinations of these. Part of the emotional content embedded in the experience of a space or building is directly related to colors chosen by the designer.

To see or feel blue may be more meta-phorically color related. With some simply viewing the color red can raise one's blood pressure, correspondingly, blue can reduce it. (From most to least stimulating, the ranking of other colors tested is orange, yellow, and green.) Shades of soft pink can quiet the agitated sufficiently that walls have been painted this way in some jail holding quarters. Associations from leisurely

1-14: Texture differences illustrated on wall surfaces

1-15: Illusion of perceived room size

periods spent gazing at water or skies, for example, might be evoked by gazing at any medium blue. Discriminating which responses to color are learned and which are innate is no more possible than determining whether new ideas are the products of unprecedented insight or of subconscious reasoning (Stockton 1983).

Psychological and perceptual effects are available in abundance to the designer studying finish choices for an interior space (1-14). A partial listing includes these possibilities:

> *Psychological/emotional effects*
> > *—encourage activity*
> > *—support feeling of well-being*
> > *—create a calming effect*
> > *—create excitement or anticipation*
> > *—opulence*
> > *—conservatism*
> > *—elegance and many more*
>
> *Perceptual effects*
> > *—increase or decrease apparent size*
> > *—focus attention*
> > *—increase or decrease apparent distance*
> > *—guide or influence circulation*
> > *—control or create distortion*
> > *—create illusions*

The previous list may be thought of as the equivalent of a set of building blocks. The psychological "blocks" consider the desired state of mind of the person experiencing the space. The perceptual set considers how materials, building elements, and space may be used to manipulate the senses of the viewer. It is also important to realize that this list is presented out of context. Employing these options happens in the dynamic of the design process and they seldom stand alone. Reality finds psychology and perception interwoven, overlaid, and subtly mixed to serve the varied goals of the designer.

Perceptual effects may be incorporated at varying levels of subtlety and sophistication. At some point, the designer may seek to create full blown illusions to support some portion of a design in progress. One of the simplest examples of perceptual effect is our previously used example of color. Another device is a wall of mirrors which increases perceived room size (1-15). On a more subtle note, early Greek designers made use of entasis in their column geometries to counter the optical illusion of a column's apparent bowing in when viewed along its length (1-16).

Views

As we consider illusion, we also implicitly consider views. While illusion supports the belief that something exists where it really does not, views are the result of sequence and orientation in a space or series of spaces. Consciously creating views is often directly linked to functional, aesthetic, and/or psychological criteria. Remember, any design creates views: they may all be internal like a clothing store tucked away in a shopping center, but views are present nevertheless. We may stand between racks

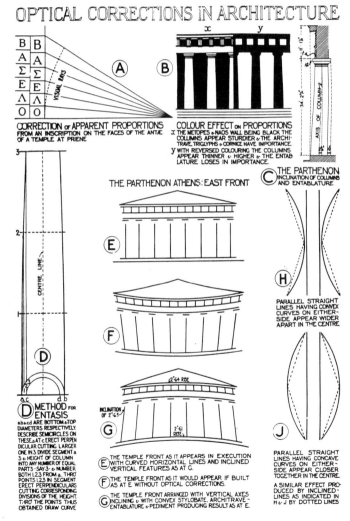

1-16: Entasis geometry from *A History of Architecture*, 19th ed., by Sir Banister Fletcher

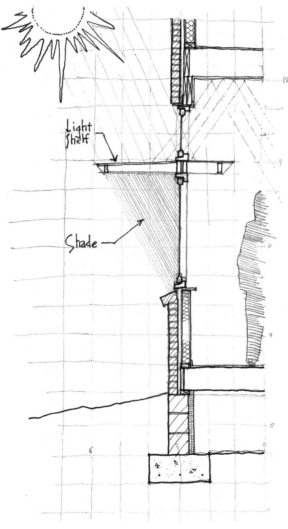

1-17: Light shelf section to provide indirect light

of coats and have our attention drawn to a flashy illuminated alcove with this spring's newest fashions or stand on a deck looking down a mountainside to a forest below: they are both views of varying scale. We can identity a sequence of scale from point to point within a space, from space to space, or from inside to outside (and vice versa). The designer chooses starting points at all scales as appropriate to the task at hand.

Light

The perception of a view may clearly be influenced by employing illusions, but the impact of light, in all its forms, has an overwhelming effect on whether a view even exists or not. Light has fascinated designers for millennia. There exists a dynamic interplay between cultural symbolism, physical phenomena, functional usage, and aesthetic options associated with light. These variables are continuously linked but weighted to different degrees depending on context. Understanding light as a physical phenomenon is the province of an introductory physics text. But understanding and appreciating the quality of light in a Gothic cathedral or an artist's studio places illumination within the complex relationships of a building's form, materials, and orientation. The cathedral and studio examples identify two primary design issues to consider in relation to light. The first is symbolism, especially prominent in a cathedral. Illumination represents divinity and purity, life and wisdom. But let us consider the converse situation: what might our cathedral have looked like from the outside during midnight mass with thousands of candles illuminating the interior? Imagine the soft, multihued glow of something so huge in the darkness. We approach and walk inside looking up at the walls fading into blackness (infinity?) above. Surely something magical exists here—the spirit of God embodied by the work of generations, of craft focused and detailed, a world view expressed in stone: past, present, and future. On the other hand, our art studio begs for the functional expediency of north light: indirect and soft, minimizing shadows. The placement of windows or skylights supports the artist's craft. The number, arrangement, and orientation of openings, and of corresponding walls and their thicknesses control the volume of direct and indirect light, shade and shadow. We consciously work light through enclosure and preserve a visual communication with the outdoors.

As we consider what a cathedral might look like at night, we find ourselves drawn to the question of how our designs may also appear in the evening hours. Can the interior illumination be arranged to create a new perception of a design solution at night? Is it possible or desirable to fashion a space that would normally not have windows, like a mall's retail shops, to have a day and night lighting scheme? Is the human body's physiology tuned to the diurnal cycle of day and night? The answer to all these questions is yes; in the correct context.

Artificial Illumination

In the universe of artificial illumination, the range of options available is overwhelming. Beginning

1-18: Lighting systems for an office

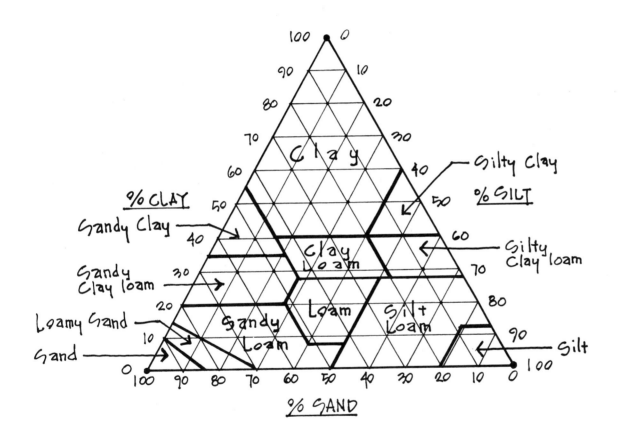

1-19: Diagram of agricultural soil types based on *Soil Survey Manual*, U.S. Department of Agriculture

with the major categories of light sources such as incandescent, fluorescent, and high-intensity discharge, we branch into tremendous variety. The range of lamp geometries and fixture designs alone fill catalogue after catalogue with a huge array of style and quality. But we can think of lighting in simple terms: lamp and fixture. The light source can be form a single point, a line of illumination, or an illuminated surface. The basic palette is straightforward. This inherent simplicity can guide our thinking as we craft each design. In both natural and artificial illumination, we may choose to "shape" the light: interrupt or control its path. If we are designing an artist's studio and are constrained by a lack of north light, the same effect may be accomplished by a southern exposure with a device, either interior or exterior, to reflect incoming sunlight to the ceiling above (1-17). The indirect light created by this arrangement is a close approximation of the quality of north light.

The quality of natural light varies continually from morning to evening and with changes in the weather. If a designer is concerned with the use of daylight to supplant artificial light during working hours, systems are available to detect the relative level of natural illumination and adjust the artificial lighting level up or down as required (1-18). There are two benefits of this approach: the user receives a maximum amount of natural light and the design is more energy efficient. The effectiveness of such a scheme rests heavily on how the space is crafted by the designer prior to the intervention of any technology. A design solution maximizing the use of daylight need not be tied to a technological support system. If the natural light level falls off, we can still get up and turn on the lights. Over the long term, the benefits of natural light continue to contribute to energy savings and the user's physical well being.

Site

In retrospect, the interior environment is rich and complex, focusing a designer's skills on multiple concerns. Not only do we think about movement in space, but also what we see and what the space is made of. We move through the negative volume surrounded by the designer's positive space: neither is separable. A successful design integrates intangible needs with a sophisticated network of design elements which the designer continually juggles while seeking closure on a problem. We have worked our way through the major components of interior space and discovered how interconnected many seemingly separate elements can be. This interconnection extends beyond interiors and enclosure: it also embraces the surrounding site environment as well. Circulation, space, materials and views have correspondence to equivalent site activities. Site space notions parallel interior concepts in many ways, but diverge in others. We find it necessary to refocus our attention as we consider elements such as climate which are not under our direct control. The automobile dominates site circulation at most scales, and site context varies constantly from place to place.

All buildings are continuously influenced by their surrounding environment. Our structures sit on the land and as such must respect the underlying structure of the earth below (1-19). Soil structure

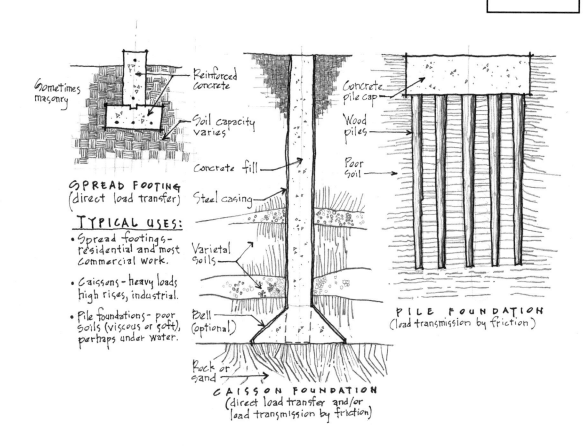

Sometimes masonry

Reinforced concrete

Soil capacity varies

SPREAD FOOTING (direct load transfer)

TYPICAL USES:
- Spread footings - residential and most commercial work.
- Caissons - heavy loads high rises, industrial.
- Pile foundations - poor soils (viscous or soft), perhaps under water.

Concrete fill

Steel casing

Varietal soils

Bell (optional)

Rock or sand

CAISSON FOUNDATION (direct load transfer and/or load transmission by friction)

Concrete pile cap

Wood piles

Poor soil

PILE FOUNDATION (load transmission by friction)

1-20: Spread footings, caissons, piles

1-21: Detail of abandoned house on Lake Michigan's southern shore—
photo by Kirby Miller

varies drastically from locale to locale. The type of foundation chosen for a building must respect the limitations of the underlying soils. There are two main categories of foundations: those that distribute loads directly (spread footings) into the soil below and those that rely on friction between an element drilled into the ground (caissons or piles) and the adjacent soil (1-20). The largest share of buildings are constructed on spread footings, but there are a number of foundation systems adapted to unusual soils. Some building types require special structural designs. High-rise structures are generally not built on spread footings: a system of drilled concrete filled caissons down to solid rock below is not unusual. Different soils have varying allowable bearing capacities due to their inherent structure and plasticity. The water content of a soil also affects how much load it can take. The critical relationship to consider is the building size versus the type of soil the finished structure will sit upon. A specialized branch of engineering studies soils and develops reports based on site testing for the use of the structural engineer and architect. When the structural engineer develops the superimposed foundation load at each column or wall, a comparison is made to the allowable bearing capacity of the soil including settlement and a factor of safety. The result is an indication of how the foundation design should proceed.

Our choice of design direction and options is also influenced by surrounding site topography. The existing topography and soil material will impose a range of possible constraints on any proposed structure. We review a site and ask where our building might sit while we simultaneously absorb information, explicit or implicit, about the character of the land. Trial and error leads through an interactive sequence where the effect of constraints are tested, judged, and accepted or dismissed. Each experiment yields more information about what may be successfully accomplished between building and site.

Each site affects our choice of building orientation, access, and views. If we are privileged to design a house on a mountainside, there is a strong chance that views will rank high on our initial menu of criteria. However, simply deciding to take advantage of a stunning vista does not guarantee that our intent will be immediately realized. How our house is oriented in addition to its interior plan arrangement immediately relates to what we see outside and from what spaces particular views are visible. Our mountainside site may have a difficult access requiring careful study for both construction and the design solution. A difficult site access may actually drive some design choices regarding materials. It would be particularly embarrassing to design gluelam wood beams thirty feet long and discover that the truck making the delivery is unable to negotiate the turn necessary for it to get on site. Changes in slope across a site can affect interior floor levels and actually create interesting opportunities for the designer. We may find that not only are changes in floor elevations required, but the actual number of floors may be influenced by a site's topography. As we reflect on our plan diagrams, we may find that the site constraints also speak to a particular foundation type. If the slope is relatively steep, a small plan

1-22: Looking across the southwest quadrant of Monument Circle in Indianapolis, Indiana

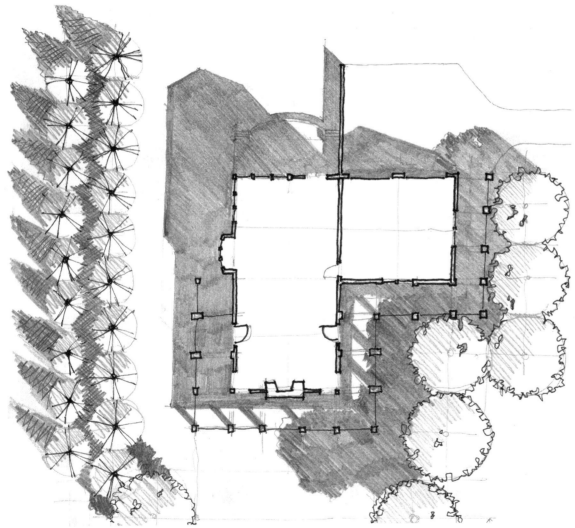

1-23: Site design to improve energy efficiency

footprint holds down the foundation cost. Instead of a single story, we entertain a multilevel approach. If our mountain house sits on solid rock, we probably will not be entertaining notions of reconfiguring the site topography to accommodate some particular aspect of the design. By the same token, if the same house were built in the rolling hills of southern Indiana, the debris left over from the last glaciers would allow us several more avenues for configuring the surrounding site and house design. How we fit a design to the land is bound up in esthetic, functional, and cost concerns. On a site, one of the costliest mistakes a designer can make is not placing the building and shaping the adjacent soils to divert water away from the structure. Many "rules" of design change with context and value shifts, but diverting surface water away from a building is as close to a constant in design as possible.

Some site environments can be actively hostile to a building. Oceanside houses may suffer the onslaught of hurricanes or typhoons. Consider the homes built on the shores of Lake Michigan from the turn of the century through the 1970's. Many of these houses are gone: swallowed up by the rising lake and subsequent erosion (1-21). This is a valuable lesson. Our surrounding environment *appears* permanent, yet it is not. We should always ask if proximate features on or near a site might in time destroy what we have labored to create. It is incumbent upon the designer to share any concerns in this regard with the client and offer as many options as possible for the abatement of the threat including another site. On a more positive note, the majority of sites offer the opportunity for us to craft the land to enhance building design features and solve general functional problems like drainage.

Landscaping

The land can be shaped to focus or control views, direct circulation, improve site acoustics, control erosion, and stabilize vegetation. Shaping the land is a natural extension of building design. Adding, modifying, and removing vegetation is an inseparable part of most site work. We may be confronted with natural sites of seemingly unspoiled beauty. When fortune smiles on a designer by presenting a pristine site, we are obliged to ask ourselves about the importance of the ecological balance within and on the land we have been given. At this point in humankind's history, I believe we can successfully argue that our designs should damage as little of a site's environmental fabric as possible. By the same token, when we contemplate building on land stripped of its original environmental cloth (1-22), we are also obligated to consider how building and environment can support each other to the mutual benefit of both. One of the more elegant features of a temperate climate is the continual cycle of the seasons. These climatic changes are mirrored by vegetation which has adapted to ensure its survival and successful reproduction. At different times throughout each year, with varying durations, we have the opportunity to fashion another compositional level in our designs. We may combine flowering plants, shrubs, and trees, creating a framework to further enhance our work. It may also be posited that vegetation contributes to our mental well-being: standing downwind from a hedge row of

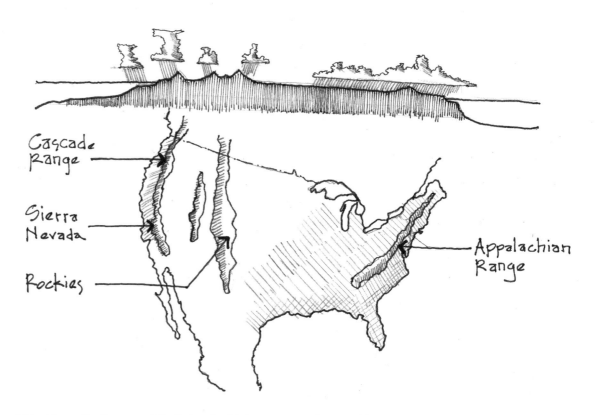

1-24: Macro climatic zones of North America (darker areas equal more rain)

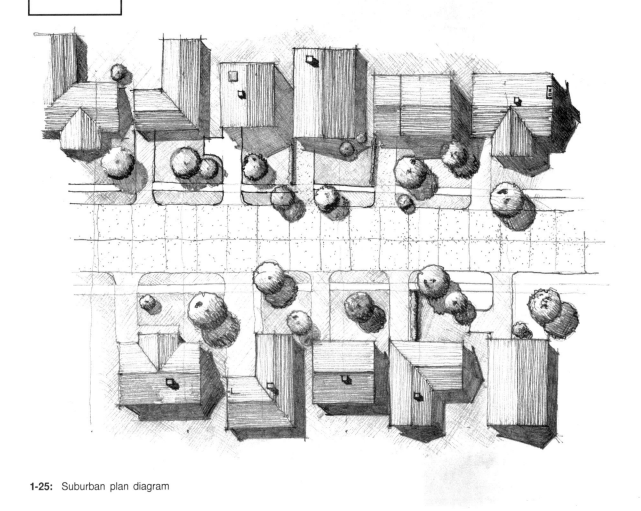

1-25: Suburban plan diagram

honeysuckle on a spring day will certainly enchant both visual and olfactory senses. In addition, we have the opportunity to arrange shrubs and trees to buffer our designs from wind and sun. Two deciduous trees, properly placed, can significantly cut a home's summer cooling bills and still pass the warming winter sun (1-23). A carefully placed row of pine trees will break the onslaught of prevailing winter winds and also contribute to energy efficiency. We have the opportunity to fashion two protective shells: the first is the building enclosure itself, and the second is afforded by the features which may be created or taken advantage of on many sites.

Climate

Control of site climate is limited at best. We protect or shield our buildings from the worst of local climate, but not the limit of possible extremes. Few structures can survive the full impact of a tornado and remain intact. Location and climate are completely intertwined: consideration of one will invariably lead to knowledge about the other. As we study the proposed location of a design, whether in city or country, downtown or prairie, it is quite possible that the climate may be very much the same in each place. Temperatures will vary within certain extremes, as will the amounts of sun, wind, and rain. The weather will exhibit a range of relatively predictable patterns, although prediction in precise detail, as we know, is impossible. Local geography makes radical alterations in climate. For example, in North America the general temperature decreases as we move from south to north. Weather systems move generally from west to east. We check the weather at our convenience, and take for granted that everything is normal. It is interesting to note that not only our climate but also our biomes would be radically different were it not for the intervention of the mountain ranges on the east and west coasts.

> ...The United States has no great latitudinal vegetational zones that reflect the decreasing temperature...Instead the north-south mountain ranges have broken the country up into an east-west series of vertical vegetational zones based primarily on rainfall differences. The two coasts are forested. The great central portion of the continent, cut off from moisture-laden clouds by mountain ranges and by remoteness from the oceans, is either desert or grassland (Buchsbaum 1957).

Climate and local environment are strongly shaped by geography often hundreds of miles distant (1-24). In addition, we also need to address the possible effect of nearby features, either natural or man made. Are we near a lake or river? Perhaps we are contemplating a building adjacent to an industrial park, power lines, or highway. The approach to site design will vary radically between the constraints posed by a nearby lake or by a 100 acre landfill.

Site Circulation

Site circulation must be considered with respect to many interrelated influences. Speaking from the

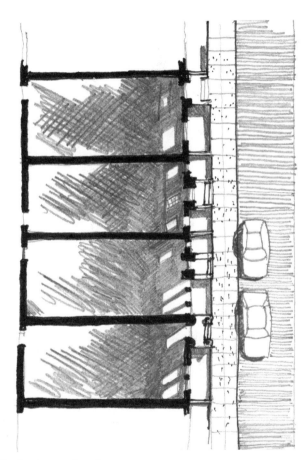

1-26: Rowhouse plan diagram

1-27: Less than successful signage—photo by Mark Platt

1-28: Effective signage—photo by Mark Platt

standpoint of overall context, we may identify two types of movement: that occurring on a site and movement occurring between sites. We also must consider our method and speed of movement. The most basic entity of site experience is the individual on foot. With this reference point, we may observe that our previous concepts for circulation, expressed with reference to built space, are also applicable to pedestrian circulation. In addition, the locale obviously makes a difference to the fundamental experience of moving towards or through a site. A country or suburban setting will probably find us moving to our destination by car (1-25), whereas an urban site gives us the opportunity to get to our destination using a variety of transportation options. Density is a prime aspect shaping site experience. For example, as density rises, the space between buildings decreases, and as a result site circulation becomes more focused and compact as well. The transitional space from site to site also shrinks while the number of exposed building elevations decreases. Consider a series of rowhouses: only two elevations are actually designed, with most of the design emphasis going to the public facade (1-26).

As we study site circulation, we must continue to keep in mind the relationship between people and these broad brush criteria: land/climate, transportation technology (automobile, bus, train, bicycle), and buildings. One series of relationships, intimately related to sequence, is how we perceive visual cues from the surrounding environment. Someone unfamiliar with a locale will desperately need information from the environment directing movement from place to place and ultimately to their final destination. We must always consider those uninitiated souls who experience our designs only once or infrequently. Since everyone, at one time or another, is a first time site and building user, we must give due consideration to making our sites visible, accessible, and understandable. This process is sequential, beginning with circulation, approach, and recognition through entry onto the site, identifying the building entry, and moving inside. This sounds relatively straightforward on paper, but let us return briefly to the idea of site density. As density rises, so does the difficulty associated with identifying circulation cues from the site environment. Therefore, the designer's inclusion of features to assist the first time user become extremely important in the urban environment. An urban pedestrian can deal with the riot of information supplied by the built environment: there is more time to fully experience the space and the option to stop and reflect on anything deemed worthwhile. However, people in cars may be hard pressed to get somewhere new without annoying difficulty.

People moving from building to building on foot have vastly different perceptions and informational needs than someone driving an automobile. While driving, identifying site access becomes a major issue (1-27). There needs to be a clear relationship between approach, site access, and circulation to the building entry. If these elements cannot be seen as a whole, individual cues must be made available as each step is completed. Signage, as a design issue, cannot be shortchanged. A sign must be of a minimum size to be successfully interpreted

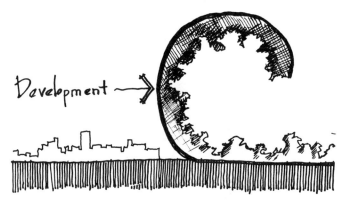

Industrial: stripping sites, wholesale habitat destruction

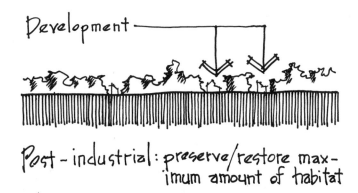

Post-industrial: preserve/restore maximum amount of habitat

1-29: Industrial and post-industrial development principles

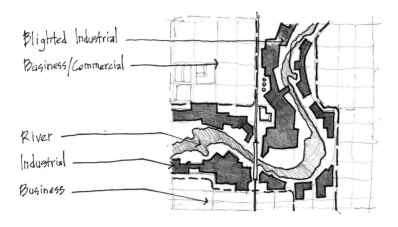

Blighted Industrial

Business/Commercial

River

Industrial

Business

1-30: Urban diagram illustrating typical 20th century development with little respect for the environment

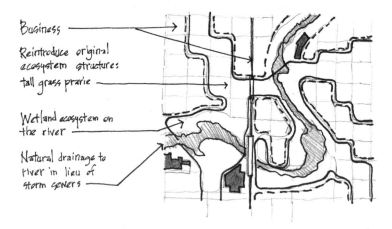

Business

Reintroduce original ecosystem structure: tall grass prarie

Wetland ecosystem on the river

Natural drainage to river in lieu of storm sewers

1-31: Diagram of the same urban area reworked to re-introduce native ecologies

by a driver and supply enough time to maneuver the car to obtain access (1-28).

Once on site, we are required to park, then navigate to the building entry. As we leave the car and become pedestrians, we are generally confronted with the uncomfortable relationship between cars and people. An environment designed for storing cars is decidedly stacked in favor of vehicular needs. More often than not, the pedestrian is left on his or her own. There is a certain lack of comfort in crossing any busy parking area. This concern is inherent in most places where transportation types overlap. For the alert pedestrian, the designer needs to ensure maximum visibility so that moving cars may be identified and avoided.

We have briefly touched on the experience of a pedestrian and the volume of information and detail someone on foot can glean from the environment. We also need to study the experience of the built environment from a moving car. With reference to design vocabulary, if a building is to be placed within an environment where many or all of its major elevations are seen from automobiles, then the scale of design features and composition may be adjusted upwards in size. This is a direct result of the speed of movement: What the eye can take in at three miles per hour versus 60 miles per hour is at a ratio of 20 to 1.

Previously, we discussed the character of building spaces. We may draw parallels between building and site space at a fundamental level. Three types of site spaces may be illustrated. The first spatial type occurs in a more or less untouched form such as a valley, meadow surrounded by trees, canyon, cave, prairie, and so on. The second kind of site space would be artificial: wholly created by the built environment. Examples like a plaza surrounded by buildings, courtyard, or town square come to mind. The final site space would be a hybrid combining natural and artificial features where the design is carefully worked into its surroundings.

Our general method of design and construction, used with fervor for well over two centuries, imposes the artificial site solution over the natural (1-29). This is consistent with the western philosophical and cultural bias of overcoming and subduing nature. Although some artificial site spaces, like the Japanese garden, are crafted to mimic nature, the net result is still displacement or disruption of the natural environment. Given the critical situation we now face environmentally and the vast resources devoted to construction, we emphasize and recommend hybrid site design solutions (1-30, 31). Admittedly, an environmentally sensitive steel mill is a bit of an oxymoron; however, in building types like residential, commercial, office, and institutional, hybrid sites are attainable goals.

Site Context

Another area influencing design direction is existing site context. The surrounding environment, natural or man made, has a particular history, use, and character. How we choose to respond to our surroundings affects the "fit" of our design. Some designers may choose an approach consciously at odds with the existing structures surrounding a site. In the right situation this may have merit: consider Helmut Jahn's State of Illinois Center in Chicago.

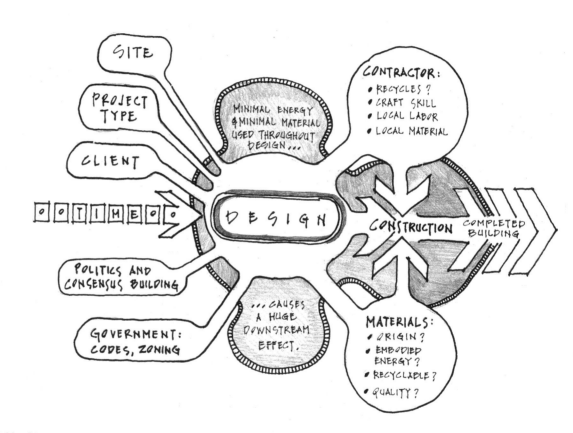

1-32: Diagram illustrating the critical nature of design choices

Environmental Responses:

Balance need for HVAC against natural ventilation

If employing natural gas, vent combustion air to the exterior

Avoid creating interior conditions where water may collect causing microbial growth

Tell your clients that no matter how good a job the designer does, without regular maintenance, sooner or later IAQ will be compromised

Use operable windows arranged to promote cross ventilation

Use natural materials employing a minimum of toxic solvents

Employ the "source reduction" concept as much as possible to systems and material choices

In site design, choose strategies that minimize destruction of trees and natural ground cover

Avoid sheets of asphalt paving and employ "grasscrete" or its equivalent

Minimize the building footprint where possible

Choose construction materials made without toxics and/or incorporating recycled material

Craft usage of building materials through detailing to minimize waste

Recycle waste construction materials or donate salvage to organizations like Habitat for Humanity

If building requires demolition of existing construction, study re-use of any existing materials in the new construction

Make energy efficiency a hallmark of design process and demonstrate the benefits to your clients

Employ renewable energy sources from the sun (passive and active solar technologies) plus wind power where practical to replace or supplement grid supplied power

Design spaces to incorporate recycling containers and collection areas

Realize that quality design embraces the ability to demonstrate the economic benefits of beautiful space

1-33: Environmental options

Everyone has an opinion, either positive or negative, with respect to the finished product. Obviously, some features of the site context were intentionally violated. Where we build can vary radically. Consider some of the following possibilities: a 300-year-old historic district, a national park, an intensely busy urban district, or an ethnic residential area. The potential variety is bewildering, but the point is that specific contexts impact our designs. Sometimes our response is an option, on other occasions, the respect of a surrounding context may be required by law or enforced by public will.

Site and Building Ecology

The last section of this chapter treats with the role of site and building ecology in design. Given the vast amount of information available, research in progress, and growing public and professional awareness, the importance of these issues to design will only be magnified as time goes on. As we consider the whole range of the built environment, we may be struck by the realization that designers appear to have little effect on environmental decisions related to building and design. This is not true! Interior designers and architects are placed at a critical nexus in the overall process of building construction (1-32). How we shape our spaces and prepare specifications has an undeniable effect, for good or ill, on the external and internal environment of our buildings. These choices reach all the way from material procurement through the usable life of a building or space.

Buildings and sites have several ecological levels requiring care with respect to design. As we have already discussed, the majority of existing buildings today are at odds with their site environment. What do we need to do to break this trend? First, we need to identify environmental goals with respect to our designs (1-33). The list in 1-33 is by no means complete: additional goals may be developed depending on the project and client. Also, depending on context, the emphasis for each goal may vary. Once again, cost becomes a driving issue as we compare first cost, life cycle costs, and environmental costs.

Indoor air quality (IAQ) is a design issue whose time has come. A few practitioners have sounded warning bells for over ten years, but only in the last three years has IAQ received the attention and concern appropriate to the magnitude of the problem. I would like to take a moment to sketch a quick background of how this new discipline was born. In 1973, the first Middle Eastern oil embargo caused a major shift in the consciousness of Americans and forced us to improve energy efficiency in our automobiles and buildings. In regard to buildings, one of the results was and is energy efficient buildings that are more tightly constructed. They do not "breathe." Lacking a steady supply of outdoor air allows the buildup of contaminants on the inside. The occupants may experience discomfort, illness, headache, chronic fatigue, and in extreme cases even disability.

This condition has come to be known as Sick Building Syndrome (SBS). Most of you have read or heard about it. People spend the majority of their time indoors in cars or buildings. The Environmental Protection Agency's initial report on indoor air

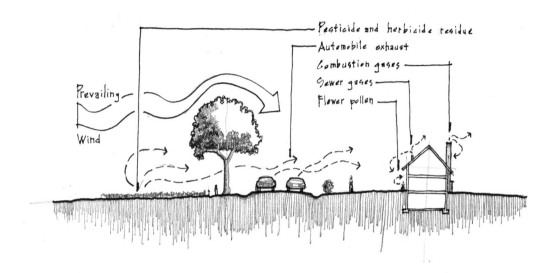

1-34: Exterior effects on indoor air quality

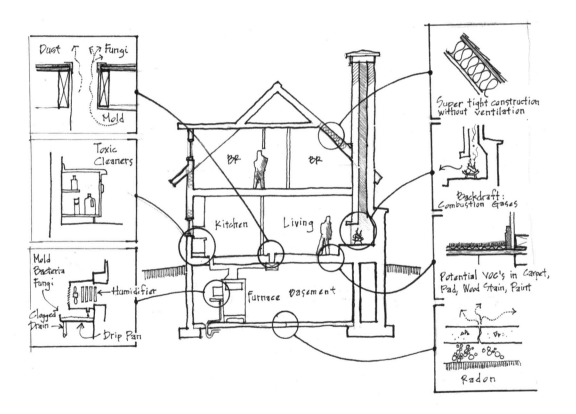

1-35: Possible interior sources of indoor air pollution

quality in 1987 concluded that in many cases our indoor environments are more polluted than the outside air. The Environmental Protection Agency's original focus on cleanup of outside air was correct: the evidence was all around us. However, our task for the 1990's and beyond will be to quantify conditions acceptable for human habitation on the inside.

Where do indoor air pollutants come from? Many come from outside a building. Substances such as dust, pollen, vehicular exhaust, re-entrained building exhaust, and radon are exterior pollutants that can be drawn inside (1-34). Another major source of indoor pollution can come from a building's ventilation system. When any form of standing water is trapped, the ventilation system may become a breeding ground for a variety of microbes and fungi. These organisms can multiply explosively in areas such as contaminated duct insulation, improperly drained drip pans, and cooling towers. Additional problems may be created by insufficient fresh air and the location of air intakes towards pollution sources. Equipment that is associated with building users can also give off contaminants. Copy machines may give off ozone, for example. Cleaning supplies may emit a variety of toxic volatiles.

The building itself can be a source of indoor pollutants. Components such as concrete (gives off radon in some cases), wood products, plastics, insulations, fabrics, sealants, and adhesives may off-gas volatile organic chemicals (VOCs). Finishes and furnishings may also be significant sources of volatile organic chemicals (1-35). The occupants themselves can be considered significant pollutant sources, particularly in respect to environmental tobacco smoke.

Who is affected? At this stage, it appears that anyone can be a victim. Certain people suffer from a syndrome called Multiple Chemical Sensitivity. This phenomenon is associated with the development of acute toxic responses that are triggered in the first place by a massive dose of a particular toxin. After the fact, sickness is brought on by minute amounts of the previous toxin in any given environment. Individuals afflicted with Multiple Chemical Sensitivity can experience life threatening symptoms and in severe cases have died as a result of their reactions. When a building or space exhibits the SBS phenomenon, the symptoms can vary from person to person and place to place. It can be obvious that a problem exists, yet its source can remain a mystery.

Radon is a pollutant no longer shrouded in any mystery whatsoever. It is a radioactive gas, colorless and odorless, which is a by-product of naturally occurring radium-226 in many soils. Prominently featured in the media in the early 1990's, radon continues to be a significant health concern highly ranked in the Environmental Protection Agency's listing of environmental threats (1-36).

The stakes within our buildings are high. User discomfort and irritation, absenteeism, loss of productivity, and disability are the results of polluted indoor environments. Increased sick leave causes higher health-care costs. Lost productivity costs business owners significant sums of money. Litigation is costly to the building team in terms of

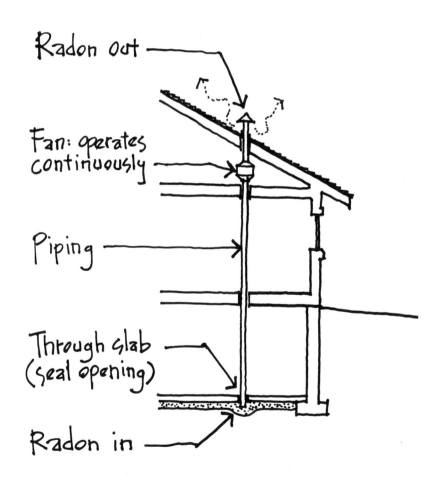

1-36: Radon mitigation system diagram

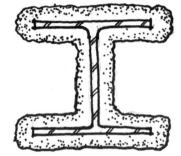

Steel fireproofing made
from newspaper

Wall insulation made
from newspaper

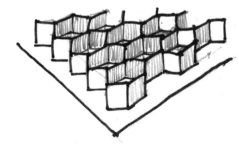

Honeycomb panel made
from paper

Brick fusing heavy metals
into inert clay matrix

1-37: Examples of recycled building products currently available

reputation, monies lost, and increased insurance premiums. In an academic or practice environment, any designer would be well advised to make serious inquiries into the available literature on indoor air issues and incorporate design concepts supportive of IAQ into his or her work.

Like IAQ, efficient use of construction materials and incorporation of recycled building materials is an idea whose momentum has grown significantly over recent years (1-37). Consider this quote from the *Guide to Resource Efficient Building Elements* (GREBE):

> *As we move into the 90's, the home building industry faces a scarcity of top quality construction lumber and durable wood products. The decline in availability and quality of these materials creates the need to develop new technologies and products that efficiently use resources while keeping housing costs within the average family's reach. These materials are available now (Loken, Spurling, Price 1991).*

The creation of any environment for human habitation uses both energy and resources. Materials themselves represent a form of embodied energy. In current construction practice, a certain volume of waste is also created during construction. As designers, *every* choice we make affects all of the above. If we understand that material resources are finite and that vast amounts of energy are perpetually available in dynamic forms such as wind (1-38), sun, and water, our environmental goals begin to look more like axioms and less like options or political whimsy.

As we continue to seek knowledge about the foundations of design, the range of materials, systems, structures, human perceptions, and environment will provide fertile ground from which creative solutions may be shaped. The variety, breadth, and potential conflict inherent in every choice is sometimes inspiring and, on other occasions, a source of limitless frustration. Working steadily to expand our knowledge base, especially with reference to the concrete, knowable features of design, is like adding colors to an artist's palette. As time passes and our knowledge grows, the painter and her work become richer and more interesting.

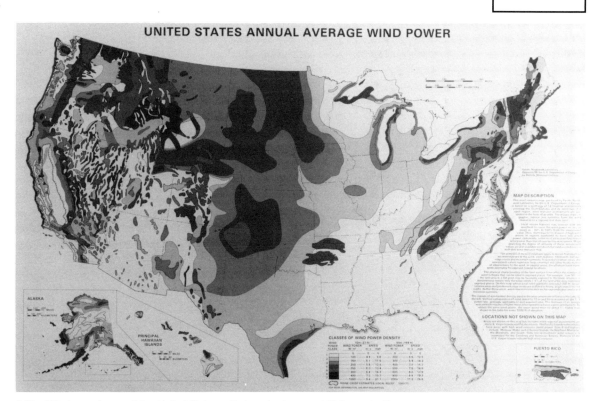

1-38: Wind speed map of the United States. Darker shades equal higher velocities— map prepared by Pacific Northwest Laboratory

CHAPTER 2

Research

Over the course of our practices, we assimilate specific project based knowledge. In school and beyond, we are confronted with the need to continually gather information. Gaining familiarity with any building type requires a commitment to acquiring knowledge of the general materials, organization, history, costs, and so on. The site provides the next area for consideration. And lastly, the client must be "studied" and understood so that a program may be developed (2-1). Programming is presented in the following chapter. This is not to imply that research is always followed by programming. In reality, they are often concurrent and intertwined, especially if the designer has little or no familiarity with the building type at hand. Research also occurs in differing contexts: chiefly, academia and the world of practice.

Information Sources

Without doubt, one of the most important aspects of research is gaining access to appropriate information. Secondly, more often than not, a particularly challenging problem is how to find what we need quickly. Obviously, libraries are a primary source of media. Federal, state, and local governments are also locations where important data may be obtained. Of course, people, in the form of colleagues, may provide valuable insight. Trade associations publish huge amounts of information on topics consistent with their agendas and missions. Architectural and design book publishers have ongoing lists of new titles. And the professional magazines publish the newest built work by designers nationwide. Lastly, with the continuing acceleration of

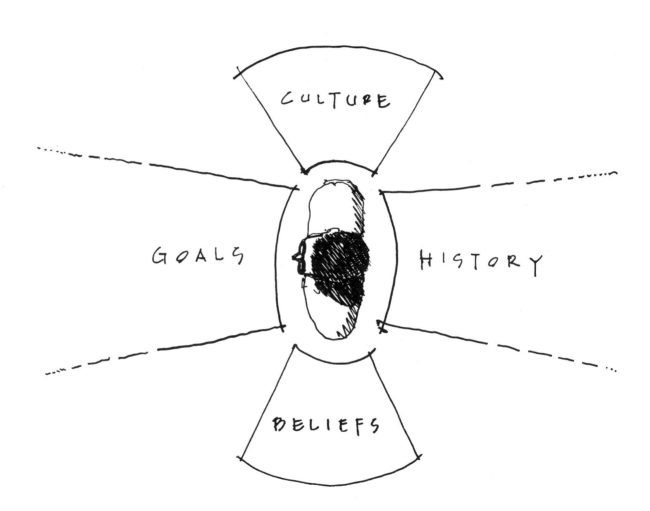

2-1: Different aspects of a client for consideration and integration

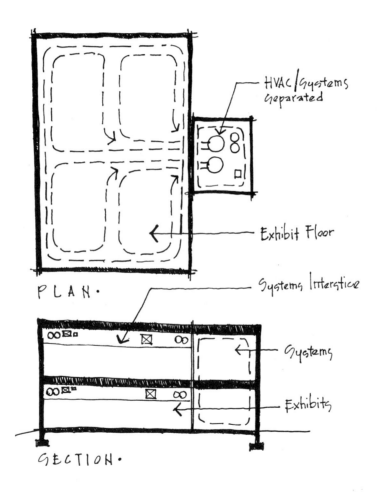

P L A N .

GECTION .

2-2: Museum systems diagram

computer use, associated on line data services continue to grow and provide even more informational options to the computer user.

As with learning any new skill, the first steps of the research process may seem difficult. But once you're familiar with even the basic information-finding resources, you'll realize that the initial time spent was an investment in the benefits you'll reap later (Horowitz 1984).

Locating information is really only the first step. Once data has been collected, we must sift through all we have obtained, then carefully work to place the material in context.

Building Types

When we study a particular building type, it is of tremendous value to gather all the knowledge we can about the history of that particular kind of building. As we collect more data, our struggle for context is slowly brought into focus by assembling knowledge about a building type's development. A building's history may extend beyond the living memory of our written heritage, like the house. At the other extreme, the established history of genetic research laboratories is quite short indeed. In the case of new building types, the knowledge base associated with them may reside in large measure within the skill of the designers specializing in these types. Therefore, to the curious designer, little public data will be available, and the process of gleaning information may be difficult or, in some cases, impossible. Conversely, if we once again return to considering the history of the house, we find a huge body of knowledge and a staggering variety of subjects.

As we conduct our research, we will find particular characteristics which are unique to any building type. Typically, these constraints are functional and essential to the baseline design parameters of the structure under consideration. A few examples will serve to illustrate this point. In a hospital or museum, the interior environment must be carefully controlled (2-2). The building systems are extremely important and significantly affect the design solution. If we consider an airport, we find departures occurring on the upper level and arrivals below. The spaces are public with high traffic volumes and dense occupancy. Functional requirements to accommodate the aircraft are stringent, and the technical requirements for routing baggage, in large installations, are a science in and of themselves. Lastly, let us briefly consider the nearly ubiquitous office building. The marketplace may create the need for a design with a particular image or "look." Lease depths, core efficiency, and vertical transportation become critical issues for the long–term financial performance of the building (2-3). Thus, we see that each building type possesses traits that require solving the functional issues in a unique manner specific to each type.

Evolution

Each type of building constructed today has come about through a period of evolution and refinement.

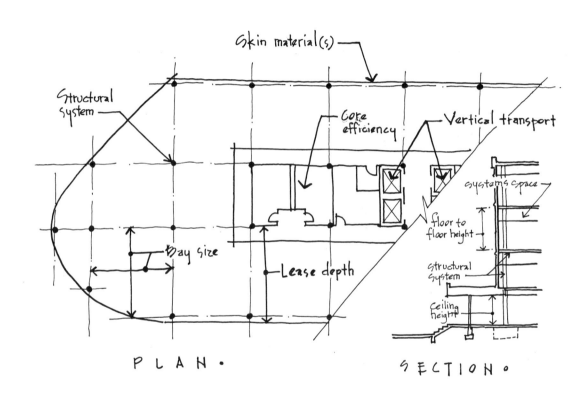

2-3: Office plan criteria

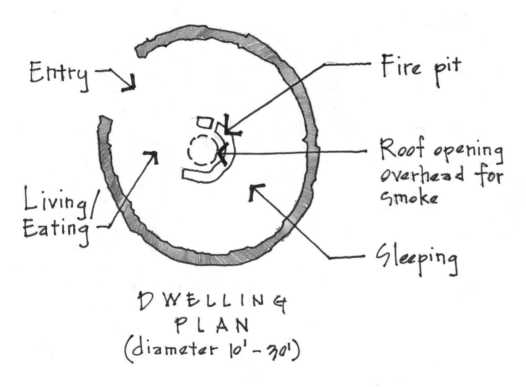

Entry →

Fire pit

Living/
Eating

Roof opening
overhead for
smoke

Sleeping

DWELLING
PLAN
(diameter 10' – 30')

2-4: Primitive house plan based on the village excavated at Ain Mallaha near Lake Hulen, Israel, circa 8,000-9,000 B.C.

This evolution is short, compared to geological time, but the term is appropriate none the less. If we return briefly to the house and open any history book, we find particular features associated with ancient dwellings (2-4). They use indigenous materials and reflect the culture and climatic constraints of their sites and times. We also notice that the basic design paradigm is already in place: there are living, eating, and sleeping areas. A modern house still incorporates these fundamental characteristics, but the design expression in the form of space, materials, and vocabulary has changed radically. The source of these changes is our cultural development and the creation of nearly limitless options via technology. Today, materials and systems are available from anywhere in the world and deliverable to our doorstep, often within days. Researching the evolution of a building type is a rich venue of pursuit. The reason for this is that the variety of solutions available puts us in a graphic environment illustrating a wide range of possibilities. The designs communicate not only the shape and character of the space but also knowledge about the culture of the times in which the structures were built. Our skill at identifying the relationship between the architecture and culture of the past is essential to grasping the nature of our culture in the present. As designers, we share a rich heritage of previous work providing an unparalleled point of departure for each design we undertake.

Understand the age you are living in so you realize what it is that you're dealing with. It's a whole different set of things, but if you can connect that to the kinds of things that have been faced in the past, you're not going to be creating buildings that are imitations of things that went before us. Not pasting together pieces of facades of old buildings, but creating something that has to do with our time, our age, society and capabilities...(Prince 1992).

Mixed Use Structures

The design of single building types is often challenging and provides the designer with difficult yet rewarding tasks. Mixed use structures combine multiple types of buildings and require the designer to research a variety of building types to gain understanding, not only of the basic functional needs of each type, but also the potential difficulties and synergies created when these types are fused into one project. The components of mixed-use projects may share similar functional traits. For example, an enclosed mall will often have retail shops, a cinema, and department store anchors. The essence of each function is to conduct sales of goods or entertainment. If we imagine a local shopping center we are familiar with, we note little functional conflict between the typical uses. In contrast, urban mixed-use projects may overlay our basic retail configuration with hotels, office buildings, underground parking, and even housing (2-5). When these additional uses are folded into our project, the complexity of the interrelationships increases dramatically. First, vertical transportation must be solved so that potential office and hotel users may

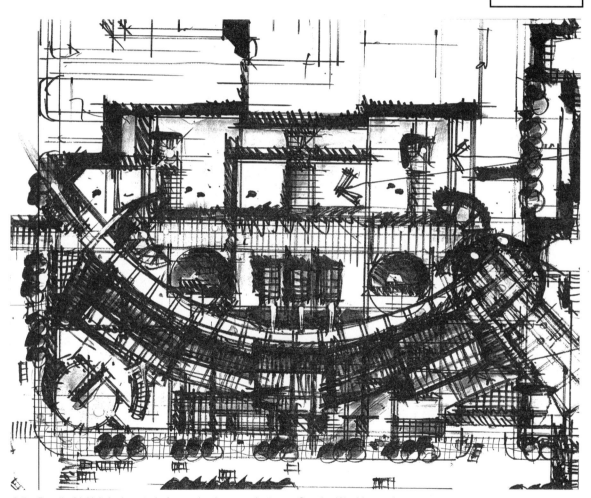

2-5: Detail of initial design study for a mixed use project near Seattle, Washington by Stan Laegreid of The Callison Partnership, Seattle, Washington

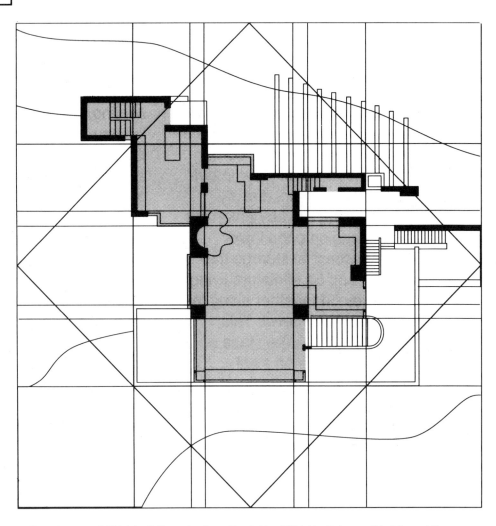

2-6: Plan diagram of Wright's Fallingwater from *Frank Lloyd Wright: Between Principle and Form* by Paul Laseau and James Tice

access their spaces from street level. Second, codes and zoning ordinances generally view each building type as a discrete, free standing entity. Adjacent uses with common space may create conflicts where usage, fire separation, and exiting must be resolved. Code issues for a large mixed-use project may be complex, requiring variances, consultants, and code reports prepared to elaborate the special systems and concepts used to satisfy life-safety issues. These reports act as a guide to functional design and as a record of building code modifications achieved through variances.

Different elements in a mixed-use project will often have overlapping and conflicting times of use. Our housing and hotel will require access 24 hours each day. An office structure and mall will be open from early morning through the evening hours. Entry and exit, plus access for the user, must be secure and uncomplicated. The spatial arrangement of the architecture contributes to successful zoning of each project element, and an active security system provides the final layer of sophistication to adequately monitor the project. The result is convenient use of the entire structure by the public and sufficient control via the security system if an emergency arises. The differing activities placed side by side in a mixed-use building may require special consideration by the designer. For example, a cinema adjacent to a department store will necessitate that the party wall be designed to provide a certain level of acoustic separation. Enclosed parking next to retail will require that positive air pressure be maintained on the retail side to eliminate any entrance of automobile exhaust. As a result of these issues, our research needs transcend the normal range of considerations for free standing buildings.

Building Examples

We have elaborated a variety of guiding concepts for undertaking research on any given building type. Our next step will be to discuss what is important to the designer in both the graphic and the real world. Locating examples of a building type in drawings, photographs, and reality is at the very heart of gaining and internalizing knowledge about designing a particular type of structure. One of our first efforts should be to obtain drawings: plans, sections, elevations, and perspectives. Even without photographs, drawings provide knowledge about a design, built or otherwise. Although drawings are useful for grasping the basic characteristics of a design or space, photography yields another avenue for acquiring a greater understanding of a design's three dimensional nature. Could you imagine Fallingwater based on the plan alone (2-6,7)? Of course, the most instructive examples for consideration in design are available when we can visit a building and experience the space first hand. If a building type is near enough to visit, go and get the full spectrum of what the designer intended. Take drawings along for reference to reinforce the connection between reality and the graphics.

Site Research

When we talk about researching a site, we entertain a place that is physical and apprehendable. The building type to be designed is placed in and on the site. This contextual interaction is a fundamental,

2-7: Photograph of Fallingwater by Alan Tucker

2-8: Contrasting site response—photo by Mark Platt

2-9: Contextual site response—photo by Mark Platt

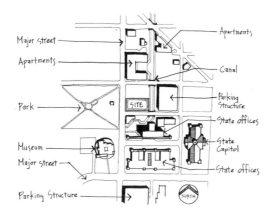

2-10: Site context

inescapable aspect of architecture. Optimally, the same building type on two different sites offers two different solutions. However, fast food restaurants and chain businesses with established marketing images are obviously an exception to this rule (2-8). But even they absorb their free standing visual identity into existing structures in an urban environment (2-9). Setting these established anomalies aside, what we are able to learn from a site is essential to generating a design solution. Chapter One discusses a majority of the basic features to consider on any site, so what I want to do here is speak to the contextual notions that drive the relation between site and building. First, our definition of site is inclusive, not only of the parcel of land on which our design will rest, but also the surrounding area. Thus, the zone of proximity and influence is large (2-10). Our process of research relates to the functional and aesthetic interest of the designer. So, on the one hand, we look to the basic knowledge of site: climate, orientation, views, and so on; and, on the other hand, we consider our surroundings with an eye towards sources of design vocabulary. A neighborhood or geographic area often has a rich history expressed within the architecture of the surrounding structures. The buildings immediately adjacent have specific histories and vocabularies. How we choose to intertwine each influence shapes the outcome of our designs.

Codes

Understanding codes and zoning ordinances, and applying them effectively, has become, for some specialists, a new division of the profession. On a day-to-day basis, designers must take new projects and use building codes as a minimum standard to insure the protection and well-being of the user. Code violations are treated as breaches of the law, punishable by the state. Extreme cases sometimes bring about criminal and/or civil proceedings.

Codes are typically divided into a plethora of sections, subsections, and chapters. The sections with the greatest effect on design include chapters covering type of building, occupancy classification, exiting, and fire separation. The remaining chapters of most codes will specify standards for construction materials and building systems. For example, you will find information on steel, concrete, and masonry construction standards. Seismic design and, in cold climates, snow loading criteria will be specified. A local code typically will also incorporate by reference standards developed by testing laboratories and agencies recognized as having expertise in specialized fields and by state and federal agencies with previously established regulatory documents.

Zoning ordinances regulate the type of building allowed to be constructed on sites wherever the ordinance has legal jurisdiction. Zoning has evolved so that the established practice segregates building types and uses. Homes are separated from multi-family apartments. Commercial and office uses are assigned to specific areas. The trend of late has been to reexamine this segregation in light of the positive results to be gained by grouping certain uses in proximity; sometimes in the same structure (our mixed-use example). With the continuing transition to an information—or knowledge—based society well developed and continuing, the original

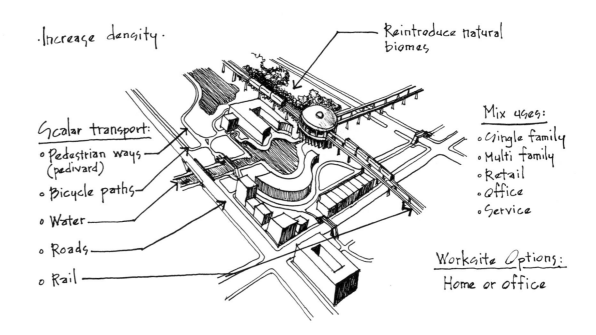

2-11: Post industrial planning paradigm

- Elimination of ornament
- Conscious rejection of the past
- Supremacy of the machine
- Standardization
- Belief in technology
- Serious tone; no humor

2-12: Corbusier's Villa Savoye and modernist principles

o Resurgence of ornament

o Interest in "image"

o Reject standardization

o Variety of materials

o Employ historical vocabulary

o Irony, whimsicality: a sense of humor

2-13: Charles Moore's Piazza d'Italia and post modern principles

concept of "zoning" is slowly being rethought (2-11). People may live in the vicinity of their offices with no impact on their quality of life. By the same token, industrial facilities are best treated in separate areas consistent with zoning's original concept. The complexity of zoning ordinances is directly dependent on the size of municipality they are designed to serve. A major city will have a reasonably complex zoning document, whereas, a small town will utilize a much simpler ordinance. Not only does a zoning ordinance specify what type of building may be constructed in a given locale; it also will address requirements such as parking, landscaping, setbacks, storm-water retention or detention, curb cuts, and so on. Zoning ordinances go hand in hand with building codes to shape the pattern of development in a municipality, and their importance should never be neglected or underestimated. A careful review of each will save many a designer time, cost, and embarrassment.

Client Research

The final, and most important, influence on the designer and design solution is the client. Research, in the context of the client, is a conscious effort on the part of the designer to grasp the client's fundamental concerns. Each person served by our craft is unique. We need to understand that not only are we required to be good designers, but that the quality of our work is grounded in our relationships with each individual client. Each person, or persons, in the context of their special needs, is also a correspondingly individual solution. Part of the foundation of the Modern Movement was the philosophy of standardization (2-12). Architectural design in the form of Postmodernism began to dismantle the model of standardized mass production (Modernism). The emergence of Postmodernism runs more or less parallel with the continuing evolution of western information-based economies (2-13). It is now possible to link manufacturing processes with the versatility of the computer. The result is the unprecedented ability to produce one-of-a-kind components for people and buildings at costs matching the mass-produced objects of the smokestack era. We have the opportunity to seek unique solutions for our clients and create designs most suited to their needs.

The last area to concern ourselves with is the context where research is undertaken. We find the academic and practice environments to have similarities and stark differences. With reference to educational circumstances, the reality of the situation is that projects generally are not built as such. The designer therefore bears no liability. Also, the client (professor) knows significantly more about design and construction than the student. In practice, the converse is true: projects are built, liability is real, and the client may know little, if anything, about design and construction. We can deduce that student needs differ from designers in practice. A student gleans knowledge from classes, peers, library (books, magazines), and immersion in the mock design environment of the studio. Research, formal and informal, happens in each of the previously mentioned places. A working designer will get information from sources largely matching the base described above for the student. We will also

add professional associations, community and business networks, clients, product representatives, seminars, and more. These research sources support additional concerns, including getting and keeping business, marketing, community service, management, document production cost, and project costs.

The final issue to concern ourselves with is time (2-14). In school and in practice, we never seem to have enough. The true value of research, conscious or unconscious, is that by garnering information, placing it in context, and identifying key issues, we make the time available to us on any project more efficient and effective. Deadlines, in school or practice, are just as real. And from experience, I know any student feels just as much pressure as a designer struggling to complete a project. Research, whether applicable once or internalized and used for a lifetime, is effort well spent.

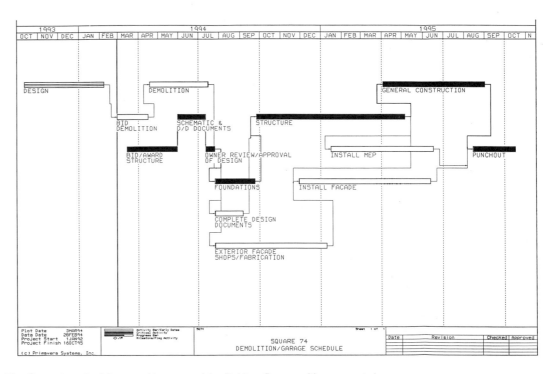

2-14: Computer scheduling graphic prepared by DeMars Program Management, Inc. using Primavera Project Planner by Primavera Systems, Inc.

CHAPTER 3

Programming

Certain types of projects, usually large or complex installations, will necessitate the creation of a formal building program. A building program identifies a problem or group of problems to be solved. Architectural programming is, at a minimum, a functional guide to the generation of design solutions (3-1). At its most developed, a program may also incorporate conceptual and symbolic concerns associated with a project (3-2).

> *Good buildings don't just happen. They are planned to look good and perform well, and come about when good architects and good clients join in thoughtful, cooperative effort. Programming the requirements of a proposed building is the architect's first task, often the most important (Pena 1987).*

Programming may be defined as an umbrella term whose result is a list of goals, problem(s) to be solved, and requirements for a design to begin, either written or unwritten. Every design, from the simplest house addition to the largest institutional work, is executed with reference to a program of some kind. The "document" is not always written out, but its importance as a foundation of design work of all kinds is undeniable. Our clients, of course, are the primary sources for programming information. The designer's task is to draw the program from the client and couple it with his or her knowledge of building. This synergy is the fulcrum about which design carefully pivots, unfolding in a continuing accretion of knowledge.

LIBRARY DIVISION

T.   Reference Area, Reading Room, Stacks

3-1: Adjacency diagram from the program for the Indiana Historical Society by The Stubbins Associates-Architects, Cambridge, Massachusetts

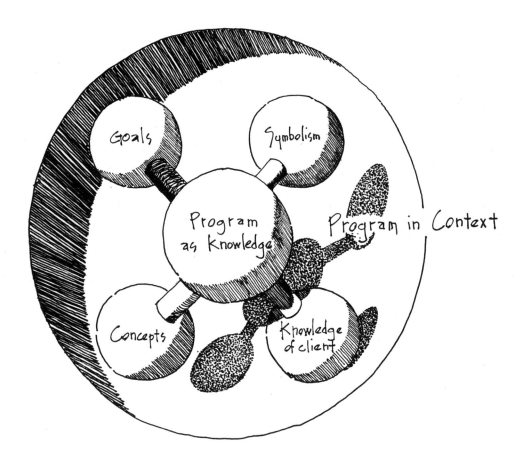

3-2: Fusing program criteria and information into knowledge

The Client

The client, in practice, is the individual or company purchasing a designer's services. In an academic setting, the professor/client is a preordained relationship established by the curriculum. In actual practice, a client comes to us based on word of mouth, reputation, recommendation, competition, formalized selection, or luck. The concept of marketing is already the subject of several excellent works, and I defer to their texts for the "how" of getting the client in the door. We will focus on nurturing the client relationship during programming and on what is necessary to create excellent service and quality design. Once the designer to client connection is made, the first, essential step is sitting down and carefully listening to the client. Identify his or her needs without preconception: ask questions, make a wish list, distinguish preferences. This is the beginning, as Mr. Pena stated above, the most important part. Care at the beginning is a must.

The designer translates a client's needs into reality (3-3). Satisfying client needs is a task that not only requires us to have a methodology for programming, but also understanding the client we service. In the existing environment of practice, we find that design is driven, on a consistent basis, by clients concerned with relating building solutions to costs. Capital expenses are an issue not from the simple perspective of construction cost, but from a variety of perspectives.

The instrumental (buildings and services as capital assets) view of build-

ings is most pronounced among business clients, including industrial and service corporations and developers, and other clients who are subject to careful budget review, such as departments and agencies of federal, state, and municipal governments. These are the clients whose entire operation is evaluated in terms of economic value. It is not surprising that they would emphasize the cost of buildings, the economic return they offer, or their impact on blue- and white-collar productivity and morale. A fact that often surprises architects when they discover it for the first time is that the instrumental view of architecture has also taken over non-profit institutions, which formerly took a more casual view of their physical plant and regarded buildings primarily as works of architectural art. This new mentality regarding buildings is especially noticeable among university and cultural organizations in the non-profit sector. With the expansion in the number of universities, museums, symphony halls, and theatres, competition for funding is rapidly becoming more intense. Curators, presidents, and other managers of these institutions are under increasing pressure to justify their building needs in terms similar to those that apply to the profit sector. The bigger cultural and

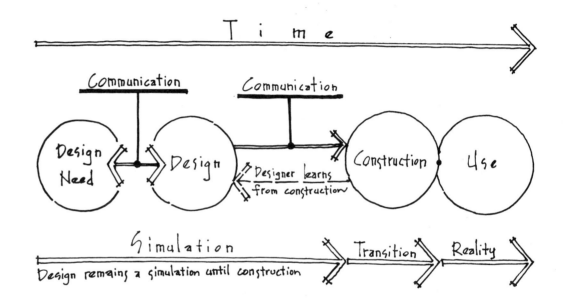

3-3: Design simulates reality

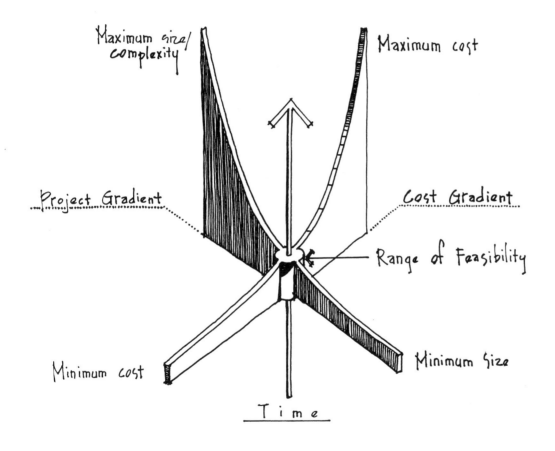

Maximum size/complexity

Maximum cost

Project Gradient

Cost Gradient

Range of Feasibility

Minimum cost

Minimum Size

Time

3-4: Design intersects cost

educational institutions now employ their own in-house architects, engineers, and facilities managers, whose functions are identical with staffs in the private sector (Gutman 1988).

The previous paragraph clearly represents a particular type of client. Regardless, across the entire gamut of practice, only on a few rare occasions will a designer provide her skills to a client where money is no object. These two extremes, and the entire range of possible emphasis along this gradient, are of singular importance to the creation of a workable program (3-4). Knowing a client's economic means will provide a gauge of whether a program, evolving or complete, is realistic and viable as a design foundation.

When we develop a formal program, we are placed in an environment where questions become the medium for our effort to determine what each client wants and needs. What we will present here are a variety of approaches. They may all be used, used in part, or not at all if the circumstances warrant, but at a minimum we should concern ourselves with being sure of our client's budget, aesthetic preferences, and functional needs (3-5).

Communication

At the outset, we should ask our client about what they like and do not like about their current building or space. Negative sentiments should be carefully noted and avoided. If we inadvertently recreate a condition with which the client is already displeased, the consequences could be anything from embarrassment to termination. It may also be valuable to ask about the client's feelings regarding other buildings similar or equivalent to the type under consideration. If the client is unfamiliar with these structures, visits may evoke more comment and useful information. The designer may ask the client to make a list of ideas, needs, wants, even fantasies without regard to monetary limits so that we may sift through a variety of possibilities and create unique design ideas that are possible solutions and continue to meet the budget. Another useful idea is asking the client to assemble an "image" book of buildings, products, furniture, fixtures, colors, spaces, and so on which they feel represents the character of the design to be created. A book like this assists the designer in discerning our client's inclination towards form, space, material, and color. At least one meeting for programming should happen on site so that the abstraction possible in another location is eliminated. A site meeting not only kindles the imagination of the designer; the client receives this benefit as well. What we presented above is the opportunity for the designer to establish a field of possibility to work within. As we determine subjective criteria, we also work through the detailed functional requirements which will provide our client with a workable space. We continue to engage the aesthetic and practical notions essential to design, and place them in the context of our client's project.

As we continue to interact with our client, the program begins to take shape. We begin comparing ideas, developing concepts, and establishing alternatives. Establishing a participatory relation-

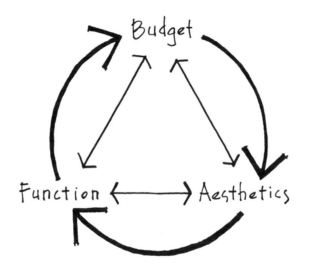

3-5: Cycle of programming and future design concerns

Fundamental Questions:

- Is the building to be remodeled and/or retrofitted?

- Will the facility also need to be expanded?

- Would the client be better served by a new facility?

- Does the environmental impact justify a new structure?

- How open is the client to new ideas?

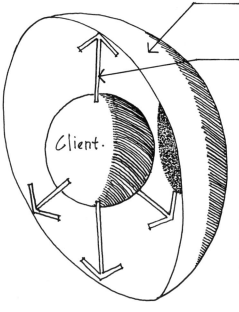

Existing space or structure

The client pushes against the building envelope with sheer size, dissatisfaction, habit, activity, and so on: these are habitual, built-in prejudices.

An existing facility may impede certain aspects of design process because it tends to encapsulate client thinking

Client.

3-6: The client in an existing facility

ship with clients has significant benefits. First, a client investing time and energy in a project is empowered with the opportunity to work with the designer to add value and quality to the design. Potential future conflicts are avoided. In addition, an involved client appreciates the amount of work required to arrive at a solution. Obviously, we do not spend every waking minute with our clients. Each meeting draws to a close and we collect our notes, sketches, and impressions for reference later. When we sit down after the fact, we have the opportunity to reflect and develop unique strategies for our clients. It is important to understand that clients are individuals: as designers, we are artists, technicians, and psychologists. One of the essential tasks of each project is to understand, then be able to respect differences among our clients.

Part of the process of beginning to understand our clients is linked to the ability to ask objective questions which will ferret out issues related to both the project and the client's mindset. We need to determine whether a client is knowledgeable in relation to the project at hand. If they are not, we may need to embark on a course of tactful education. We also need to get a feeling as to whether they are clear in their needs. Are the functional issues articulated in a usable way? A designer is an interpreter, a translator of language and the circumstances that our clients exist within (3-6). By far, the biggest source of information to designers resides in the language, verbal or written, that is generated in relation to a project. Therefore, the designer's grasp of language must match or exceed her design skills. In a way, language is an extended form of design process: words codify and support our three dimensional creations. One of the most useful skills for a designer is the ability to "trade places." The idea is to put ourselves in the client's shoes, making an effort to think like he does, then bring that knowledge to bear on a design problem. For the majority of practitioners, the programmatic requirements of each building type are slowly embedded in the designer's mind through a process of slow, steady education in the buildings each particular firm undertakes. Part of the trust established between designers and clients rests in this tacit understanding of needs. It is important to note that often situations will vary from project to project, and the designer will need to extend her base of knowledge to include some new aspect of the work at hand.

In the realm of large projects, regardless of the firm or reputation of the designer, the need for creating a quality program is paramount. Complex projects, regardless of size, will identify the development of a program as a separate phase of work. The programming document becomes the point of departure for the evolution of design concepts and their subsequent connection to building forms. Research often continues during programming. In fact, if a firm has little or no experience with a particular building type, research may continue through the complete phase of programming and beyond, as a guide and supplement to the discoveries that programming engenders.

Multiple Clients

The client and designer are key participants, but around this fundamental relationship swirl a num-

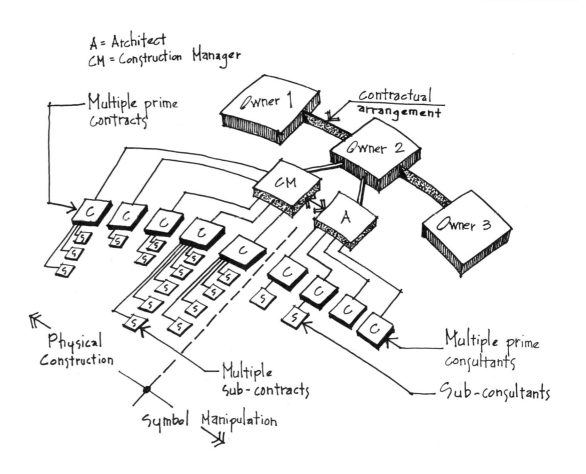

3-7: Project organization illustrating multiple clients

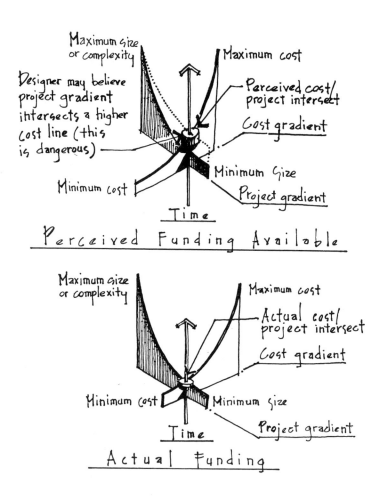

Maximum size
or complexity

Designer may believe
project gradient
intersects a higher
cost line (this
is dangerous)

Minimum cost

Maximum cost

Perceived cost/
project intersect

Cost gradient

Minimum size

Project gradient

Time

Perceived Funding Available

Maximum size
or complexity

Minimum cost

Maximum cost

Actual cost/
project intersect

Cost gradient

Minimum size

Project gradient

Time

Actual Funding

3-8: Program versus funding

ber of external influences which can significantly alter the program document and the subsequent design. For example, there are political relationships between clients with multiple representatives (3-7). This particular type of environment is complicated when no single individual is identified to make final decisions binding to all parties involved. With multiple clients or client groups, the result can be close to chaos. Reaching consensus on even simple issues can be difficult at best. The designer is occasionally forced to make decisions graphically, then present them to the group for feedback. It is fairly safe to say that changes always result, but if the designer can work quickly and establish alternates for review prior to client meetings or on the spot, this approach can be coupled with persuasive verbal skills to move a project ahead. Programming and design are tightly interwoven, with each bearing on the other. Bear in mind, any number of constraints established by a formal program may be shattered at any time after the design begins to evolve (3-8). The key is to reconcile the rearrangement of parameters so that the form of the building continues to serve the root needs of the client (3-9). Uncertainty with respect to the guidelines established by the program allows the designer to work within a volume where the rules may be stretched in the interest of defining options for the actual form of the buildings. Like music, architecture subscribes to a variety of rules and guidelines which, when broken in the proper context, may yield results of singular elegance. Decision making is critical to the refinement of a building program. The owner may make determinations, the client and architect may reach consensus on issues, or the designer may make decisions. If we, as the designers, take it upon ourselves to make programmatic decisions, we must be prepared to justify our reasoning to the satisfaction of the client.

The program should include a brief section on any significant building code or zoning criterion which will have an impact on the design. The concerns of life safety must be codified by the designer to determine the extent of their effect on the design. On occasion, a large or complex design will afford the designer with the opportunity to rethink code issues, or the design, by its nature, will challenge the written code document so that variances will need to be sought.

A Performance Document

The program is a performance document: it specifies what the physical form of a building must enclose and arrange to make a workable environment for the user and owner. The definition of "workable" varies from building to building or space to space, but in each case the designer must use a mental or written construct to guide the implementation of a design. We may embed the programmatic necessities in our minds over time for simple buildings or building types produced frequently by a firm having a reputation and track record for a given kind of building. Conversely, one-of-a-kind structures require the creation of a program document to guide the designer and provide a check for inclusion of the various needs identified by the owner. For these unique projects, a separately identified phase of work prior to or

overlapping the beginning of design activity proper is best. Lastly, a program is the most organized way to list the baseline criteria for a building or space. It affords us the opportunity to check our work and provides essential guidance as we struggle with bringing our designs to fruition.

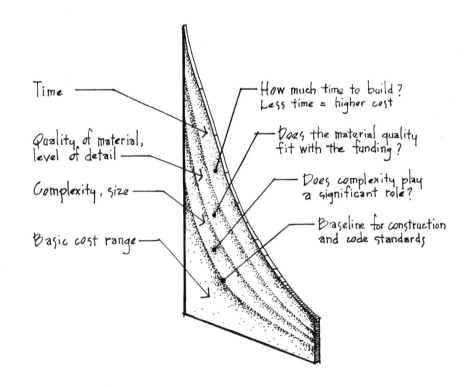

3-9: Breakdown of project gradient components

CHAPTER 4

Concepts

With each new project, we enter a mental state to nurture creative designs. There are many ingredients: we have discussed the basic knowledge required of building and site, the necessity of programming spatial functions and relationships, and research to learn more about the specifics associated with unfamiliar building types. The next essential step is concept elaboration. What are concepts? Concepts are ideas identified by the designer as a foundation for giving form to a space, building, and/ or site. These unique observations are intertwined with a building's function, providing interest, subtlety, and richness. It is also quite possible and acceptable to derive form from spatial functions, relationships, previous structures, and even other cultures. This process of search, identification, and fit are part of the fun of architecture and design. Architecture has a playful component amidst the serious tone of the profession. Academia provides the opportunity to stretch this aspect to the limit. On the other hand, actual practice imposes the balancing weight of the practitioner's obligation to public welfare, cost, and the standard of care. Regardless of how serious we tend to be as we are confronted with each empty sheet of paper or the blank gaze of the CRT, we reach into our base of knowledge for ideas and symbols that will connect the pragmatic and the artistic.

Symbolism

Each major building type has characteristic symbolic concepts that may be associated with potential forms. For example, an airport may evoke words like movement, travel, speed, and technology (4-1).

4-1: Underground tunnel connecting Concourses B and C at O'Hare International Airport, Chicago

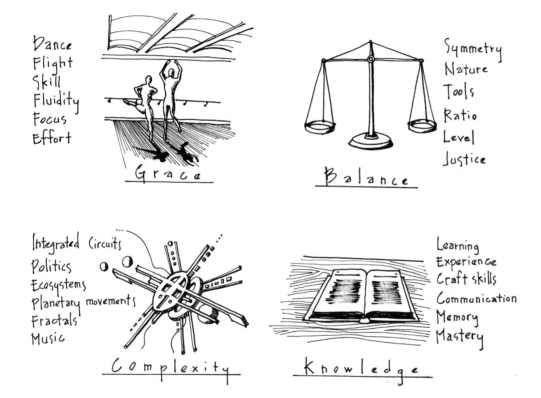

Dance
Flight
Skill
Fluidity
Focus
Effort

Grace

Symmetry
Nature
Tools
Ratio
Level
Justice

Balance

Integrated Circuits
Politics
Ecosystems
Planetary movements
Fractals
Music

Complexity

Learning
Experience
Craft skills
Communication
Memory
Mastery

Knowledge

4-2: Concept translations-visual and verbal

A library may bring words to mind like teaching, learning, wisdom, knowledge, security, and information. We seem to rely quite heavily on words as descriptive sources. Our language is one method we use to communicate with our clients. If we step all the way out of the design context, we see that language serves as the principal foundation of design ideas. The meaning associated with the words begins to suggest form (4-2). Words as givers of meaning, then form, are half the equation. The other realm for exploration is that of the visual: concepts may be taken from existing structures and studied in the rich venue of drawings. They may represent ideas for literal built form or be abstractions that merely suggest possible forms or even emotions. Two valid methods to design vocabulary and organization are available, and neither should be slighted as we seek quality work.

To create a base of concepts useful for a project, the following simple method has value. First, list all the symbolic adjectives, nouns, and images identified by the client and designer as having a bearing on the project. On one hand, we continue to balance the considerations of site, site context, and building function against our now active search to apply meaning. Next, we may choose any number of symbols for use in the search for translation to form. The choice of symbolic link need not be shrouded in complex philosophy: simplicity more often yields an elegant connection between design and form. There are endless ways to apply concepts to the material of architecture including the use of multiple concepts applied to various pieces of a project, additive concepts that build to support a master principle, concepts applied with reference to project scale, or separate concepts overlaid on the site. Indeed, our options are many with a magnificent array of possibilities.

Sources

Concepts are drawn from a variety of sources. The designer is an important source of ideas and in addition acts as the interpreter throughout the gestation of a design. The client provides a broad palette of notions for consideration by the designer. For instance, does a particular company have a "mission" or image to portray in the architecture? If so, it must be considered side by side with other concerns in the design. Each site contains unique qualities both within and around its limits. What if a site is in another country or culture? We must consider the relative value of blending or contrasting with the indigenous architecture, along with the availability of specific materials and skills. The building type, its functional requirements, history, and extant examples are concept generators. Lastly, the user may suggest possible considerations for inclusion at many levels of a project.

Consider this project for the Indiana Historical Society. The building will be a headquarters for an institution over 160 years old. To seriously begin studying the design, the architects have talked at length with the client about what the Society means as an institution, the history of the State of Indiana, the context of our time, and what the longevity of such a facility might be. The client and the designers are very concerned with history; how it links with the present and the future. The preoccupation with

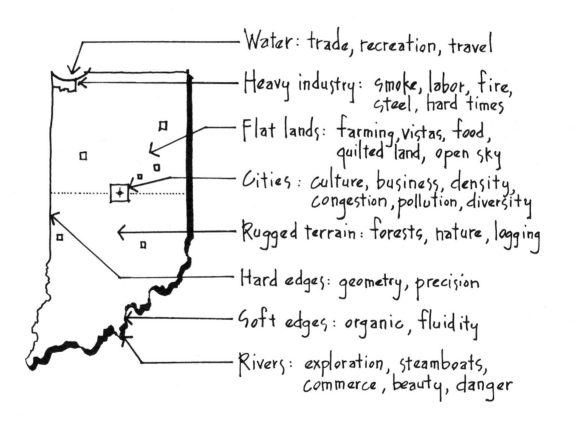

4-3: Major features of Indiana with beginning concept translations

Water: trade, recreation, travel

Heavy industry: smoke, labor, fire, steel, hard times

Flat lands: farming, vistas, food, quilted land, open sky

Cities: culture, business, density, congestion, pollution, diversity

Rugged terrain: forests, nature, logging

Hard edges: geometry, precision

Soft edges: organic, fluidity

Rivers: exploration, steamboats, commerce, beauty, danger

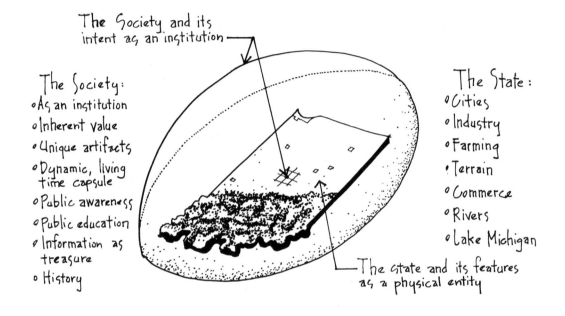

The Society and its intent as an institution

The Society:
o As an institution
o Inherent value
o Unique artifacts
o Dynamic, living time capsule
o Public awareness
o Public education
o Information as treasure
o History

The State:
o Cities
o Industry
o Farming
o Terrain
o Commerce
o Rivers
o Lake Michigan

The State and its features as a physical entity

4-4: Diagramming physical forms and symbolic intentions for the Indiana Historical Society

the future comes from the realization that over the last 160 years overwhelming change has swept across our planet. Surely the exercise of asking what the next 100 years may harbor is not trivial, especially since the anticipated life span of this new structure will quite probably exceed 100 years. The thought process also considered the State of Indiana as an entity with a distinctive character, landscape, and contribution to history. The state is largely flat farmland in its northern half; the south is hilly and forested. The largest urban center is located at the state's geographic center. Also, the most concentrated heavy industry is in the northwest and, ironically, sits adjacent to the Indiana Dunes on Lake Michigan, where the science of ecology was elaborated. The southern border is formed by the Ohio River. These physical characteristics are a broad substructure to underpin the creation of form (4-3,4). As we apprehend these various features, we also weigh in various functional requirements such as the stringent environmental control required for the library stacks, the staff offices, exhibition gallery, and public space. As we consider the potential life span of this new structure, we realize that environmental concerns should be applied to the design process. How much will energy to heat and cool the building cost 100 years from now? What are the most durable materials for a long-term building? What kinds of information systems are being envisioned or developed as we design in these waning years of the twentieth century (4-5)? These are not easy questions, but their answers must be sought to fairly appraise the issues confronting the client and incorporate them successfully into the design.

What we intend to do is search through these broad interests and select a range of images and words to serve as the platform for a particular design. Our stack of ideas may be enormous. We may seek to list each and every adjective and image we feel is important to a given project. As we study the possibilities, we look for a fit between concept and function, often on many levels. This may be done via sketching, in a strictly nonverbal, almost nonrational way. Sketching allows access to some of our most sophisticated problem-solving skills and provides an efficient vehicle for the integration of potentially huge volumes of information. Our verbal abilities may be challenged by a request to explain what we have done, but oddly, as others study our drawn work, they may intuitively grasp our intent without benefit of extended explanation. The concepts we choose act as seedlings for inspiration that may come quickly or with extended effort, but regardless of the time involved, the concepts we embrace will be the lattice that channels the growth of our designs. Concepts are the ideas behind a project, giving it art and interest. They are unspoken and live in the finished architecture. Interest, even through a casual glance, is aroused by these unspoken but resident notions.

Objective to Subjective

Concepts are the point in the design process where we tentatively begin to leave the realm of the objective and venture into the first wisps of the subjective. If you have been reading this book in order,

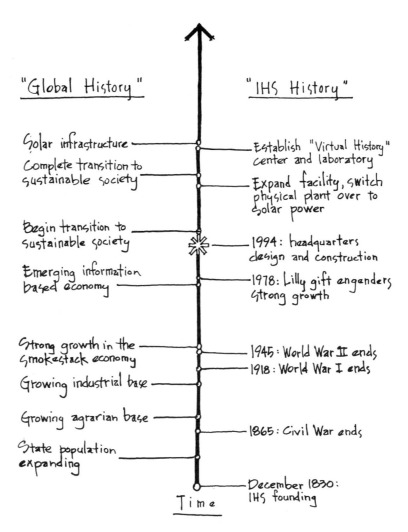

4-5: Diagram of temporal concerns for the Indiana Historical Society

CHAPTER 4
CONCEPTS

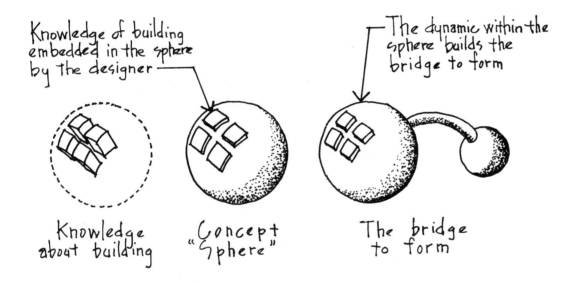

Knowledge of building embedded in the sphere by the designer

The dynamic within the sphere builds the bridge to form

Knowledge about building

"Concept Sphere"

The bridge to form

4-6: Concept sphere diagram

front to back, the first three chapters stand quite firmly in an area of design that we may safely term "objective." There is a little ambiguity, but generally we can agree on the characteristics of a site, how materials work, the arrangement of spaces, and the history of building types. These things are mostly tangible and apprehendable. However, when we begin to construct ideas for breathing life into a design, our interest turns to sources of form. While a design may be executed with no effort to identify or ground concepts as givers of form, buildings lacking this care are easily identifiable and contribute little, other than shelter, to enrich their users. Conversely, designs whose development hinges on a careful incorporation of ideas from site, client, user, and building type stand gracefully for expert and layperson alike. We embody our wills, perceptions, even dreams in the spaces we create.

Concepts may do many things for us. First, they can organize a plan, elevation, and/or section. They may lead to the incorporation of particular materials, design vocabulary, and detailing. As we mentally study possible ideas for inclusion in a design, one worthwhile way to value each idea is to check how it fits with the proposed function or functions where it is to be applied. We blend and interpret concepts to mesh with the functional criteria described within the program. For example, if we return to the Indiana Historical Society project, the intent expressed by the client is that the facility represent the entire state of Indiana. One possible way to translate this idea is to use the shape of Indiana to roughly define the perimeter of the building plan. Obviously, this is not the most subtle application of concept translation, but if it is coupled with other ideas, there may be some preliminary value in this approach.

Concepts do not necessarily stand alone. They more often work with one another and the building function to lead us from fragments to a loose scheme. We take our knowledge about building and site, then place it in the context of a "concept sphere" (4-6). Living on the concept sphere are the designer, client, and user. The objective knowledge of building and site are connected to the surrounding concepts and become the bridge to form. These exercises become the basis for a working schematic design. As a design begins the process of evolving detail, knowledge is constantly added to the functional and conceptual drivers of a project. As a result, design seldom becomes fully fixed until very late in the course of working drawings and perhaps even construction.

Changes

If, over the course of a design, any of the objective criteria change, it is essential to determine if the previously developed concepts are still valid. Usually, when something changes or new information is revealed, some part of the concept lattice will wither. Sometimes this is unavoidable, and on other occasions we may have latitude to maneuver out of harm's way. As a general rule of thumb, the larger the change, the more damage is incurred to the concept sources for a given project. For this reason, it is important to look for master principles to guide a design at the level of overall scale. Allowing the supporting ideas to branch from a guiding principle

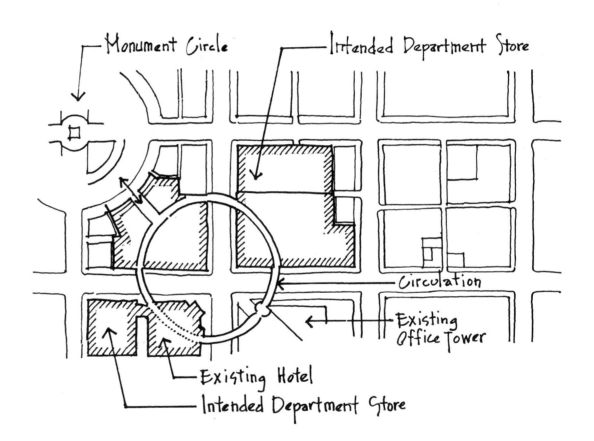

4-7: Circle Centre Mall—abstraction of the original plan diagram, design architect The Jerde Partnership, Los Angeles

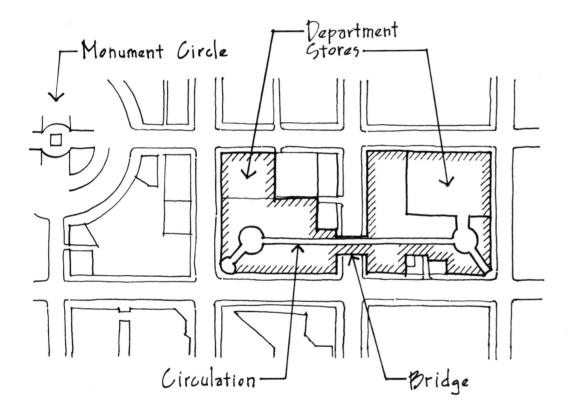

4-8: Circle Centre Mall—abstraction of the constructed plan diagram, design architect Ehrenkrantz and Eckstut, New York

assures us of maintaining some of our original approach intact as a project evolves. On the other hand, the changes occurring during a design's development often nurture and elaborate the original ideas (4-7,8). It is rarely possible to establish a concept structure that will stand immutable through the complete process of crafting a building. It does occur on occasion, but with the steady diet of changes associated with the majority of built work, restructuring or discarding of driving concepts occurs on a regular and continuing basis.

Concepts knit the practical components of a project to observations about what a design is with reference to itself, surrounding context, and global parameters brought on line by the designer (4-9). This process may guide the initial translation to form and inform our priorities throughout the creation of a building. These choices are made in a dynamic environment and are subject to revision or replacement during design. We tend to try to freeze our solutions in some optimum form, but when the functional parameters change, the conceptual substructure must be reexamined to determine whether a working fit still exists between what the designer intends to portray symbolically and the newly generated criteria for the functional design. We make "rules" to guide and organize our work. This playful interpretation's only caveat is that we stay alert and review whether our concepts still work when changes happen, as they always do, in midstream.

The Hannover Principles:

1. Insist on rights of humanity and nature to coexist in a healthy, supportive, diverse, and sustainable condition.

2. Recognize interdependence. The elements of human design interact with and depend upon the natural world, with broad and diverse implications at every scale. Expand design considerations to recognize even distant effects.

3. Respect relationships between spirit and matter. Consider all aspects of human settlement including community, dwelling, industry, and trade in terms of existing and evolving connections between spiritual and material consciousness.

4. Accept responsibility for the consequence of design decisions upon human well-being, the viability of natural systems, and their right to coexist.

5. Crate safe objects of long-term value. Do not burden future generations with requirements for maintenance or vigilant administration of potential danger due to the careless creation of products, processes, or standards.

6. Eliminate the concept of waste. Evaluate and optimize the full life-cycle of products and processes, to approach the state of natural systems, in which there is no waste.

7. Rely on natural energy flows. Human designs would, like the living world, derive their creative forces from perpetual solar income. Incorporate this energy efficiently and safely for responsible use.

8. Understand the limitations of design. No human creation lasts forever and design does not solve all problems. Those who create and plan should practice humility in the face of nature. Treat nature as a model and mentor, not an inconvenience to be evaded or controlled.

9. Seek constant improvement by the sharing of knowledge. Encourage direct and open communication between colleagues, patrons, manufacturers, and users to link long term sustainable considerations with ethical responsibility, and reestablish the integral relationship between natural processes and human activity.

The Hannover Principles should be seen as a living document committed to the transformation and growth in the understanding of our interdependence with nature, so that they may adapt as our knowledge of the world evolves.

4-9: An environmental perspective—William McDonough's Hannover Principles

CHAPTER 5

Predesign Summary

We practice design and in so doing, take the many layers of knowledge essential to building from the point of little understanding to an expanding, inter-disciplinary base of knowledge with each passing year. This embodied knowledge is represented, in part, by our basic grasp of building, research, and programming. Each area of skill is a study in and of itself, with important relationships among them informing and affecting each.

Basics

Knowledge of materials, systems, assemblies, and site ground each and every choice made during the course of design. Learning the "basics" alone is daunting, compounded by the explosive advance of technology. While new building system tech-nologies are being created regularly, other areas such as information systems and environmental concerns promise to affect our craft as surely as the invention of reinforced concrete (5-1,2).

The frantic pace of technology begs us to look beyond the concerns of buildings as objects on the land and place our work in the context of a rapidly changing society: not just in the west, but in the developing countries as well. The developing coun-tries of the third world may well leap from preindus-trial to postindustrial societies in less than fifty years. Buildings conceived by their architects should respond to societal and contextual design con-straints, rather than solve problems from the smoke-stack era. In the future, western designers will be called upon to build more frequently in other coun-tries. It will be essential to conceive quality designs in different cultures. Technology, at home and

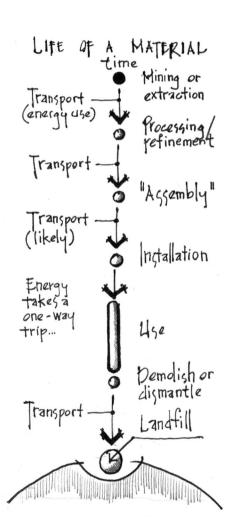

5-1: Unlimited resource use diagram

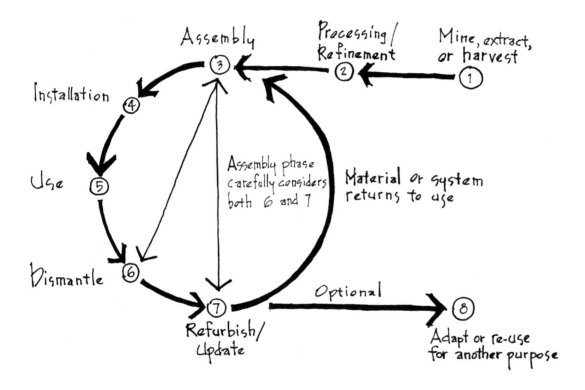

5-2: Resource use diagram modeled after natural systems

abroad, must inevitably be placed in context. Without this care, buildings of poor quality, wasting precious resources, will contribute additional damage to ecologies and cultures already under massive stress. This same mistake has happened in the west as well: we are not immune.

With the emergence of the global economy and greater codependence among what were once separate states, our options begin to emerge as obligations. We have begun to question our past choices with respect to materials, energy efficiency, indoor air quality, zoning, and urban planning. Many of these issues cross boundaries far from the notion of the basics applied to creating buildings. Conversely, others are intimately tied to our understanding of the physical materials employed in our structures. Design thrives on the idea of unlimited possibilities. However, from an ecological standpoint, the infinite elasticity of the earth to absorb humankind's abuses is a fading myth. The possibilities of design are still unlimited, but there is little doubt that respect for our biosphere must step from design option to mandate. How we use our most basic knowledge of building reflects and amplifies our priorities illuminating our most personal beliefs and agendas.

Research

When we research a building type, we broadly assimilate background in a cultural and functional framework. From a preindustrial standpoint, many building types display elegant adaptations to the requirements of climate: New England saltbox houses, bedouin tents, adobe structures of the southwest United States, and Native American tepees are a few examples. In a world view where energy efficiency becomes a cornerstone of quality design, these timeless structures work with the surrounding environment and display a deep grasp of ideas adaptable to present-day designs. When we consider building a conceptual bridge to a postindustrial design paradigm, the responses of preindustrial cultures are instructive. The rub seems to be combining the best of preindustrial design with many of the useful technologies from the last hundred or so years (5-3). Technology in support of the well-being of the user, such as nontoxic building materials, is a good example. Another would be the use of computers for building systems optimization. There are many more applications whose best fit may be found by identifying a series of goals for both research and programming. Goals provide focus and direction by making explicit statements about what we intend the building or space to accomplish. Also, whenever we design, a substructure of goals for the work is inherent in our beliefs and experience. If we codify as much as possible at the outset, then add, delete, or modify as each project develops, the result will be better suited to the client's needs and completed more efficiently overall.

Research is the foundation of programming, and the two, as mentioned previously, often occur at the same time. The place for a statement of goals to guide a design is within the program. In a way, the heart of a program is the problem statement and goal summary. The fledgling pro-

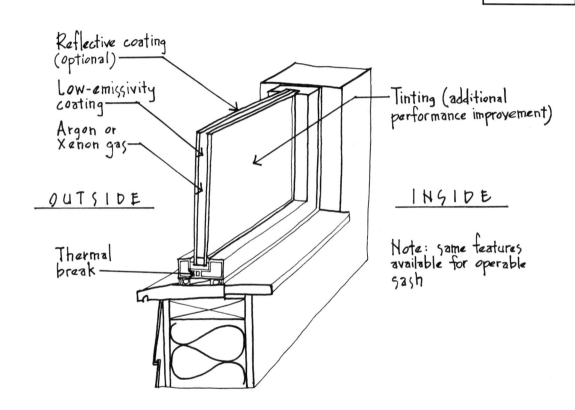

5-3: High performance window components

Reflective coating (optional)

Low-emissivity coating

Argon or Xenon gas

OUTSIDE

Thermal break

Tinting (additional performance improvement)

INSIDE

Note: same features available for operable sash

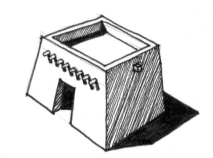

Adobe Structure:
thermal mass

Mandan Indian Mound:
thermal mass

New England Saltbox:
wind

Bedouin Tent:
sun, heat

5-4: Design solutions distilled from the structures of indigenous cultures

gram also directs research and asks questions of the goal structure. A continuous interplay occurs between basic architectural knowledge, research, and programming. As we study a building's history, timeless relationships manifest themselves (5-4). We gain understanding of the general functional issues and see how the design of, say, the windows in Jefferson's Monticello is based on technology available two hundred years ago (5-5). Assuming the previous example appropriate and that we are embroiled in designing a building, we would then compare our knowledge of present-day window systems and weigh the esthetics of another time against the use of an off-the-shelf unit or custom design.

Programming

Programming also defines a range of specialized facts. Some of the information will be hard data defining specific items with exacting certainty: the capacity of a laboratory exhaust hood or classroom size. Other types of knowledge will allow a tolerance from maximum to minimum for particular objects, features, or spaces. Loosely held approximations may take the form of well known "rules of thumb" and also be strongly influenced during design by other variables of the process. As we perform research, areas with a larger range of options will often be illustrated, showing how the designer chose to limit or extend the program schema in the finished design.

In addition, the program will identify adjacencies between functions to enhance a variety of qualities. These adjacencies are implicitly tied into parts of the goal structure relating to efficiency and convenience of operation. Many possible guidelines may shape adjacencies, depending on the building type. A jail will be largely driven by security issues, whereas a library will focus on the relationship between reading areas, stacks, and light, with security control at the entrance/exit. External influences can play into the arrangement of adjacencies by virtue of considerations such as natural light, the desire to have a space accessible by the public, formal considerations exterior to the proposed building—e.g., urban axis—and the physical limitations of a site. In research, we look for information, relationships, and context to inform an ongoing design effort. As before, this background provides potential examples of how external concerns can shape a project to its benefit or detriment, depending on the situation. Part of the difficulty lies in the ability to recognize when various portions of a program support each other and when they conflict. Sometimes these surprises remain hidden until schematic design uncovers the problem. When this happens, we loop all the way back to programming and disassemble the problem area for study, looking for reintegration. This may correspond to the "dead end" phenomena to be described in the chapter on creativity and refinement.

As we study program spaces, their assembly into larger units, the definition of relationships between each, and identification of associated activities, we find a hierarchy composed of first, building blocks with simple, well defined functions, followed by conceptualization of increasing complexity and abstraction. It is relatively easy to work

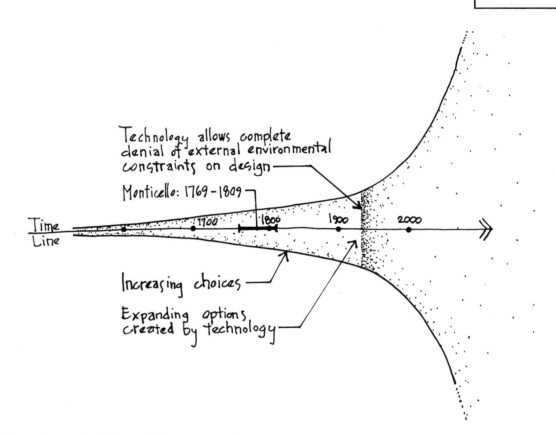

5-5: Technology is a fundamental player in the design process

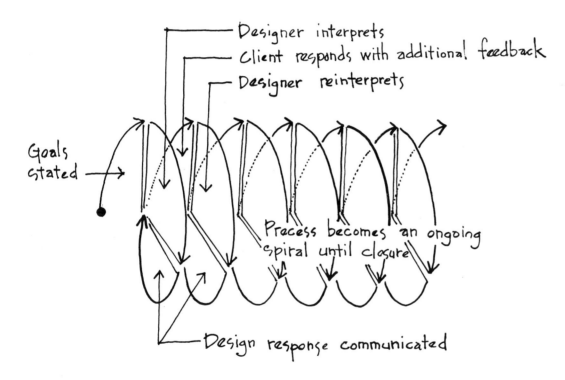

Designer interprets
Client responds with additional feedback
Designer reinterprets

Goals stated

Process becomes an ongoing spiral until closure

Design response communicated

5-6: Cycle of design, communication, and response

with a client and make a list of existing spaces and activities. To make that list into a fine design is quite a different story (5-6). Part of the solution, aside from decades of experience, is the practical listing of what a client has now and how she envisions her new facility coupled with a statement of goals: these aspirations may take the form of ideas such as increased productivity, embodied symbolism, history of a company, quality of environment, and untold numbers more. In my experience, building the conceptual bridge from the aspirations of the client to the designer sets up the opportunity for the resonance essential to quality design (5-7).

Limits: Functional and Economic

So far, we have studied the triad of basics, research, and program in a broad spectrum. One aspect of placing each activity in context has been implied but not fully explicated: understanding the limits inherent in each. With respect to building materials and systems knowledge, the physical limitations are fairly easy to grasp. They are a function of physics: cause and effect, thermodynamics, compression, and tension. Research is ultimately limited by the time available within the project budget, in respect of the fact that if we spend our fees learning about every last aspect of a building type, there will not be any money left to complete the remainder of the work. And as we briefly touch on the notion of money, we may also conveniently connect our fee structure to overall building cost and realize that part of the program document must include data on the ultimate limit for architecture: how much the client has to spend.

Ignoring the client's piggy bank has led many a designer down the path to disaster (5-8). It happened on a project I worked on in my first job. The office was delighted to be designing a high profile bank and office building, yet little effort was expended to ascertain what the final building would cost. We were well along in working drawings when someone from the construction manager's office put pencil to paper and determined that the building as designed would cost at least twice as much as the client had to spend. Within a month, my employer was fired from the job, highly embarrassed in both the community and the profession. As far as I know, there was little effort made by that office to realistically cost the design. Ultimately, disaster was the result. Understanding the fiscal limits of any project, from a single-family house to a billion-dollar high rise, is essential.

Concepts

The last step in the formative areas of the design process is concept development. We may derive our pathway to the first wisps of physical form through application of social, cultural, philosophical, contextual, precedent, or historical influences. These concerns grow directly from our understanding of client, site, research, and program. We compare our knowledge base, sifting and assembling myriad ideas in a search for resonance to structure a quality design. The conceptual choices we make become the jumping-off point for the elaboration of mass, organization, vocabulary, and future detail. As we continue in this vein, we shadow possible form translations with our understanding of the project

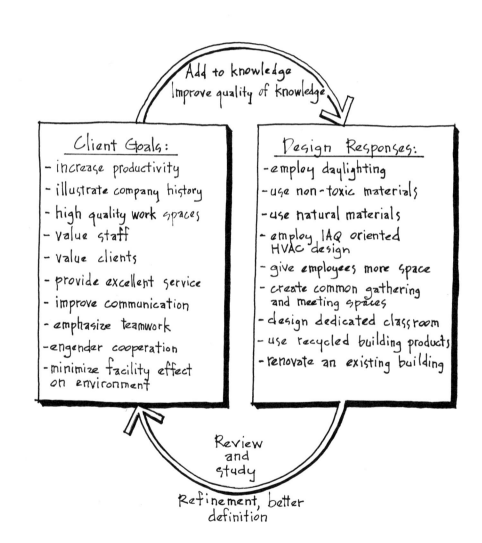

5-7: Client-designer resonance

budget. Care and attention inform the architecture and serve the best interest of our client as well.

Design is a scalar phenomenon that includes simple activities linked to a nearly infinite number of variables. A finished building or space is indicative of the long-term result of design process: closure at the largest scale. At the other extreme, the big picture acts simultaneously to distill the work into closing cycles of short duration, continuous throughout the process. These tiny representative microprocesses metamorphose into completed work for the designer to learn from, reflect upon, then set out again. Our preparations, via basic material and systems knowledge, research, and programming, allow us to engage the creative component of design with the sound underpinning essential to producing quality work (5-9,10,11).

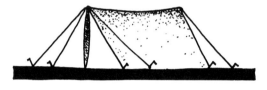

What the client
could afford

What was designed

5-8: Don't ever forget the monetary side of the design equation

Research Summary:

1. Information sources
-access to information and required time
-types and sources of information
-transforming information into knowledge
2. Building types
-history
-unique functional characteristics
3. Evolution of building types
-timeless relationships
-impact of technology
-culture: past and present
4. Mixed use structures
-combining multiple building types
-complex interrelationships
-potential conflict
5. Building examples
-study of drawings and photographs
-the value of an actual visit
6. Site research
-understanding building site & surroundings
-application of basic site knowledge
-potential sources of design vocabulary
7. Codes and zoning
-standards for life safety
-identifies minimums for construction and systems
-codes dedicated to standards for building
-zoning establishes urban relationships
8. Client research
-understanding needs and attitudes
-unique individuals requiring custom solutions

5-9: Research criteria summary

Programming Summary:

1. The client
-concerned with costs
-particular aesthetic preferences
-distinct functional problems to be solved
2. Communication
-study & assimilate existing conditions
-ask for ideas, needs, wants, even fantasies
-create an image book
-meet on the site to discuss the project
-establish a particapatory client relationship
-ask questions, questions, questions
-the designer is an interpreter, a translator
-the importance of verbal and written skill
-programs are not always written out
-a quality program is essential to a quality project
3. Multiple clients
-complex politics
-diffusion of responsibility
-consensus building becomes the designer's job
-the rules may be broken
4. A performance document
-an embryo of form and spatial relationships
-may be embedded or customized
-a separate phase of the work
-grounds the evolution of a design

5-10: Programming criteria summary

Concept Summary:

1. Symbolism
-building types and symbolic associations
-create a listing of symbols for a project
-choose a number of symbols to inform the design
-simplicity has value
-multiple, additive, and/or scalar concepts
2. Sources
-designer as source
-client as source
-site sources: immediate and surrounding vicinity
-culture should not be overlooked
-the building type and its attendant history
-do not forget the user
-collect and sift
-employ verbal and nonverbal study
-use language for organization
-use sketching for integration
-concepts are the ideas behind a project
3. Objective to subjective
-concept assembly begins the trip into creativity
-concepts may organize space and form
-concepts may suggest material, vocabulary
-check conceptual to functional "fit"
4. Changes
-change is inevitable
-objective changes may effect concept structure
-the importance of master principles
-design is a dynamic environment
-be prepared and remain flexible

5-11: Concept criteria summary

PART TWO

The Unknown

When we design, the mind is challenged with an incredible variety of problems. It is no surprise that the territory of creativity is mostly uncharted. We can say, however, that at this stage of the design process, the synthesis of basic knowledge, program, research, and concepts occurs full force. It must be understood that the business of design is undoubtedly complex. Yet, careful preparation in defining the nature of the problem will simplify the designer's task. Chaos in a project with no clear limits or definition will not yield a good solution. The seed of quality process is planted as the designer gains knowledge about all aspects of the task at hand. With a grasp of the initial requirements of a design, we can now work through approaches to enhance and help organize the creative process. Begin flexible, stay flexible, and persist.

CHAPTER 6

Sketching

The first half of this book has been devoted to preparation. The second half puts all the previously accumulated knowledge into use. The fine arts, crafts, and even sports are characterized by extensive preparation, both in school and in the real world. Individuals defined as excellent in each discipline share similar habits: they practice, work steadily, research the state of the art, and continue to learn. We have accumulated a vast pool of knowledge to begin designing a particular project. The very first step for most of us will be either putting pen to paper (6-1) or sitting down at a computer terminal (6-2). In either case the concept is the same. What we are beginning to do is sketch. Sketching is a prime tool. Many practitioners would probably argue that sketching is *the* tool for the production of most designs and built work of all kinds. If we embrace the previously mentioned notion of excellence, immediately we realize that practicing sketch technique is of critical importance. Most courses of instruction emphasize sketching of existing objects; buildings, natural features, and living things are typical subject matter. One of the leaps that occurs in the mentality of a designer is translating knowledge of drawing real objects into knowledge about how to draw from the mind's eye or imagination.

Tools

We refer to sketching as a tool, but we are still one step ahead. We must briefly consider what we sketch with: what are the fundamental tools of drawing? Generally, drawing tools take the form of physical devices like pen on paper and electronic media like

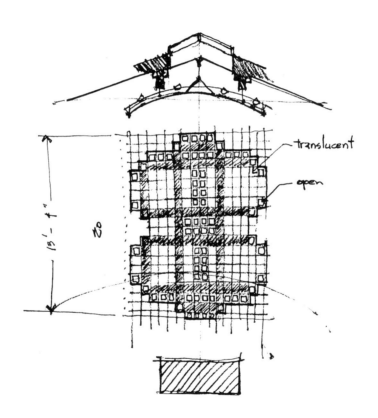

6-1: "Parasol" suspended light - Test House

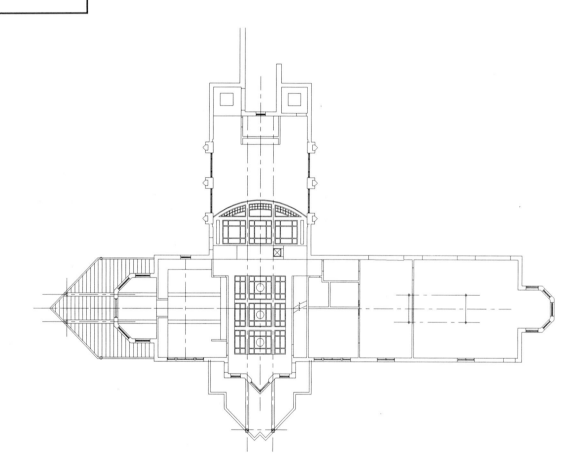

6-2: Reflected Ceiling Study - Test House

computer aided drafting systems. We design with these tools: their very use affects the design process. Hand drawing and computer media are the two current modes of graphic representation. A third system is under development even as this text is written. The next wave of electronic media for designers will be computer based virtual reality (VR) systems (6-3). Virtual reality will have many applications in business, communications, entertainment, science, art, and design.

...The idea of using architectural walk throughs as one of the "driving problems" for VR development is that the main thing architects do is envision models of three-dimensional structures. This is a complex cognitive and perceptual task, exactly the kind of problem that humans still solve better than computers... Because they spend a lot of time thinking about three dimensions, architects tend to have better skills at envisioning three-dimensional spaces from two-dimensional renderings. But there are many aspects of any design— the effects of different kinds of lighting on complex spaces, or acoustics, or seismic stress, for example—that are beyond the abilities of even the most skilled mental modeler. A three-dimensional model large enough to walk through could boost the architect's ability to conceive of three-dimensional spaces and could make it easier for

clients to understand something of what architects see in their imagination (Rheingold 1991).

Although virtual reality is taking shape in research laboratories and private industry, quite some time will pass before VR makes its way permanently into the day-to-day activities of the designer. Therefore, the physical and electronic media previously described will continue to be the mainstream choices of the vast majority of designers.

The traditional combination of pen and paper is nearly an archetypal example of the designer's tools. If we look at the nature and substance of drawing as a craft and how physical media affect design process, certain features of hand drawing are inherent: for example, it is time-intensive. Any developed level of detail commits us to a fairly long stint at the desk. Drawing is also a craft skill. The designer, through years of practice, develops a vast internalized knowledge about relationships between pressure and line weight, how fast the pencil moves, options for positioning the hand, how choice of paper affects the quality of drawing, and more. It is difficult, and in some cases impossible, for the designer to explain the subtleties of drawing by hand. We internalize this knowledge by doing. The choice of physical media affects how any sketch or study is perceived and judged. For example, we prepare a schematic perspective of a design idea in pencil, then carefully highlight the background with blue pastel chalk and overlay the major buildings faces with additional pastels. Pastel has the ability to be worked over the drawing below and

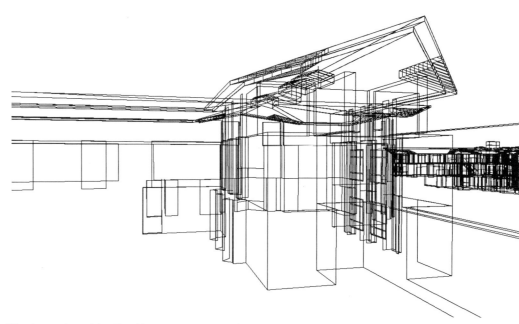

6-3: Wire frame view of the Test House

6-4: Porte Cochere addition to an existing corporate center

maintain transparency. Combining the two materials can yield a suitably "fuzzy" drawing with a good feel for design intent, (6-4,5) but lacking in significant detail (therefore taking less time).

Drawing is a mechanical process, and as a result, there is a consistent relationship between drawing size and time to completion. Large drawings require more time: we need to consider our intended result and adjust the drawing size to an appropriate scale. Results are not only dependent on size, but like the example in the previous paragraph, depend on intangible qualities related to our training, background, experience and prejudice. The word *style* seems to distill these intangible qualities into one idea for reflection. Style varies radically from person to person and often evolves over time. Do your drawings from five or ten years ago look like your work today? Four years ago, I had never touched a CAD system. Now I use a computer daily and agonize over the three dimensional possibilities of our in house system. My "drawings" no longer look like anything I prepared in the past because of the computer (6-6,7).

Using pen on paper, we are confronted with a purely two dimensional medium, but as we begin to use computers for drawing and design, we look into a three-dimensional electronic medium. As a simple drawing tool, the computer is as time-intensive as drawing by hand. Its advantages lie in its use as a media system. Electronics become a media chameleon creating:

—Sketches and schematics
—Three dimensional models

—Working drawings
—Word processing
—Desktop publishing
—Video animation and drawing

It is possible to obtain linkage between all these features. They are transparent, interchangeable, and may be combined to any end we see fit. This flexibility, combined with a knowledge of the equipment and an active imagination, yields a huge array of creative and timesaving possibilities. For example, the majority of high-end CAD applications now include modeling along with basic three dimensional wire framing which ties back into two dimensional drawing. These programs also are designed to allow the importation of word processor text from external sources. Conversely, word processing and desktop publishing systems typically incorporate the ability to import and place graphic drawing files. The computer will not replace drawing, but at a basic level transforms how the interaction between the mind and the tool take place.

Visualization

Our drawings are the external expression of an invisible mental process. In many ways, internal visualization is the genesis of design ideas. Therefore, actively using visualization reinforces the creative process expressed via drawing. Imagine a space you have experienced and particularly love. What makes it great? What did the space sound, smell, feel like? Set aside a little time each day. Start with just five minutes: you will be surprised at how long (and short) the time can be. Then exercise your

6-5: Loggia and entry alternate for an existing corporate center

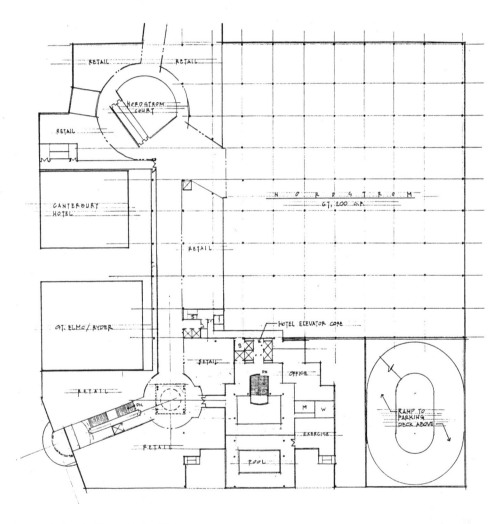

6-6: Hand sketch, Circle Centre Mall

imagination (6-8 through 12). I have been lucky enough to imagine spaces of elegant beauty, and saddened by the fact that they will never be built. We all have the ability to imagine literally unlimited possibilities. How much would the built environment benefit through a careful, continuing application of the power an active imagination can wield? Five minutes, or whatever amount of time you can make available, will energize the basis for each design you conceive. I close my eyes and visualize a new space. My next step is to draw this vision. As this process proceeds, we find that the development of a particular design proceeds from broad notions down through to details as the solution unfolds.

I am presenting the shell of a process concept. The linear nature of reading makes the presentation *appear* linear. It is not. This book does not have to be read from beginning to end in order to provide insight. If we approach a design from a base of general ideas, we find an implied bias toward the "big picture." The general trend is to work from the largest elements of a design through a series of refinements. At each stage, we elaborate a slightly higher level of detail. A rule is implied in this statement: that design proceeds from big pieces that are separated, crafted, defined, and detailed to make a building. In the most general sense, this is probably true. However, we must ask: will we be rule-guided or rule-governed? There is a subtle but significant difference. As we design, the best solution may not evolve from a strict adherence to the big to small sequence. If our process is solely governed by an inflexible rule, then each choice faces automatic limitations as it proceeds through to success or failure. We must select A or B, up or down, good or bad. If instead we approach design from a rule guided viewpoint, a constant variety of options are sought: A, B, C, D, L, Q, or Z becomes available. It seems our chance of success rises exponentially, does it not?

Starting a design exploration at the extreme level of detail is another possibility. Perhaps the client has a preference for a particular letter or symbol, which could become the basis for a piece of ceramic tile, a wainscot, a column capitol, on the building plan or section. Each beginning suggests myriad possibilities as we translate our interior vision into graphic form (6-13).

As you experiment consciously with imagination and visualization as a source for design ideas, some inherent problems will surface. One of the most difficult aspects of sketching from the mind's eye is conflicting scale and how the designer controls the mental image compared to an actual measured drawing or sketch in progress. Imagination does not readily grasp defined scale and allow the "pilot," if you will, complete control as he or she imagines a space. A space, or elements and their interrelationships within an imagined space, may conflict when rendered graphically. This discovery is often quite annoying, especially after what appeared to be an initial flash of brilliance provided by imagination. However, a conflict at hand does not imply failure. Using imagination as a creative tool requires care. For example, create a mental space 40 feet by 20 feet in plan and 20 feet high with a mezzanine at plus 10 feet. We decide to place a stair

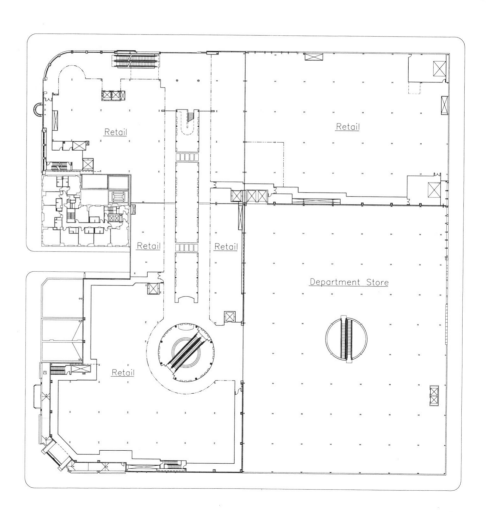

6-7: CADD Schematic, Circle Centre Mall—Centre Venture Architects, copyright City of Indianapolis 1993

6-8: Marina Project

6-9: Marina Project

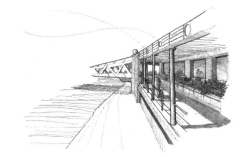

6-10: Marina Project

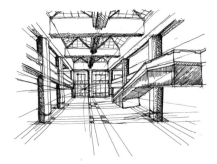

6-11: Ballroom Space study

6-12: The "Flying House"

to the mezzanine on the far wall (6-14). If the stair is parallel to our view, will it fit? Logic, math, and some basic knowledge of building codes can assist at this point. Ten feet from floor to mezzanine is 120 inches divided by 7 inches per riser equals 17.14 risers rounded up to 18 risers at 6 5/8 inches each. This leaves us 17 treads at 11 inches for a total stair run of 187 inches or 15 feet 7 inches. If the stair is 4 feet wide, a four foot landing at top and bottom totals 23 feet 7 inches. Therefore, the mental space is too narrow. So we increase the plan size to 24 feet by 40 feet. Now we can sketch our plan idea, test its success in relation to additional criteria, and try other options such as spiral stairs or a straight stair run parallel to the room's long axis.

We may practice our craft using imagination fueled via sketching and vice versa. We act as creative detectives and look for "evidence" suggesting solutions, materials, spaces, and options. Often, speed becomes an issue. In a charette, or whenever time is limited, the ability to quickly sift and assemble ideas is an invaluable asset. With this in mind, I often use the following approach to obtain reasonably accurate scale drawings quickly in sketch form. Draw a grid in pencil and determine an equal dimension for each grid section. If we assign an arbitrary dimension of 1 inch to each grid segment, the work will be at a high level of detail (6-15). Conversely, if we assign a dimension of 20 feet, we are ready to study a site. With the grid drawn, it is now possible to develop a sketch with some measure of confidence as to its scale. Also, Mylar and vellum sheets of varying sizes are manufactured with a nonprint grid that can assist in preparing sketches.

Plans

Designers seem to prefer to begin their solutions by laying out potential plans (6-16). How plan arrangements fit together is a careful balance of the internal, external, and physical factors identified in Part One. Beginning with a layout of a potential plan, placing large functional pieces in relationships that make sense for adjacencies and general circulation is an acceptable approach to diagrams solving internal requirements. One way to approach design process is to imagine the scheme as successful but undifferentiated, a spatial solid to be sculpted into a solution. In concept, we begin to mentally sculpt, separate, and reassemble this mental clay. Loose parallels can be drawn between the development of biological life from fertilization to birth. Biological differentiation is both similar and dissimilar to the design process in terms of concrete physical comparisons, but conceptually they are equivalent. Each is creative and follows a pattern from formlessness to a complete, detailed "organism." Designs tend to grow and become more elaborate as they move toward integration.

Keeping a biological viewpoint, the first step in development includes dividing the design into major functional pieces. Plan iterations beginning with diagrams allow some preliminary choices about general organization and adjacencies. Designs often require many different plan levels. The result is an immediate demand to think in three dimensions. Suddenly, we have cycled back to the rich landscape of imagination. Frank Lloyd Wright was attributed with this observation regarding his designs: consider the space first, and craft the interior/

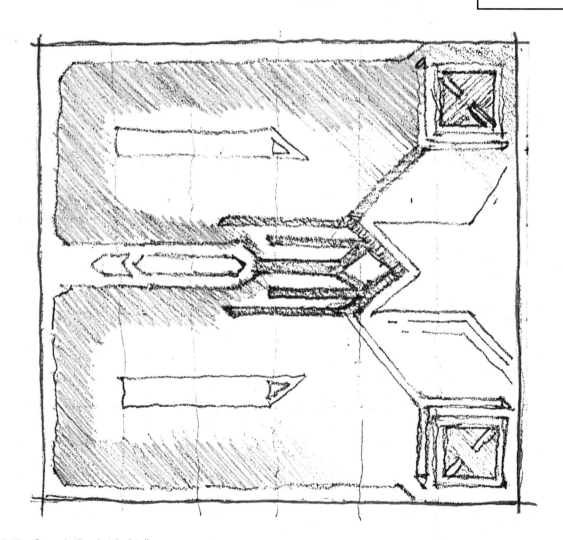

6-13: Ceramic tile sketch detail

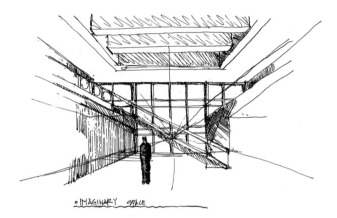

• IMAGINARY SPACE

6-14: Visualization experiment

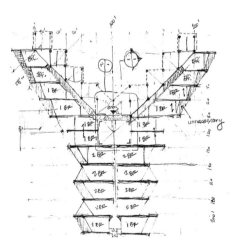

6-15: Pencil grid for more accurate quick sketching

enclosure to match a vision of what each space in a design should accomplish. The idea of what is inside, the negative or void we inhabit as opposed to the positive structure of any design, is often referenced in the available literature. But a thorough review of negative space's value as a reversal of the standard approach for developing a design solution is seldom stressed. An interesting resonance begins to emerge. On the one hand, using visualization tends toward the three-dimensional and therefore creates an automatic bias towards considering a design from the standpoint of negative space. On the other hand, as we sketch, the drawing medium creates lines and reinforces the positive, concrete elements of a design.

Sections and Elevations

After an initial plan concept is developed, take several sections to begin differentiating shapes of the various spaces (6-17 through 19). Trade orientations between plan and section on paper and in imagination as well. Look for both synergy and conflicts between working relationships. Spend extra time studying the section diagrams and think about negative space and how light, both natural and artificial, will affect your creation. What might it look like at night from the inside; from the outside? Sections allow us to address more than just the proposed profile a space might take. With reference back to the plan(s), one-point perspectives are fairly easy to create and contemplate (6-20). A section also creates the opportunity to sketch interior elevations. We continue this reflective process: aspects of plans and sections are studied simultaneously.

We refer back to conceptual guidelines, physical constraints, and programmatic constraints. At each point, we check for agreement or conflict, then determine our relative level of success. As we spend more effort considering sections and the spaces these profiles create, we generally begin to fold in possibilities for exterior elevations. Keep in mind, plans organize spatial and activity relationships. Sections and elevations are what we see. The finest plan, solving every functional requirement, will be an unmitigated disaster without concurrent attention devoted to sections and elevations. Therefore, even in the highly variable context of solving a design problem, we can successfully conclude that a balanced study of plans, sections, and elevations is essential to a quality solution.

With experience, many criteria, overwhelming when first introduced to the novice, become internalized. A transition from explicit to implicit occurs. Parallels can be drawn between acquisition of craft knowledge and the internalization of design criteria. This may be especially pronounced at firms with design specialties. A new employee or a student fresh out of school will struggle with the learning curve required for a brand new building type. Over time, the various team members come to share a body of knowledge about a particular type of building, and this unspoken agreement guides their work.

Design Constraints

As we saw in Part One, literally thousands of criteria may bear on any given design problem. The volume of information can be staggering. Given this diffi-

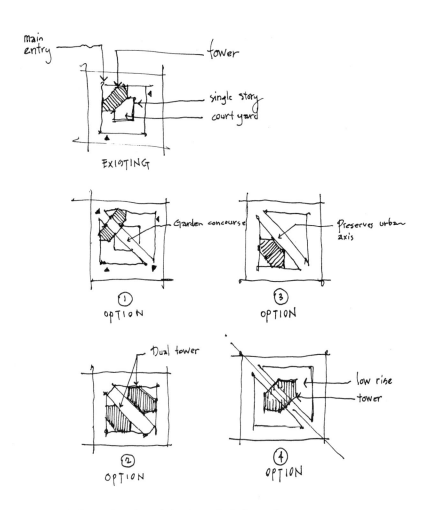

6-16: Additional plan options for existing tower in Indianapolis, Indiana (existing as shown in first sketch, top left)

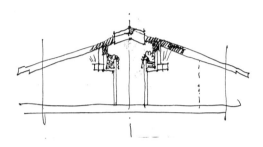

6-17: Section of corridor - Upper level of Test House

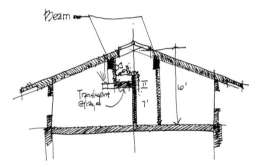

6-18: Section integrating structure, planter - Test House

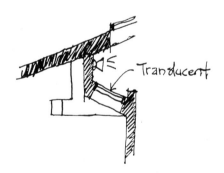

6-19: Section at glazing - Test House

culty, designers may tend to sift and identify a key issue to guide a design's growth.

> *These early ideas, primary generators or organizing principles sometimes have an influence which stretches throughout the whole design process and is detectable in the solution (Lawson 1990).*

A design proper may be thought of as a core or center point. Surrounding this center are multiple partial spheres of influence (6-21). Each has a varying density depending on the strength of constraint. The design reaches from the center point and engages the various constraints. Designs may be crafted in as many ways as there are people to address any given problem. Primary choices about how a design engages constraints will guide a solution. We have made various observations about the essential relationships between sketching, visualization, and constraints. I have always struggled with what I call first solution preference. I would strongly recommend the designer strive to create more than one solution, a minimum of two and preferably three. Why? Because the struggle to generate the secondary and tertiary solutions is like digging further in a mine shaft. As we get deeper, a secondary line of creativity may show itself and lead into a new level of quality. How do we break a first solution preference? Initiating an alternate approach to the problem may generate the beginnings of a new scheme. Here are several suggestions from a multitude of possibilities and options:

—Select a new organizing principle.
—Sketch in negative space only.
—Work from a different viewpoint: say, sections only for awhile.
—Study one aspect or constraint: natural light, for example.
—Ask questions; be critical.
—Consider other disciplines' constraints.
—Consciously design in a different style.
—Ask a child.
—Work in a new medium: marker instead of a razor point; watercolor instead of pencil.
—Employ a creativity tool like the Creative Whack Pack *(6-22).*

Sometimes our internal dialogue in the creation of any level of solution can become strained: talk to other designers and to people in related disciplines such as engineering or interior design because their problem solving perspective varies, and as a result, may provide additional insight.

Comparison and Review

The first concentrated round of mental hand wringing is over: we, in principle, now have multiple solutions, ideas, and approaches for a given design. A careful and serious review of the attributes, advantages, and disadvantages of each solution should be undertaken. We create a sort of mental ledger or balance sheet. One side will be positive, the other negative. What does each scheme do well? What

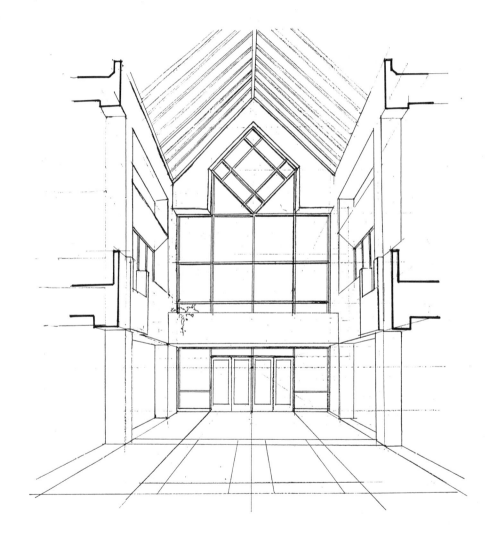

6-20: Section developed into one point perspective

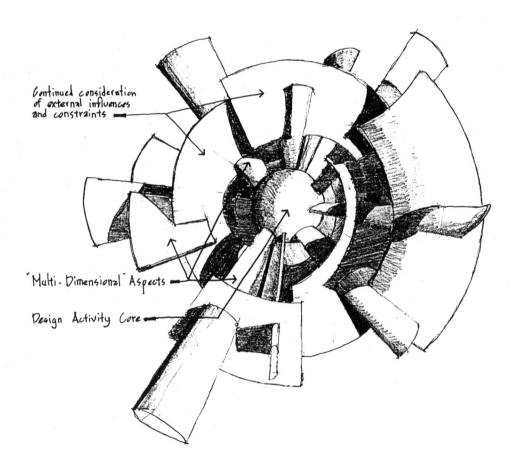

Continued consideration
of external influences
and constraints

"Multi-Dimensional" Aspects

Design Activity Core

6-21: Spheres of influence

does each scheme do poorly? Do any of the schemes suffer from a fatal flaw? Do any of the solutions stand out among the others? What appears to be a promising idea may often benefit greatly from hybridization with features from another scheme. Scheme A has a great entrance; scheme B contains a successful master bedroom suite. Does their combination create a better solution than either of the original ideas? We proceed from the loosest notion of a design through the beginning of schematics that appear to solve the majority of critical constraints. We have created plans, sections, and elevations. The next litmus test is to create "thumbnail" perspective sketches. The scale may be adjusted to embrace a range of size from overall massing to particular details of interest to the designer. There is an advantage in making small sketches, derived from the size of the drawing. As we mentioned previously, larger drawings take more time; smaller drawings are less demanding. Also, detail begins to be limited by the medium itself. This is good because we are still in schematics, and "nuts and bolts" generally should not come into consideration until the design is more refined. If we are comfortable with our plans, sections, elevations, and thumbnail sketches, we proceed to the next level of detail.

Sketching encompasses many activities; degree and intensity vary. Discovery, conflict, synthesis, and synergism are all process activities. One series of events that we experience in varying order are assembly, failure, anxiety, reassembly, partial success, reflection, and inspiration. A designer's sketches are a visible record of his or her initial approaches to problem solving. Depending on graphic approach, a fair portion of the design process may be visible for consideration. This visibility is a curious glimpse into the designer's mind. The iterative nature of design provides clues for novice and seasoned practitioner alike. Creativity and judgment are intertwined at each step. Breakthrough or disaster always looms just around the corner. We begin to discover that the design process is not neat. In practice, it often skirts division and confuses categorization. We see that as we sketch, we tap and develop the designer's primary creative tool.

6-22: Cards form the *Creative Whack Pack* by Roger von Oech

CHAPTER 7

Modeling

As our designs continue to be studied and differentiated, one valuable method for promoting their evolution is the creation of study models. At this point, we do not want to confuse marketing or presentation models with the study model approach. Study models are yet another tool to enhance communication, available for presentation to a client as needed, but even more useful in assisting the designer as he or she begins the translation of ideas, needs, and goals into space (7-1 through 3). A designer begins making models early on, especially to address the general issues of site and building shape. This kind of experimental form giving helps address a variety of issues, including views to and from a site, relationships with other structures, visibility, and general massing. Such a model may be based on as little information as a gross square footage, outline program, and a potential site. We will focus on models for use during schematics to help the designer see the three-dimensional implications of our two-dimensional graphic studies.

Modeling and Sketching

Up to this point, we have spent a tremendous amount of time thinking in three dimensions and sketching in two. In principle, we should have the beginnings of a working plan. These statements imply that we sketch, then model. However, modeling can run parallel to sketching from the outset of any design effort: the choice of approach is solely up to the designer. In essence, the time is always ripe to build an approximation of what we have in mind. The miniature construction of a project allows a design to move into three dimensions straight off. You, as

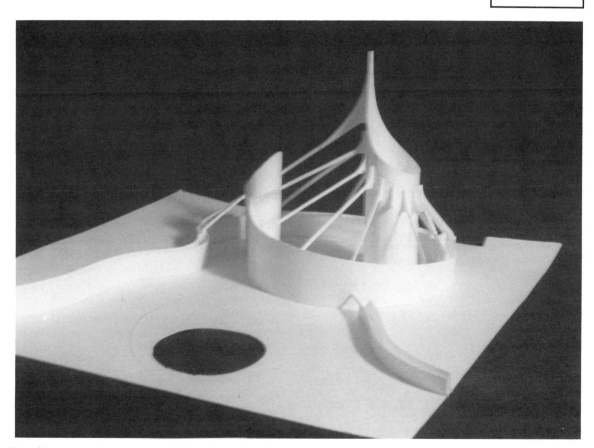

7-1: Church massing study, model and photo by Mark Platt

7-2: Elevator screen study model by CSO Architects, photo by Mark Platt

the designer, can now see possible forms. This allows a visual, and tactile response to these newly created volumes and their intersections.

Internal visualization without a three-dimensional reference, for most designers, often leads to and exacerbates errors in size and space relationships. Models help avoid these problems, as they assist and enhance visualization. The construction of a model may also identify an unanticipated conflict that previously was not apparent in plan, section, or elevation. As a design evolves, so may the models employed to support the overall process. The first studies are relatively crude masses that inform the broadest level of site concerns. As we begin to lay out more plans and sections, we have the opportunity to, in principle, carve away at the initial solid masses. At this point, the model materials change from masses to planar or linear forms. We begin to build the walls, cut experimental openings, and consider roof lines, skylights, and interior voids. A model of a room or group of rooms may be instructive. Building a model of a section profile illustrating the general line of the interior space and simultaneously integrating it with a complementary exterior form may be illuminating as well. As a design continues to obtain additional layers of detail, corresponding models will probably assist in improving the work at more than one level. What we model is limited only by our imaginations and the particular goal at hand.

Models and Clients

Our clients are also the beneficiaries of three-dimensional studies. Most people are unfamiliar with reading drawings. Reading certain plans, sections, and elevations can be difficult even for a seasoned designer. Models help the client begin to understand a design's evolving form. In addition, a model in conjunction with drawings will lend greater comprehension of the various views we have chosen to draw. In general, plans, elevations, and sections are often vexing to the untrained eye. The wide variety of graphic techniques used by designers, some quite excellent and some done in extreme haste, further confuse the client's chance of understanding a design. The vagaries of line weight, shading, and scale, although familiar to designers, often appear more like a form of abstract art to the layperson. Drawings and models are synergistic communication tools. A client may actually pick up a model, hold it close, and peek into any number of potential views while simultaneously comparing it to the corresponding drawings.

When a design begins to come together, there is a certain inherent excitement on the designer's side of the fence. Clients will find this "electricity" more contagious if they are provided with the opportunity to more fully understand what the designer has in mind. There is a flip side to this scenario too: if your client does not like what she sees, you will be returning to the office to rethink what needs to be done. As a general rule, a designer does not face total rejection of a scheme. However, with the dynamic climate inherent in design, a proposal seldom leaves a thorough review unchanged. In the overall view of bringing a project to fruition, it is better to suffer a setback early on and correct it than to complete the contract documents

7-3: Facade study model by CSO Architects, photo by Mark Platt

7-4: CAD model of the Anhui International Trade Center at night, Hefei, Anhui Province, People's Republic of China by The Stubbins Associates-Architects, Cambridge, Massachusetts

and show the final rendering or model to the client only to be told that extensive rework is necessary at your cost. The potential margin for error is much smaller when a client sees a model, reacts, and provides immediate feedback.

Relying solely on drawings for presentation, because of time or budget constraints, clearly has its pitfalls. Earlier I mentioned the notion of models being built to follow the evolution of a project. Although one model may be sufficient for a presentation, having a number of models available may be even more valuable. When it is time to meet with the client, take the study models, put them in a box, and bring them along. They help every participant in a project every step of the way.

Color

An often neglected but critically important aspect of design is color. It is possible to use study models to create and review proposed color schemes in miniature. For example, by using typing paper as a base we can color an exterior elevation, interior wall, or whatever is appropriate at the time. Then we cut the miniature rendering out and apply it to get a feel for our ideas. In addition, photography may be used to address both color and material.

Photographic techniques are used by model makers...A marble facade, for example, can be represented by a photograph of a real marble slab that is then reduced and reprinted on paper with an adhesive backing that can be attached to the model. Likewise, in interior models a carpet with a texture that is especially difficult to reproduce or a wall paper with distinctive patterning might best be represented through photography (Busch 1991).

Another approach to both renderings and color studies is to project slides of a model onto paper, and to draw the image. Using vellum or Mylar allows us to run blueline or blackline copies and color to our heart's content.

Color not only affects the psychology and feel of our buildings but may also directly influence the perception of form. Dark colors make objects and spaces appear smaller; light colors make these same objects and spaces appear larger. The psychology and perception of color is a subject in and of itself, with several excellent books available. Any designer will be well served by an inquiry into the nature of color, including knowledge of color symbolism, interaction, false perspective, and illusion. It is also interesting to note that color symbolism varies from culture to culture.

The use of indigo as a dye is so old and so widespread that cultural traditions have grown up around its use everywhere, many of them calling upon blue's preponderance in the environment in water and sky. In China blue was associated with the east, and in Tibet, with the south. In Japan blue connoted spring and also victory in battle. Because blue was thought to keep poison-

7-5: CAD model of the Anhui International Trade Center during daytime, Hefei, Anhui Province, People's Republic of China by The Stubbins Associates-Architects, Cambridge, Massachusetts

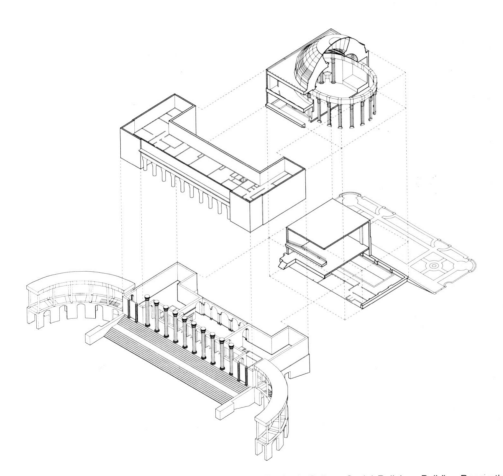

7-6: CAD wireframe model of the Vanderbilt University, Peabody College Social Religious Building Renovation and Addition, Nashville, Tennessee, by The Stubbins Associates-Architects, Cambridge, Massachusetts

ous snakes at bay in Japan, it was often used for work and traveling clothes. The Egyptians, who used indigo as early as 4500 B.C., colored the sheets used to wrap mummies blue (Stockton 1983).

If we were preparing a commission abroad, we would be well advised to gain knowledge about color and its symbolism in the culture that would be the recipient of our skills.

Model Construction

Study models need to be built quickly: designers seldom have sufficient time to do all the drawings needed, let alone models. Regardless of the demands of each deadline, the value of models within the design process is certainly proven. So how do we take advantage of modeling, yet avoid spending hard-earned fees? First, the materials chosen for the model are absolutely critical. Lightweight paper stocks like oak tag (manila file folder paper), construction paper, typing paper, and poster board allow us a wide range of material options that are simultaneously easy to fabricate. Clay and styrofoam blocks for massing studies may allow an extremely quick study to be completed. Size is also an issue because, just like a drawing, a larger model uses more material and takes longer to build. Therefore, study models should be fairly small. As a general rule of thumb, the model should fit on an 18" x 24" base at the largest, with 11" x 17" or smaller even more desirable. These sizing constraints are not hard and fast by any stretch of the imagination, but are merely presented as a guide. The primary criterion is to balance the demands of available time against having a physical representation of the design solution.

Another way to construct study models is within the environment of the computer (7-4 through 8). There are advantages and drawbacks to computer modeling. On the positive side, if we are already working on computer, we work directly with our design in progress. The drawing files are downloaded into the modeling program and no additional construction tools are required. If the client comes to our office, we can show them the model on screen taking any view as appropriate. If our meeting is away, we need a portable computer or to print out a number of views for our client. It is important to bear in mind, buildings become physical realities: things we can touch. The computer, regardless of its power and potential realism, does not provide that hands-on experience. However, the computer model, once "built," is both an interior and exterior representation of a design. A physical model, on the other hand, is hard pressed to become both. Plus, the computer model can be further developed and detailed as a project proceeds. I believe there is a place for both options in our process, but like so much of design, our choices are influenced by available equipment, time, and context. Ultimately, the computer may provide more advantages than disadvantages as we seek a timely methodology for the creation of study models.

Models in Context

We always want and intend to build models. The reality is that tight budgets coupled to tighter dead-

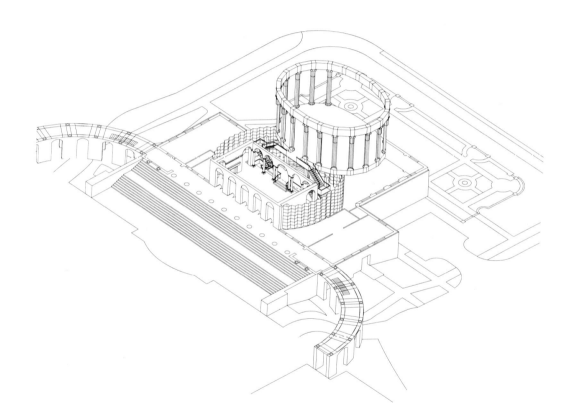

7-7: CAD wireframe model of the Vanderbilt University, Peabody College Social Religious Building Renovation and Addition, Nashville, Tennessee, by The Stubbins Associates-Architects, Cambridge, Massachusetts

7-8: Rendered CAD model of the Vanderbilt University, Peabody College Social Religious Building Renovation and Addition, Nashville, Tennessee, by The Stubbins Associates-Architects, Cambridge, Massachusetts

lines sometimes push the modeling option to the side. When a time crunch looms, pen or pencil on paper becomes the refuge of choice. Like so much of design, the need to model serves many possible ends. As a result, we need to gain an appreciation of what our models are for. When we consider our client, we need to ask if they are graphically literate: a bank's board of directors is probably hopelessly confused by plans and sections, while a project manager for a major developer may know more about building than the architect sitting across the table. The project itself will begin to bring the need for models into sharper focus. A $250,000 shopping center is not likely to have modeling as part of its design process (although you are certainly welcome to build models if you like). Conversely, a high-rise in a major urban center will benefit from the application of a variety of modeling techniques including study and presentation models (7-9).

The proposed site may also determine the decision of whether modeling is a necessity or not. If a site is in a city or on complex terrain or if the design has specific concerns with views to and from a parcel of land, the result may be the need for a site model ready to accept possible building forms. Obviously, materials for site models need to have some thickness to account for topographic variations within the existing site, if any. Thicker materials such as mat board tend to be difficult to cut and time consuming as well. Other materials like foam core have thickness, but the foam center makes them easy to cut.

If we build models to supplement our drawings, a dialogue begins to emerge from the abstractions we create on paper or computer and the tiny physical simulations that we build. Ideas grow from the sketches, while a model gives them form. The model forces the abstractions of design into a different medium, closer to reality. Each model may support original design ideas, identify conflicts, or suggest new avenues of inquiry. These notions feed the continuing design process. Models assist in the internal process of design, supporting our efforts toward effective communication with our peers and clients. The experience of making buildings and space tells us that the knowledge that our clients have about architecture, building type, and site is tightly bound to our personal comfort level within the process: the design quality we are capable of achieving without the use of models. I believe the majority of practitioners would derive tangible benefits from modeling in the course of developing schematics and beyond until the design is well defined, both in the mind of the designer and of the client. Generally, once a project is at the stage of working drawings, the need for study models is minimized. But while we are embroiled in translating program and design ideas into possible forms, building models becomes an invaluable tool throughout the early phases of a project, adding richness and quality to the activity of design.

7-9: Study model of Rincon Center, San Francisco, by Johnson Fain & Pereira Associates

CHAPTER 8

Creativity and Refinement

The essence of creativity has defied quantitative analysis for decades. In fact, the scientific community has expended relatively small effort to illuminate this realm.

> *The creative process has been the subject of a great deal of intriguing speculation but very little research, and for good reason: part of the process—very likely the most important part—takes place outside consciousness and can neither be described by the persons in whose minds it happens nor observed by others. The product of the unconscious cerebration emerges into the light of consciousness, but what takes place in the dark before that emergence remains unknown; cognitive scientists, thus far, can only speculate and make a few inferences about those unseen events (Hunt 1982).*

Just what makes a creative mind remains a conundrum (8-1). Personally, I rather enjoy the fact that such a mystery continues to elude the realm of science. In architecture, the quest for new ground and distinctive solutions seems to constantly dance above and below the consciousness of the designer.

I contend that a good portion of the activity expended from the very first moments in the life of a design are creative. The effort of designing space and creating buildings proper is circular and open-ended. (Cuff 1991) We may spend as little or as much time as we are able to integrate a solution, but

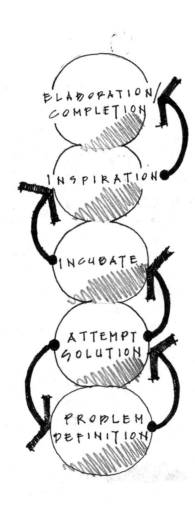

8-1: An oversimplified diagram of the creative process

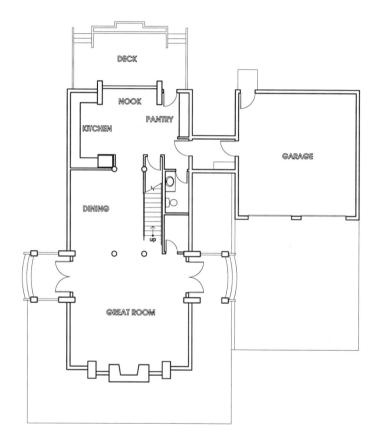

FIRST FLOOR PLAN STUDY

8-2: House plan sketch study (early CAD schematic)

the time required to arrive at a workable scheme always seems to exceed what we had originally planned. Real-world commitments with respect to a project's budget will constrain the ultimate amount of effort possible. Of course, if we truly believe that maximum effort is necessary, we can forego sleep and charrette until we drop; however, there is a point of diminishing returns. Creativity and the generation of options are time-dependent. That is, regardless of what we are designing, simply to prepare the drawings and models associated with a scheme will demand a given volume of time plus the effort required for exploration of options prior to focusing in on what appears to be the best solution.

Dead Ends

The issue of time becomes critically important when our search for a successful design stalls: the dead end. We reach these impasses most often when a design is in its infancy. Schematics are the trial runs without guaranty of integration. In addition, we may quickly assemble a scheme, then while presenting what we have in mind have our client react and revise the constraints, add some new twist, just plain not like the work, or change the scope of the project. The circular pattern described previously develops and becomes a constant. It is not unusual for any of the new parameters to force a violent shift in one of the root concepts of a design. These root or guiding ideas are often difficult to release, as they are not only ideas but form givers as well.

We may redefine our notion of a design at a variety of points during a project. In sketching the first ideas for a solution, it may become obvious that little is emerging from our "concept engine," and each avenue we try evolves slowly, then staggers to a halt. When we circle around a problem in this manner, we have yet to achieve the synthesis leading separate ideas to closure in possible built form. One approach that can be very useful is to carefully pick apart what we have and ask questions about what is and is not successful. Bear in mind, it is extremely unusual to face an insoluble problem. If such is the case, then something is amiss in the program and needs to be ferreted out, then eliminated or redefined.

Besides the political and interpersonal conflicts possible in any design effort, the designer faces the program and her own internalized design prejudice. We seek to express a personal vision which coincides with the design challenge. Our intentions often do not fit the relationships identified as essential. Conflicts that stonewall the process can be surmounted in a variety of ways. We can shift plan relationships or change approach, emphasis, and especially *artificial constraints* that designers tend to use in an effort to shape building and spatial forms (8-2). Often, difficulty may center on an artificial constraint. The task is to recognize the situation, scrutinize options, then create a way to remove or redefine the constraint (8-3).

If a design is stuck in a cycle of little or no progress, we may benefit from taking a break and setting the work aside. Perhaps we can work on another aspect of the design or think about the site plan or detailing. Another project may be in need of attention and consideration. We may also take what we have put down so far and share it with others

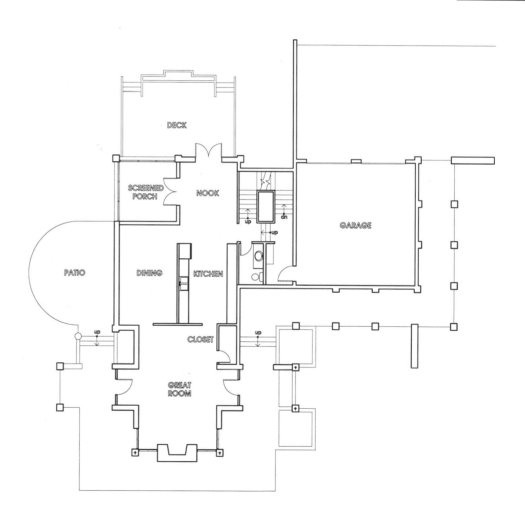

8-3: House plan sketch study with constraints revised—stairway taken out of the main mass and moved to the garage connector

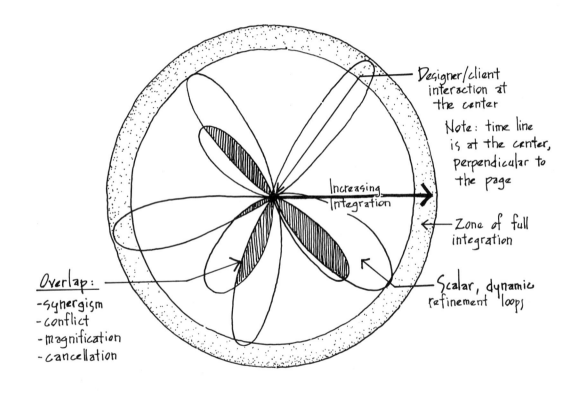

Designer/client
interaction at
the center

Note: time line
is at the center,
perpendicular to
the page

Increasing
Integration

Zone of full
integration

Overlap:
-synergism
-conflict
-magnification
-cancellation

Scalar, dynamic
refinement loops

8-4: Refinement loop diagram

for a different perspective in hopes of breaking our mental "log jam."

Subconscious Mind

As we reflect on the intricacies of our craft, the sheer volume of information and problem complexity leads us to consider the importance of the subconscious mind in design. Without reference to any empirical evidence, relying on the testimony of my peers and my own experience, I believe that the subconscious is very important, if not essential, to the process of design. A method for fully engaging the subconscious lies in the effort to saturate the mind with data pertaining to a project. It is not unusual for this point of saturation to coincide with our dead end. At this point, we will set the work aside and let our subconscious gnaw on the apparent design paradox.

Our internal deliberations synthesize the data we collect, then using our graphic skills, we transform these myriad ingredients into a proposed design. The transition from not having a solution to a working scheme may take many forms, depending on the project and the experience of the designer. Occasionally, the problem may be especially difficult and frustrating, compounded by a lack of sufficient time. Some of us find that sudden inspiration wells up from our unconscious after working on a problem for a while: the subconscious may present a design solution in minute detail. Or, the design solution may come about in a simple step-by-step pattern as we work through a scheme. In another light, the transit to a working scheme may require a methodical, almost tedious attention to the assembly of many ideas jigsawed together. The subconscious is the organizer, the field that floats our conscious efforts. When conscious effort fails, yet the goal and commitment remain, the unconscious takes over to assimilate and reveal a solution.

Continual Discovery

Our creative efforts are inevitably bound up in the real-world constraints imposed by each project. Progress from the program and initial design concepts proceeds on many fronts at differing levels. One way to think of the combined activities in a project is to imagine a varying number of refinement loops: parallel tracks running simultaneously. Each loop is a microprocess addressing some aspect of a design with relationships between loops and the intent of designer and client. The loops themselves are dynamic, and change in relative size and importance depending on the status of the project and focus of the designer and client (8-4). Refinement proceeds in fits and starts, moving ahead in one area, sometimes lagging in another. In addition, there is an ongoing process of constant discovery. (Cuff 1991) New information is continually revealed as the design is studied by the architect, client, and others (8-5). The center point for these activities is the relationship between the designer and client, which moves through the continuous dynamic of time. We use the tools of communication, both verbal and written, sketching, drawing, and model making to shape and evolve the architecture. And we find that we continually use our communication skills as we respond to the influences that focus or frustrate the elaboration of the design. Lastly, the

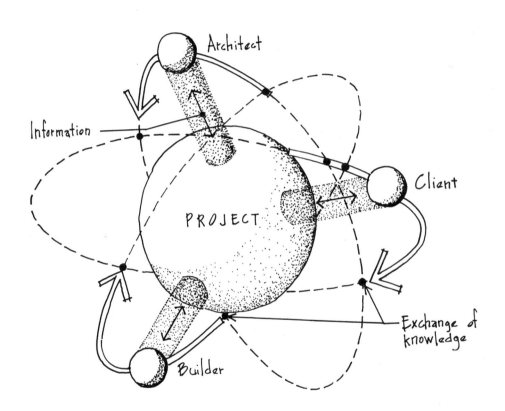

8-5: Continual discovery

8-6: Exterior elevation of Rincon Center by Johnson Fain & Pereira Associates, Los Angeles

overarching connecting concept is the designer's creativity used as an applied skill in this context.

Tangibles and Intangibles

The influences on a loop may take both tangible and intangible form. Tangible aspects include any of the physical forms we know such as site concerns and context. A more subtle and interesting area for study resides in the area of intangible effects. Politics, in both the relationship between designer and client and project to community, may play a large role in the design of a project. For example, Rincon Center in San Francisco is a large mixed-use project that had to answer to concerns beyond the goals of the architects and developers (8-6). The city of San Francisco and its agencies were actively involved in the design process. A brief example is instructive:

> *Both the architect and the developers were chafing over the extensive and, in their minds, intrusive involvement of the redevelopment agency staff. One of the most significant and stubborn debates was over the color and density of the glass for the curtain wall. The developers wanted gray glass and the redevelopment officials wanted light green glass. They were very alarmed that the gray would be a dark and dull blot on the city's skyline. And anyway, there were no gray-glass buildings in San Francisco, a fact that caused the bureaucrats untold consternation. The decision had been made that the only*

way to resolve the debate was to set up a display of the actual types of glass proposed for the curtain wall. Then maybe the staff could be persuaded that the color and density of the gray were acceptable and the project could move forward (Frantz 1991).

The example above shows us an interesting and not uncommon situation. Not only do we see that outside forces may affect the design of a project, but also that an exterior conflict on some aspect of a design decision can *stop* or significantly hinder a project. The idea of creativity begins to take a new shape as the designer transcends the need to simply craft material and space. The issue metamorphosizes into what will be required to convince a third party that our vision is legitimate and appropriate.

Each player acting on the design process is possessed of a special "world view." This is a personal notion of what a project's primary issues are. From the standpoint of the designer, a knowledge of these prejudices has practical value (8-7). I will make an effort to identify some of these concerns, but I must stress that there is little substitute for experience in these matters. First, the goals of the designer are numerous, but for the sake of brevity let us say that quality of space and its experience by the user are fundamental concerns. A developer may be little concerned with anything but profits and costs. Consultants bring a specialized and sometimes narrow view of priorities, focusing on certain systems or functions. The best of each party is the individual who can successfully view the context of

Owner:
"I never thought I'd be so excited and terrified at the same time."

Designer:
"I'd better start talking to these people and gauge their reactions."

Facilities manager:
"Will the exterior materials need a lot of maintenance?"

Engineer:
"How am I going to make the framing work?"

Construction manager:
"We're really going to have to watch the budget closely."

Code official:
"It'll need several variances."

User:
"I hope our work stations are sized adequately."

8-7: Diagram of differing perspectives focused on a design

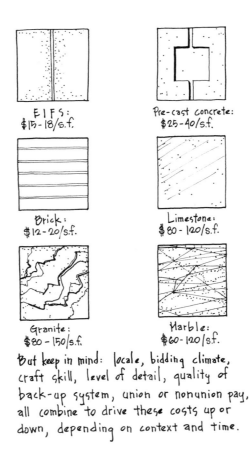

EIFS:
$15-18/s.f.

Pre-cast concrete:
$25-40/s.f.

Brick:
$12-20/s.f.

Limestone:
$80-120/s.f.

Granite:
$80-150/s.f.

Marble:
$60-120/s.f.

But keep in mind: locale, bidding climate, craft skill, level of detail, quality of back-up system, union or nonunion pay, all combine to drive these costs up or down, depending on context and time.

8-8: Typical exterior materials and an indication of their relative costs

the other. Architects, for their sanity and sometimes survival, are expected or forced to understand the needs of each group as a project proceeds. Our understanding of these matters has direct bearing on how we apply our creative skills, especially when we sit down face to face and present work for review and/or approval. We prioritize our communications to satisfy the root concerns of the particular individual or group at hand. If we ignore the needs of the other participants in the design process, we will find extreme difficulty in obtaining any successful execution of our proposed work. A working understanding of the views of others during design must be cultivated from the earliest moments of a project. And if we have any doubts about the mindset of our client or secondary political influences, we will find lasting value, and perhaps more peace of mind, in gathering some intelligence on each group. Partial or little information may be available, and as a result, the designer will fold the effort of learning about a particular group or individual into the active design process as we communicate with each entity. This effort has to be active and conscious: much more value is obtained than relying solely on intuition or happenstance. To a certain extent, our knowledge of both our client and external influences is evolutionary. The redevelopment official we considered an adversary one day provides an insight of true value during the course of a project. There is always the opportunity for surprise and growth. These intangible contexts are inherent and essential to every project.

So how do these intangible, but all too real influences effect the creativity focused on a project?

Some examples may prove enlightening. I would also recommend talking to others with experience on a variety of projects. Let us first consider a developer who wants to build an office building shell for $52.00 per square foot. Several things happen immediately to our approach to the design on receipt of this information. First, at this price, a cap on the cost of exterior materials emerges. Focusing on the exterior skin of the proposed building will be instructive (8-8). We will not be using granite, limestone, marble, or any kind of custom exterior skin system. More realistic materials are brick, precast concrete with simple articulation, and off-the-shelf curtain and window wall systems. The plan geometry will probably be square, rectangular, or some combination of these. The detail, depth, and articulation of the skin will need to be restrained. This may begin to sound a little bleak, but that is not the case. There are many opportunities within these constraints to do a quality building. It may not be a transcendental experience for the user or trailblaze a new vision of design, but it need not be a complete disaster either.

Another, and more disturbing example comes from my own experience. In 1990, I was asked to design an office headquarters for a national chain of retail stores. Our client was a developer working with the retail chain. A site had been selected, and some very preliminary plan options had been sketched and presented to the developer. Preferences regarding a particular plan schematic had been tenetively identified, and at that point I came on the scene. I was given all the documentation up until that time and told that the developer wanted to

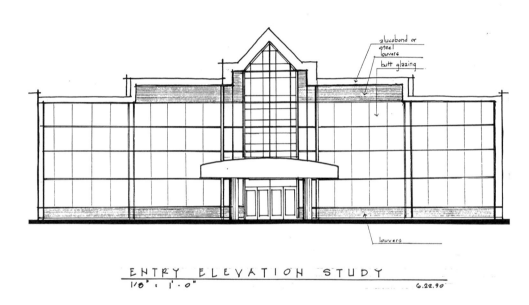

ENTRY ELEVATION STUDY
1/8" : 1'-0"   6.22.90

8-9: Sketch elevation of the ill-fated office building

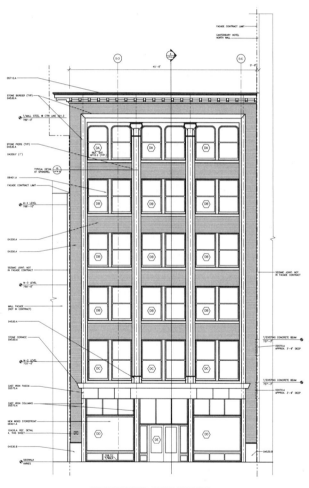

8-10: Elevation of historic facade to be reassembled on the exterior of Circle Centre Mall—Centre Venture Architects, copyright City of Indianapolis 1993

build the building shell for $27.00 per square foot. This is a scary number: you probably cannot build warehouse space for that amount, but I was told that we were to create a solution which would support this dollar amount. I went to work early and stayed late. I did volumes of sketches. I built models. I had a vision of what I thought the building should be (8-9). Unfortunately for me, the developer was not impressed with any of my solutions and as a matter of fact, was somewhat perturbed. I did some research on building costs and discovered that, for all intents and purposes, it appeared impossible to build an office shell for $27.00 per square foot. I asked the principal in charge about this and was told that the developer had "connections" that would allow them to accomplish this feat. To my detriment, I continued to cling to my scheme when I should have revised my approach to the design. Finally, another designer was brought in with a different perspective and a new scheme was developed. Much to my dismay, his scheme was chosen by the developer for further study. What went wrong? This is a prime example of my ignoring basic constraints imposed by the client. The developer wanted a simple, cheap, no-frills solution. This particular client has broad experience with the development of office buildings. As a result, we can safely deduce that numerous prejudices and preferences had been created over the course of their experience. Another interesting aspect of this example is that I never made any face to face contact with the client. In essence, my client was another architect. My recommendation, having dealt with a "middleman," is to at least be in the same room when designs are presented. Work hard to get the opportunity to attend design-review meetings. You may not have the opportunity to say anything, but you will get a feel for the dynamic of the relationship and the client's reaction to your work. In retrospect, as I reflect on this experience at the time, I realize that I wanted desperately to do some creative design. I was driven very much by my own personal vision of what I wanted to accomplish. Unfortunately, my venue was extremely limited and a tough if not impossible solution even for a designer who knew much about the intricacies of creating a quality design on the thinnest of budgets.

Projects built in urban areas are complex on many levels, but one area of concern that can provide rich contextual opportunity is also a potential nightmare: historical restoration, facade preservation, facade disassembly/reassembly, and the political complexities created by dealing with the people representing historical interests. Circle Centre Mall, in Indianapolis, Indiana, contains a number of historic facades. Their disassembly, restoration, reassembly, and final locations on site were subject to the review of a local consortium of historical organizations. In addition, federal money for the project was dependent on their approval of our plans for the facades and adjacent mall elevations. Lack of their approval would have had serious consequences for the project's schedule and finances. It is clear that criteria of this nature had a pronounced impact on how the design was executed. The historical issue demands respect of the context, materials, detailing, and proportions used in the old structures (8-10 through 14). A direction was established using the historic facades as points

8-11: Historic facade supported in place prior to shell construction of Circle Centre

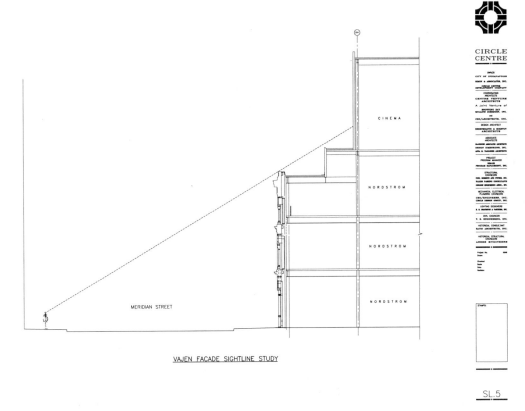

VAJEN FACADE SIGHTLINE STUDY

CIRCLE
CENTRE

SL.5

8-12: Presentation drawing for historical agency review—Centre Venture Architects, copyright City of Indianapolis 1993

of reference for the creation of the exterior elevations. The Indianapolis Nordstrom Store illustrated in Stan Laegreid's sketch is a good example of a careful response to the design challenge posed by four historic facades placed about dead center on the store's primary elevation (8-15). You may be hard pressed to identify exactly what is historic versus new construction based on the sketches shown.

Being creative in a political environment is a continuing challenge. And, regardless of innate talent, the intent to be creative coupled with an astute awareness of external issues goes much of the distance necessary to begin what may evolve into quality work. In complex projects, the odds against creating excellent design rise exponentially with the size of project and number of external entities involved. The designer is enmeshed in an environment demanding almost continuous creativity as a result of the fact that the "rules" may change weekly, daily, or hourly on any number of components within a design. If our process stalls, we are forced to scramble for new ideas, often with insufficient time for a complete exploration of options. Dead ends in the creative efforts on a design often center around the essential duality of architecture. A simple definition of this duality lies at the heart of the craft: on the one hand, practicality, and on the other, art. Conflict may arise when either part does not lend itself to the other. Also, there is no guarantee that an excellent practical solution will be amenable to the art we seek in quality buildings. As a general rule, the more cost is constrained, the larger the struggle to create the artistic component becomes. Be aware that a majority of projects with

small budgets will demand serious effort from the designer to forge a creative solution. In fact, the tighter a budget becomes, the more difficult it will be to devise any solution at all. It is essential for our work to evolve consistently with respect to the continuous play of influences surrounding each project. This context shapes the direction of our inquiries and focuses our creativity toward the aspirations we embody as each design takes shape, first in imagination, then in drawings and models, and finally in built form.

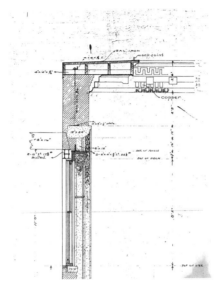

8-13: Original detail of historical facade. Rubush and Hunter Collection, Indiana Historical Society Library

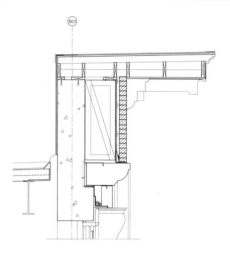

8-14: Reconstructed detail of historical facade—Centre Venture Architects, copyright City of Indianapolis 1993

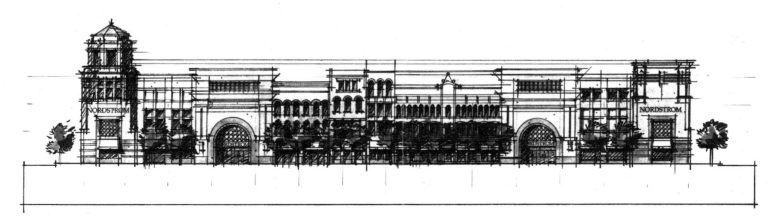

8-15: Meridian street elevation of Nordstrom Store, Indianapolis, Indiana by Stan Laegreid of The Callison Partnership

PART THREE

Return to the Known

We emerge from the creative phase of design, in theory, with a working scheme. This labor becomes the object of intense scrutiny whose goal is to test the success of the work. Testing a design takes several forms, all dependent on communication for success. Success in this context is defined as the transfer of project understanding to those besides the designer with a stake in the work. An iterative dialogue emerges between the design, architect, client, government, and community. A project moves in stages from the "privacy" of the designer's office to public study and comment. This process of exposure and feedback often returns the designer to creative effort, seeking resolution of these external influences. Many projects will have several cycles of input followed by response and additional input. The point of true closure arrives when a project is completed and provides us with the opportunity to experience our efforts in the flesh, adding yet another layer of practical knowledge as we begin again to embark on new design challenges.

CHAPTER 9

Completion

At some point in the design process, we are either forced or choose to embrace a given level of "completion." The notion of closure on a design is sometimes problematic, but we would be well served by agreeing to a deadline, either real or imaginary, for a design review (9-1). When we have plans, sections, and at least a couple of elevations complete, we array our work and test the success of our scheme. What basically happens is a thorough question-and-answer session, which follows through the two major phases of design we have presented so far: assessing both the known and creative components that we have navigated to create a schematic. This dialogue may be private and internal, or formalized and presented to a group for comment and criticism. As we test our design, we immerse ourselves in a microcosm of the whole design process—a flyby looking both at the known, then creative cycle of evolving detail.

Functional Requirements

The first and potentially least painful portion of our review would be a check of functional requirements. First, we consciously check through the requirements and limitations imposed by our basic knowledge of building. Does the structural system make sense? Do the internal circulation paths work successfully? Does the building's orientation and fenestration maximize energy efficiency? Is the design within budget? It is possible to ask myriad questions, but generally more constructive to focus on problem areas, major or minor, that come to light. Previously, we made reference to knowledge about building components and architectural concepts as

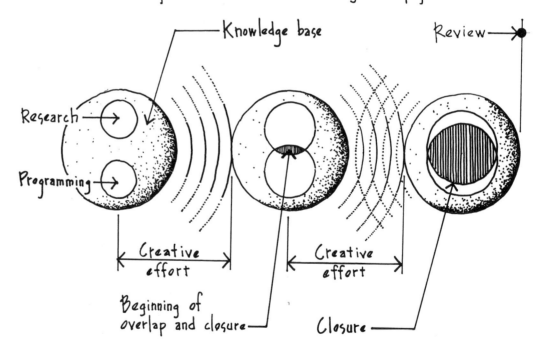

Note: apparent closure can, and often does, disintegrate at review. The result is reflection back to partial integration. This oscillation may occur innumerable times throughout a project.

Knowledge base

Review

Research

Programming

Creative effort

Creative effort

Beginning of overlap and closure

Closure

9-1: Cycle of project design

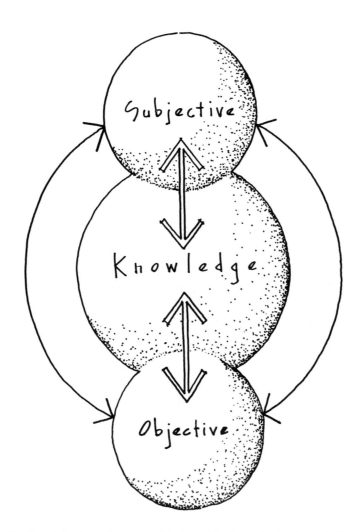

9-2: Knowledge base is compared to both objective and subjective criteria

a palette, a source from which to draw. It may be argued that what we choose to apply in our buildings or spaces is based on our knowledge foundation. The potential success or failure of our work and its embedded quality are fundamentally linked to this architectural and spatial knowledge (9-2). When we create a program in conjunction with research, additional knowledge is the result. In addition, program and research focus the design effort. Linkage is established between knowledge translated into form and space and the programmatic document describing the architectural and spatial goals. At this point, it is interesting to note that as we conduct the first level of our review, the possibility for disagreement, between designer and designer or designer and client, is minimal. As we proceed, the possibility of conflict escalates. Why? Because we steadily translate from objective into subjective levels of consideration.

Symbolic Constraints

The next level of completion review is a check of symbolic constraints: Do the semantic, contextual, cultural, and client concepts create a reasonable fit to the design? Are these vocabulary sources consistent with the program? If not, problem areas need to be rethought and interpreted to more successfully respond to the symbolic framework established for the solution. Since the intent of conceptualization is to create a mental framework for the execution of a design, adjustments will change the appearance of our work. This is not to be taken lightly. Consciously or unconsciously, we make choices about how our buildings and spaces appear. Few designers can arbitrarily create an aesthetic that fools the trained observer. Even a lay person will sense a vague ambivalence towards a design without a conceptual "undercarriage." Consider the visual power of the Acropolis or the Great Wall. These structures are thoroughly grounded in the culture and philosophy of their creators, countries, and time. Designs well fitted to the environment solve both the functional and contextual sides of the design equation.

Aesthetics

Testing the success of aesthetic considerations is probably the most rarefied activity a designer undertakes. Every participant in the design process has a variety of preferences with respect to the composition and arrangement of design vocabulary (9-3). Our clients are sometimes not sure about what they want. As a result, an unusual dichotomy begins to unfold. The designer solves the aesthetic component of a design to his or her satisfaction. Completion is achieved at the individual level of the designer with the implicit belief that we have successfully translated our understanding of the client's needs and preferences into a solution. With design in hand, we toddle off to the client and test our interpretation. Sometimes we get it right or close; other times we scrap our work and reformulate our understanding of what the client wants. Previously, we discussed the value of bringing the client into the design process and posited that there were clear advantages to doing so. As we consider testing our designs and the varietal communication requirements associated with a working solution, we may

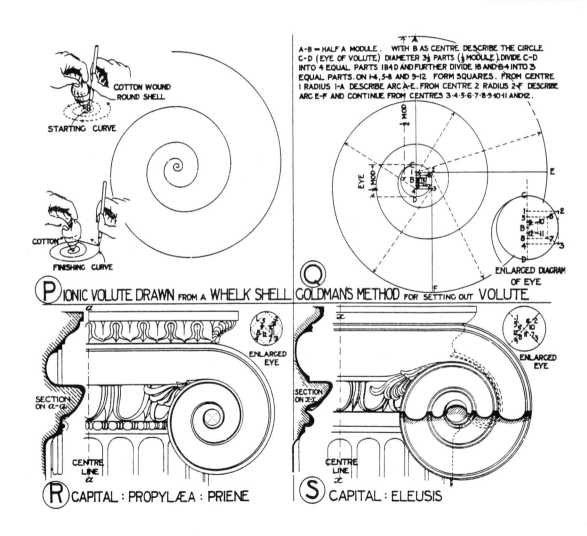

9-3: An ancient example in the elegant proportions of the Ionic Volute from *A History of Architecture*, 19th ed., by Sir Banister Fletcher

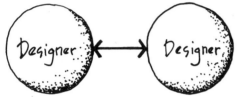

- Shared knowledge base
- Common background
- Graphics may outweigh words

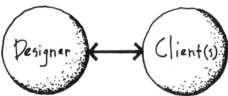

- May be graphically illiterate
- Words may outweigh graphics
- Different priorities than designer
  • Cost
  • Schedule
  • Maintenance
  • Financing

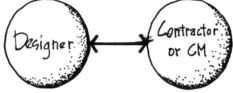

- Words and graphics about equal
- Different worldview
  • Serving "Owner's interests"
  • Controlling/reducing cost
  • Maintaining schedule
  • Organizing and directing work

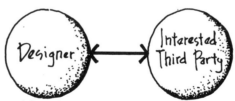

- May be graphically illiterate
- Specialized focus and agenda
- Possibly antagonistic
- May influence design process

9-4: Communication diagrams

also argue that having our clients actively involved at the schematic level and beyond will increase the likelihood of minimum "downtime" and rework. The client's participation guides, supports, and improves the general design quality.

Communication and Completion

As we work, we constantly test and judge what we create until we achieve inner completion. This relationship may be described as "designer to self" and is the fundamental pivot around which all creative endeavor turns. But the designer's interior dialogue is only one-half the process of achieving and verifying completion. We must shift our focus from the internal considerations of what is being tested to how designs are tested person to person. We are confronted with important communicative tasks transcending our internal dialogue. Testing our designs does not occur in a vacuum: it is an interpersonal process. To a large extent, success at conveying our designs is closely knit with our ability to explain what we have done and why we chose to do so to others.

We move from satisfying our internal analysis and dialogue to external communication (9-4). The simplest form is one-on-one interaction: designer to designer or designer to client. Each situation is grounded in a different context. When we explain our work to another designer, we share an implicit knowledge of the standards, techniques, and conventions used within our craft. However, when we elaborate the nature of a given design for a client, we are faced with a task that may be significantly more difficult and subtle. The assessments we made in regard to clients in the programming chapter are in many ways the tip of the iceberg. Design is often thought of as a visual medium, and this is true within the shared knowledge of the professions. But demonstrating how a design serves our clients' needs demands proficiency in visual, verbal, and written media. In addition, the dynamics of a group presentation vary markedly from the one-on-one situation first described. As designers seeking effective communication, our goal must be full understanding of how our clients may best appreciate and perceive our work, plus the facility to enhance any graphic presentation with verbal skills that make the design truly come alive in the clients' imagination. Consider the richness, emotional impact, and mental images evoked by a well written story and that most people read and listen to huge amounts of information on a daily basis. Our clients draw meaning and context from these media.

Quality designs that meet the needs of our clients are our implicit goal. For example, consider any project you have worked on recently. Can you successfully explain how the project meets the needs, wants, and desires of your client? When we present our work, we simply cannot put up our drawings and sit down. No graphic presentation, no matter how complete, will stand alone without explanation (9-5). Not only is explanation essential, but context and connection to the client are paramount. Let us place ourselves in the mind of our client. The designer makes a presentation in this form: "Looking at the building plan, we see the entry. Once inside, we are in the central atrium with vertical transportation on the left and a water feature

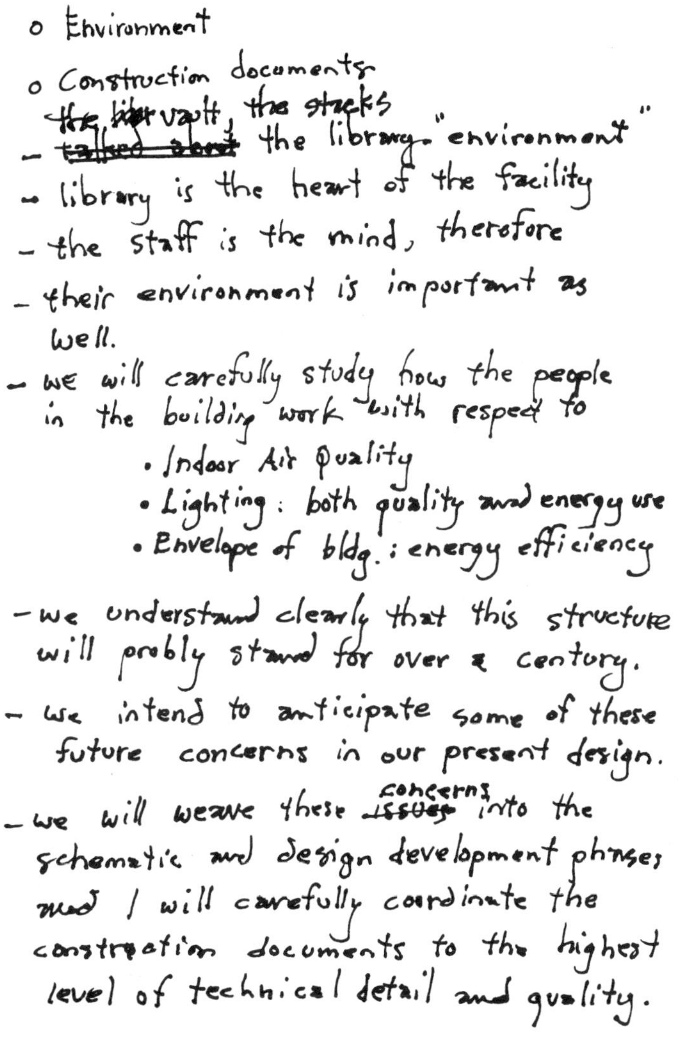

o Environment

o Construction documents

~~the library vault, the stacks~~

~~talked about~~ the library "environment"

- library is the heart of the facility

- the staff is the mind, therefore

- their environment is important as well.

- we will carefully study how the people in the building work with respect to
   • Indoor Air Quality
   • Lighting: both quality and energy use
   • Envelope of bldg.: energy efficiency

- we understand clearly that this structure will probly stand for over a century.

- we intend to anticipate some of these future concerns in our present design.

- we will weave these ~~issues~~ concerns into the schematic and design development phases, and I will carefully coordinate the construction documents to the highest level of technical detail and quality.

9-5: Rough notes for a presentation

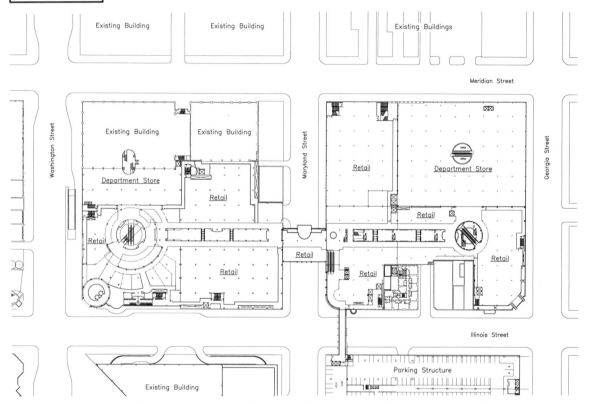

9-6: Circle Centre's overall project plan—Centre Venture Architects, copyright City of Indianapolis 1993

on the right." Consider the same presentation when conveyed like this: "As we approach the entry, we notice that it is designed based on the idea of shelter and community, consistent with this company's corporate philosophy. We move through the entrance into a softly lighted atrium filled with plants specially chosen to contribute to the quality of the indoor air and enhance the feeling of interior comfort and well being..." There is a powerful difference between a simple recitation and demonstrating that we have given careful thought to creating a design with depth and quality. A designer who works steadily to improve her grasp of written and especially verbal skills and to incorporate client knowledge and understanding will find more satisfaction, anticipate and head off problems before they happen, have a lower stress level, and do higher quality work. In addition, she will quite probably have repeat clients who recommend her to others.

Occasionally, a designer will have multiple clients on a single project. This particular animal may take several forms: for example, a group of people from one organization, such as a board of directors, or separate entities committed to the same project. Circle Centre Mall, in Indianapolis, is an example of fully separate clients consisting of the City of Indianapolis, a limited partnership, and a private developer (9-6). Separate clients may have wildly differing needs and agendas, which the designers must successfully integrate. There may be conflict between clients requiring an architectural solution or the creation of compromises satisfactory to both parties. Local organizations may object to a project or have control over some financial aspect of the work. In either case, the designer will be called upon to accommodate the concerns of third parties, then formally communicate how these accommodations were made to the satisfaction of those concerned. Sometimes, an interested third party wields significant power over a project and requires the designer to take the utmost care: treating this person or group like a client on a one-time or continuing basis. In each of the previous cases just described, the designer generally faces a group of people, often with different backgrounds, needs, and expectations. A focused effort to grasp the context of each situation and tailor our presentation to fit this specialized audience will communicate the nature and intent of a design with the greatest clarity.

Client-Designer Relationships

The intent and agenda of designers and their clients often mesh. On other occasions, this symbiotic relationship may diverge and conflict (9-7). Over the course of any project, there will be a dynamic flux between the designer's interpretation and the client's goals for any project. It is quite possible to work with a client who has no business providing aesthetic direction to an architect or interior designer. Sometimes this individual will hand over all matters of taste and aesthetics without a fight. Other times the designer will be forced into a nightmare where the client insists on imposing his or her will on a project without compromise. In a difficult economic climate, the designer is left little choice in these situations: survival, completion of the work, and paying the bills become a necessity. More often than not, a cooperative relationship exists

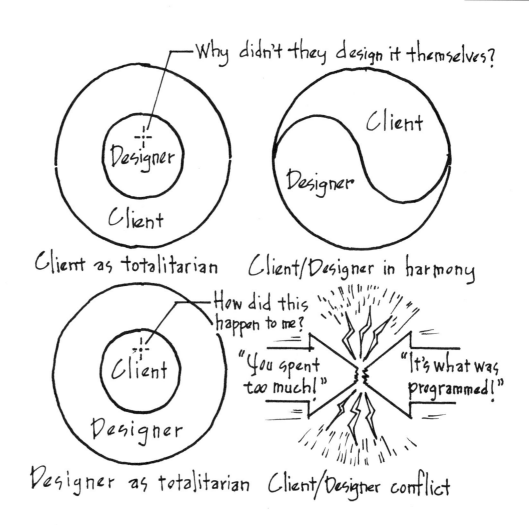

9-7: Varietal client-designer relationships

① Listen to your client

② Translate what you believe
has been said – get feedback

③ Take notes, ask questions
If you don't understand, say so

④ Return to item number 1 ...

9-8: Don't forget the "input" side of the communication equation

between client and designer. The participants agree and provide mutual support for the development of a given design.

A cooperative relationship is established at the beginning of a project: the pivotal time period is during the development of a program. The quality of the programmatic document sets the stage for the subsequent interactions between designer and client. Unfortunately, the majority of projects undergo little, if any, programming. Therefore, the designer's ability to interpret the client's needs with a minimum of client input and strong background knowledge becomes key to solving a given design problem. In the course of dealing with any client, the designer must bring several communication skills to the table. The first and, in my mind, foremost skill is the ability to listen. Another requirement is taking the time to translate and restate what the client has explained. Translation allows the client to verify the designer's understanding of a given problem statement. Finally, the ability to ask questions often allows a client to refocus attention on a previously unconsidered aspects of a program (9-8).

There are times when clients will provide direction to the designer that is clearly unwise. In these instances, the designer is placed in a situation requiring finesse and tact. The logical thing to do is explain why a particular idea might not be in the client's best interest. Bear in mind, an objection of this sort must be presented from the client's point of view. Why? The reason is simple: presenting from the standpoint of a purely design-oriented position makes our concern appear to be more for the sake of our convenience and less in the client's interest.

Couching our concerns in terms a client can understand will have a much larger chance of succeeding.

The potential conflict just described is often solved with little difficulty. In rare instances, we will be faced with an adversarial result instead of the solution we are seeking. What are the sources of conflict in a project (9-9)? Actually, they are quite straightforward. First, a mistake of one kind or another was made. Second, a project budget was overrun and too much money was, is, or will be spent. Never forget: we must always know what our clients have determined to spend on a project. Design is the opportunity to exercise tremendous creative latitude, but if the designer's creation is over budget, all effort to the point of discovery may well be wasted. Third, a deadline is or will be missed. Obviously, we never intend to place ourselves in these situations, but sooner or later we face a client demanding an explanation and a solution. What is the best way to calm an angry client? First, and this is sometimes hard, admit a mistake was made. Then be prepared to offer a solution to the problem.

Influencing Others

We are continuously immersed in an environment in which our interactions are made with equals or those we serve. We intend to act in their best interest, but many times our perception of what is best may not be shared or understood by our peers or clients. We are placed in a situation requiring us to exercise influence without authority.

Every day, architects have to influence people over whom they have no author-

 You made a mistake

 You spent too much of someone else's money

 You are unable to make a deadline agreed to in advance

 Primary rule of survival: tell the truth. Admit your error, offer a solution, and fix the problem

9-9: Classic project faux pas

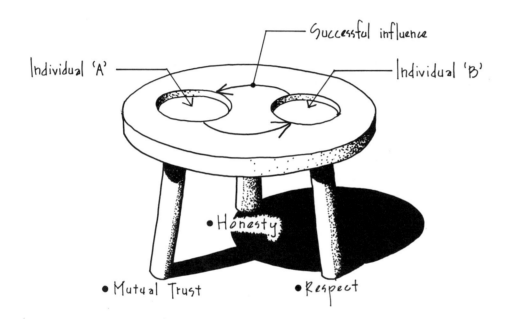

9-10: Foundations of successful influence

ity. This happens within the firm when you have to work with colleagues or supervisors. It happens on simple building projects when you have to work with clients. And it happens on complex projects when you have to work with interrelated, sometimes hostile, factions to achieve the desired results.

The goal of influence is to get others to give support and share their valuable time and resources. At first, it may seem that the other person holds all the cards, because he or she has what you want—time, money, staff, support, information...

There is a way to balance the situation, however, if you remember that the other person involved also has needs, wants, and desires. If you can determine what they are, you may have resources that will help him or her meet those needs (Kaderlan 1991).

Influencing without authority rests on the foundation of any working relationship (9-10). First, we must be honest and clear with the other person. Once again, communication is the front runner in our efforts to express our needs and serve others in return. Second, there must be mutual trust between the parties involved. In this case, there must be some personal history extant between participants. And lastly, we must respect, and be respected by, the person we intend to influence. This is harder to codify as it reflects the culture, background, and experience of the "players." If any of the above are lacking, creating influence of any kind may well be impossible. It is important to review our goals in a delicate negotiating situation and, if necessary, be prepared with a variety of potential options.

> *When making the exchange, the most obvious things you can offer the other person are goods, such as budget dollars, time, equipment, and personnel. But other people have needs for things other than goods—you can offer services, such as a faster response time, information, or public support. You also can offer sentiments such as gratitude, praise, and appreciation (Kaderlan 1991).*

The result is that we obtain what we need and the other party is "paid" in kind: both people receive mutual benefit from the exchange.

The presentation and sequencing of this chapter might lead one to believe, from a cursory read, that functional, symbolic, and aesthetic considerations in design may be conveniently separated. Nothing could be further from the truth. In design, it is possible to place final finishes after the fact, and with the practice separation between interior design and architecture, this position seems to be borne out by reality. In the existing climate of fragmented, a'la carte design services, it is unusual for a single individual to have control over all aspects of a design. However, a single design professional or firm often coordinates all disciplines working to create a building. Therefore, communication, not only between designer and client, but designer and design team, takes on critical importance. We find that each design is subjected to scrutiny, beginning with the designer herself, followed by the client or clients in the continuous process of seeking completion and communication on any project.

CHAPTER 10

The Presentation Environment

Over the life of a project, the most important times, aside from the creative moments that form and direct a design, are when we present our work to another person or group. Each presentation is a snapshot of our ongoing fusion of design's subjective and objective elements. The finest design will not be successfully communicated without an accompanying presentation of the same quality. Making a presentation requires a variety of skills: from the ability to read body language to fielding questions for which the designer is completely unprepared. We must also make an effort to think about our audience and adjust our approach and content to suit the knowledge of the group at hand. Presentations are milestones. Many will be small and informal, but a few take on the status of theater and demand careful, painstaking preparation.

Methodology and Scale

Being aware of the fact that presentations are inevitable and regular invites us to spend time reflecting on exactly where we will discuss our work (10-1). One environment we are all familiar with is the desk crit. From the microcosm of the desk, the scale varies across a wide range. This variety of scale demands that we consider the methodology used in the creation of our graphics. Beginning at the desk, we have the designer and one or two other people review what is happening on a project. Interpreting each and every nuance of the work in progress is relatively easy. As a result, the designer can choose to work in just about any convenient medium.

The next jump in scale is to room size, with a corresponding increase in formality. We take our

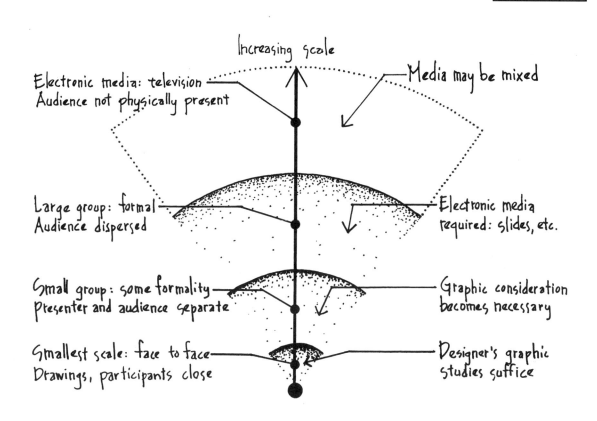

10-1: Scalar aspects of presentation environments

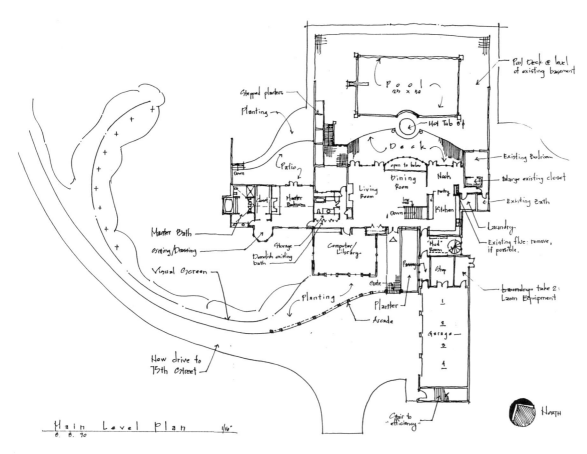

10-2: Presentation using basic linework

work and pin it on any uncluttered wall. Our audience is quite probably seated and may now number from three to ten people. From this point, whoever prepares or is responsible for the graphic component of a presentation must consider whether the drawings will read successfully (10-2). The critical distance is from the plane of the drawing to the person seated farthest away. If you take this seat and successfully read what has been posted on the wall, then you may be sure that every person in the room can interpret the graphic content of the design.

If the drawings are not readable, we need to review how they can be revised to achieve more "punch." The options are fairly simple. First, we may increase line weights. Second, we can begin to shade rooms or zones of concern (10-3). The next level of complexity adds color to lines, zones, rooms, and/or circulation paths depending on what the designer deems crucial to the communication of the design. It is important to understand that, in drawings at whatever size, there is a maximum level of detail attainable in presentations to larger groups. If we have achieved a certain level of detail impossible to communicate with the graphics being used, yet still feel it essential for the audience's understanding of the design, two options are available. We may add details blown up in scale or distribute a separate handout. In a business situation, handouts are useful tools. They are most often used for agendas, but may also incorporate information on a firm, fee structure, and/or graphics. In addition, we must realize that when our presentation is complete, we leave the room with our drawings and models. Nothing physical remains of what we have attempted to communicate, save for the impression made in the minds of our listeners and, if used, a thoughtfully designed handout.

As the size of room and group increase, paper media no longer suffice. Slides or an overhead projector becomes the primary tool for communication. One advantage of this kind of media is that the original document may be at any size. We may customize the image size to any room we use. With reference to slides, I recommend using a 100 slide tray in lieu of the 140, as the larger tray has closely spaced dividers more prone to jam. In addition, bring a back-up projector and an extra lamp. A second heavy-duty extension cord may also be a lifesaver on occasion. When we rely on technology, a certain level of paranoia is truly wise because some perverse law of the universe causes machines to break down when we need them most.

Computers and Presentations

The highest veneer of technology currently available for presentations uses computer and video. The newest generation of hardware, coupled with state-of-the-art software, time, and someone knowledgeable about both, can create astonishing results. Originally, three-dimensional representations on the computer began with simple "wire frames," then moved to planar illustrations, light and shadow, and luminance and reflectivity. Animation has been used in high-end systems for over fifteen years, but with the continuing decrease in cost and rising system capability, all of the above options and more are now available to the mainstream practitioner. Our designs can exist in the virtual reality of a

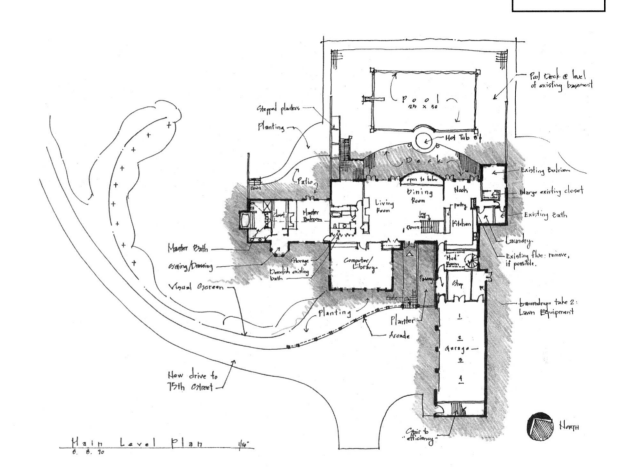

10-3: The same presentation with additional graphic emphasis

10-4: Nordstrom Men's Concept interior—The Callison Partnership, Seattle, Washington

computer before ground is ever broken. Some businesses and institutions have literally created a building within a computer prior to construction.

When Sitterson Hall (University of North Carolina at Chapel Hill) was in the planning stages, the VR researchers who were going to work in the multimillion-dollar building after it was completed converted the architect's plans to a full-scale 3D model—that existed only in cyberspace. When the people who were going to spend their days in the building "walked" through the model, many of them felt that one particular partition in the lobby created a cramped feeling in a busy hallway. The architects didn't agree until the future occupants of the building used the 3D model to give the planners a walkthrough. The partition was moved. The building was built. (Rheingold 1991)

Our work can come alive via the use of color renderings, animation or, in unique situations, virtual reality. As we discussed in Chapter Six, virtual reality is still in the future for day-to-day use, but high quality computer graphics are available now (10-4 through 9). We have the opportunity to view building and site from any position, time of day, and season, inside or out, with accuracy and a fair amount of ease. These three-dimensional capabilities give the client a preview of the design in an appearance that mimics daily experience. It is now possible to remove the abstraction of two-dimensional drawings from the presentation process and leave the client with a videotape in lieu of paper.

The sophistication and power of computers continue to increase while their cost falls. I have spoken to designers who have scorned these devices as useless to the "essential" process of design. Since we have successfully fashioned edifices of all kinds for several thousand years without our digital friends, this point is well taken. However, as we close the twentieth century and scan the vast horizons visible and waiting, it is obvious that computers and information technology are already knitted into our lives. For those of you who still view computers with a wary eye I have some simple advice: get one and learn how to use it, or be left behind.

Speaking

We have talked about graphics and technology, discussing a basic approach for achieving communication at the level of the drawings. When we present, we also speak: if we use our verbal skills well, what we say enriches the tapestry of each design. However, if we speak poorly with little confidence in our work, the best graphics in the world will not save our project from potential rejection. This is especially true in actual practice where an audience of lay people lacks the graphic literacy to read a set of drawings. They rely on the verbal part of the presentation and less on the content of the drawings. Generally, most of us are probably average speakers. Some of us are significantly less than gifted in this area, while others are polished, comfortable, and eloquent. The majority of designers are expected, perhaps required, to speak in reason-

10-5: Mission Valley Center—The Callison Partnership, Seattle, Washington

10-6: Boeing Customer Services Executive Training Offices—The Callison Partnership, Seattle, Washington

ably coherent terms about design at each stage in a project's development.

I consider myself an average speaker, but I make a conscious effort to boost the quality of my presentations by using a few simple methods. The first thing I always do is organize what I intend to say. Then I write key words on a little card to jog my memory and allow for a spontaneous style. I never memorize a presentation, no matter how important. I may identify key ideas or phrases during my preparation, but that is the upper limit of my formal memorization. What if you are required to speak and the situation is positively terrifying? Do it. An old Spanish proverb says: someone who fights a bull and is not afraid has done nothing. Someone who is afraid and does not fight a bull has done nothing. Whereas, someone who is afraid and fights a bull has truly done something. If you fear speaking, pick a subject in which you passionately believe. Take your area of interest, assuming that it is related to design, and create a little presentation. Give it to your team or department, a small group. Work on it some more, add material and look for a larger audience. The idea is to "fight the bull" in a less threatening arena, then slowly increase the scale and gain experience. Repetition as we learn a new skill removes uncertainty and apprehension.

Preparation

Up to this point, we have discussed the ingredients for a presentation. An important line of inquiry resides in how we take the various pieces of a presentation and assemble them into an effective package: our preparation, no matter how casual, has impact on the presentation event. Let us also up the ante by placing our preparation in the context of actual practice where competition is fierce and success or failure can hinge on misperception or a casual comment. This is within the zone of time prior to receiving a commission when many firms may be competing simply for the opportunity to be considered, via interview, for a project.

The following is an example of how to approach a fairly detailed preparation. It may be used during design as well to support a working understanding of the client and their concerns. The first thing to do is get organized and start gathering intelligence. We need to know about our potential client, both personally and in the context of his institution or business. We may approach the people in question directly by calling and arranging a meeting. In fact, meeting face to face, if possible, prior to a formal presentation may provide a wealth of information in subjective areas such as level of comfort, psychology, and personality. In addition, gaining even the tiniest bit of familiarity adds to our effectiveness later. We need to talk to the client and also to people familiar with our potential employer. Here we have a situation analogous to gaining insight into the contextual issues related to a building site. The people who know our client will help identify secondary concerns for consideration as we make our preparations. We should work to learn about the client's organization via facility tours, if available, and printed matter explaining the organization, its operation, and history. The goal is to gain understanding of the client's project, current situation, and mindset. One or two people can easily

10-7: Boeing Customer Services Lobby—The Callison Partnership, Seattle, Washington

Dining Area

10-8: Boeing Customer Services Dining Area—The Callison Partnership, Seattle, Washington

undertake this aspect of the work.

As we gather intelligence, we will concurrently be assembling a team for the project. This group will consist of a small number of key people committed to obtaining the work, focusing project expertise, and seeing it through completion. This group takes the project intelligence and studies it in detail to develop a presentation strategy. This concept, or series of ideas, structures the presentation in an effort to demonstrate competence, understanding of the project, understanding of the client, and the process proposed for completing the work. Initially, the demonstration of competence is often accomplished by the written proposal. Assuming that the proposal brings us to the next step, in the form of an interview, we gather more intelligence and make final preparations for the presentation. A day or so before the "show," we check our strategy and rehearse the event. For large projects, more than one presenter is not unusual. Therefore, we need to know in advance what each person's role will be and the basic content of what will be said. Rehearsals allow us to make these decisions and critique general performance for consistency with strategy and our knowledge of the client. We practice, and, like other performers, hope it makes perfect.

The day of the presentation may be fraught with anxiety or calm (for the old hands). Actually making the presentation may be something of an anticlimax, while judgment of the outcome is often murky at best. Murphy's Law may intervene to the amusement or chagrin of the participants. Sometimes we receive good news, while on other occasions our effort is wasted. When we contend unsuccessfully for a commission, it is essential to gather information after the fact regarding the reasons for the client's choice. Understanding why we were not chosen helps us to prepare more effectively for future efforts. Each cycle in the process of obtaining projects is an opportunity to learn: the schooling can be quite painful. Applying this wisdom to future work makes us more effective as practitioners and mentors: the "school" of real life continues uninterrupted even after we receive our degrees.

In closing, presentations often require a variety of approaches depending on the intended result, and we use a wide spectrum of technologies to get our message through. Successful communication should always be the goal of our preparations. To enhance communication, we must consistently look at the context grounding the presentation and ask a steady stream of questions of our clients, potential clients, and ourselves. If we choose to work in a vacuum, we will be consistently disappointed. Presentations are where projects surface for formal examination and comment. Each presentation event shapes the design and moves our projects one step closer to completion.

10-9: Rogue Valley Medical Center aerial view—The Callison Partnership, Seattle, Washington

CHAPTER 11

Postdesign

At this point, we have completed the cycle of the design process. The professional designation of work phases—schematics, design development, construction documents, bidding, and construction—describe the standard nomenclature, but the reality of making buildings at best approximates the accepted sequence. At this stage our current position in the design process is near the end of design development, preparing to make the transition to construction documents. Although the largest share of the creative effort may be over, the possibility of unexpected surprises still looms large. Preparing construction documents is a continuation of the contextual and political complexities inherent in any project. Each stage of each project is open-ended with the designer both seeking and solving problems. And lastly, we must not forget that designers and builders have an enormous effect on the usage of precious resources, our culture, and the future. We are presented with the opportunity to reflect on a myriad of design aspects throughout the entire continuum of creating buildings. This chapter attempts to achieve closure on the overall process and prepare us to begin again.

External Influences

The transition from design development to construction documents is often fuzzy. With CAD use, this distinction is further blurred (11-1). External influences continue unabated as a project proceeds into and through construction documents. These effects can be exerted by the owner, institutions of government, and even civic groups. Each and every one can blindside the design process, changing the

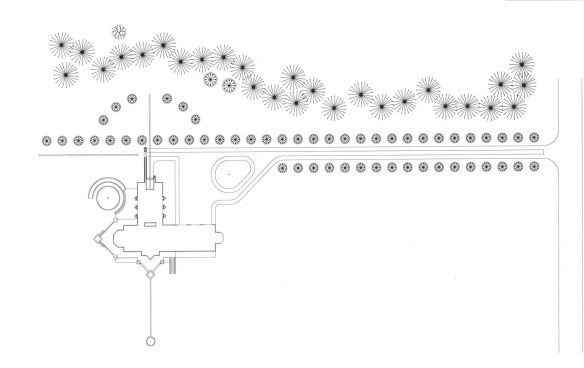

11-1: A CAD schematic looks deceptively complete

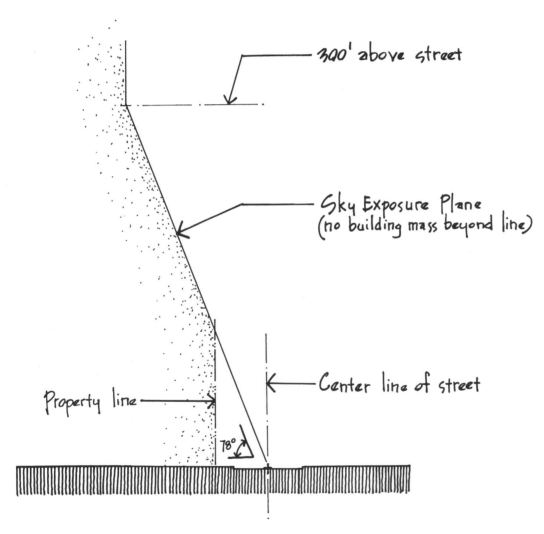

300' above street

Sky Exposure Plane
(no building mass beyond line)

Center line of street

Property line

78°

11-2: Skyplane section diagram based on the City of Indianapolis zoning ordinance for the Central Business District

direction of a project minimally or dramatically. Urban projects in particular are vulnerable, since the approval process is complex. The requirements of building codes and zoning ordinances are at first glance rigid standards to protect the public welfare, the vision of planners, and government as to how the urban fabric should be molded. Some flexibility with respect to codes is available throughout the design process, but it must be understood that codes defining fire protection criteria are of serious consequence. The request for a variance should be backed up with careful research and a demonstration of equivalency with respect to the rule we wish to reinterpret. New interpretations of the code to fit a design concept should be presented to building officials early in the design process. To do otherwise is to court disaster. As we consider the massing of a building, we should also refer to the corresponding zoning ordinance for potential conflicts (11-2). Cities have ordinances for signage, canopies, massing, skyplanes, shadows, design review, and more. Each and every one can alter or cripple a designer's vision depending on where in the process the regulation intervenes. Proactivity on the part of the designer will save time, money, and heartache.

Historical Concerns

Many a building in the United States and abroad now falls under the purview of historical concern or direct supervision to protect design integrity and preserve these structures for future generations. Federal guidelines may be further restricted or modified by local historical groups. Local historians focus specialized knowledge of urban or regional structures: they may not have the power of law to back their valuation of a historic building, but they will definitely present their views in a professional or strident manner depending on the situation. In cases where a developer and his architect are seen as conspirators planning the demise of a priceless structure, the historical community can be expected to use a variety of tactics including the media to bring pressure to bear on the offending design.

The scenario above hints at an interesting environment for the designer to work in: a new building in a historic district. The biggest challenges are meeting the needs of the client, developer or otherwise; creating a solution sympathetic to its surroundings; and convincing any local review committees that the design is a suitable addition to the existing built environment. James Stewart Polshek's Washington Court in Greenwich Village, New York is an interesting case in point.

The design of this apartment house in New York City's historic Greenwich Village today epitomizes contextual urban design, but it caused an angry public debate in 1984. Community groups saw the building—the first major new construction since the Village became a landmark district in 1969— as an opportunity to set a precedent for future development. Architect James Stewart Polshek's philosophy is that "new buildings must reflect the future as well as the past." The architect's initial concept was admittedly modern-

11-3: Restaurant prior to remodeling

11-4: Restaurant after remodeling—photo by Mark Platt

ist, which, due to neighborhood pressure and negotiations with the Landmarks Preservation Commission, evolved to reflect more "historical" references, but in an abstract way (Shoshkes 1989).

Input from the community had a significant effect on Washington Court. Presentations to the community continued regularly throughout the process to "monitor" the progress of the design. Clearly, the practice environment we work in today is far removed from the idea of the heroic architect working in isolation. Design is a social as well as a physical and artistic process.

Experience

Experience is a steady and sometimes brutal teacher of the working designer. Over time, brilliance will not prosper without practice: the conscious, day-in, day-out curiosity about design, buildings, and what creates quality in both. Each individual has preferences of aesthetics, media, work environment, and so on. These tendencies are connected to varied goals. Part of our individual development is finding a comfortable niche consistent with personal objectives. The search for excellence is coupled to personal desire and the environment in which we choose to practice. Finding a supportive niche to practice and grow within is quite possibly as important as a commitment to pursue quality design. Both are mutually supportive and synergistic.

As our design skills evolve, it is worthwhile to experiment with a variety of illustration media. Two possible scenarios present themselves: the first is the consistent use of a particular medium in every possible nuance; the second is the use of different media depending on the situation. Using a variety of media increases the designer's options but simultaneously dilutes the focus and hence the ultimate graphic quality. Our options are always open and adaptable to the situation. Experience coupled to commitment, environment, and tools are the key drivers of quality design process.

Completed Projects

Completing a built project is always a milestone for the designer. In our practices this event is the opportunity to see the final translation of our simulations. We get to check our work and to see the reaction of the end user, the public. Sadly, many designers seldom return to their work after it has been in use for awhile to obtain realistic feedback from the occupants. Often, the closest we come to study a design after the fact is the one-year warranty inspection, which generally focuses on complaints or problems requiring contractor attention. Each completed project offers the opportunity to continue the interaction with our client and reflect on how reality compares with the paths of imagination (11-3,4). Practice does not make perfect but rather allows us to continue learning and approach a greater understanding of the complexities inherent in our work. Standing within one of our designs, we are still confronted with the fact that subjective issues and personal preferences color each and every person's perception: one critic's genius is another's disaster. From a programmatic stand-

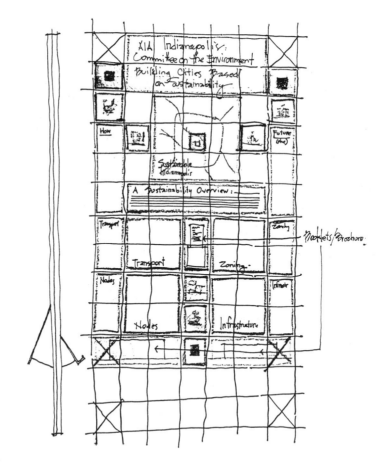

11-5: Design graphic study for an exhibit

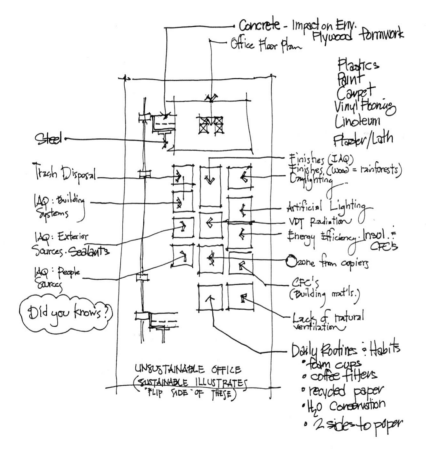

Concrete - Impact on Env.
Office Floor Plan Plywood Formwork

Plastics
Paint
Carpet
Vinyl Flooring
Linoleum
Plaster/Lath

Steel

Trash Disposal

IAQ: Building Systems

IAQ: Exterior Sources. Sealants

IAQ: People Sources

Did you know?

Finishes (IAQ)
Finishes (wood = rainforests)
Daylighting

Artificial Lighting
VDT Radiation
Energy Efficiency. Insol. = CFC's

Ozone from copiers

CFC's (Building mat'ls.)

Lack of natural ventilation

Daily Routines & Habits
• foam cups
• coffee filters
• recycled paper
• H₂O Conservation
• 2 sides to paper

UNSUSTAINABLE OFFICE
(SUSTAINABLE ILLUSTRATES
"FLIP SIDE" OF THESE)

OFFICE PANEL •

11-6: Design graphic study for another exhibit topic by a different individual

point, less gray area exists, but some ambiguity always remains. Users almost universally shake their heads and think, "If they'd only done it this way..." The way to minimize these concerns lies within the careful, perhaps painstaking programming undertaken at the very beginning of the design process, which then must be followed through to completion so that user needs are not subjugated to whim or ignorance. Success in programming ties directly back to knowledge of building types: a useful understanding of how a building should work for its users is then coupled to a program document that explains the details, needs, and broad-brush issues in a manner understandable to the client and designers. In making buildings we both act as generalists and apply specialized knowledge to the task at hand. Our skill is honed by the accumulated experience we glean over the course of our practice: knowledge is truly power.

While programming is generally thought of as problem seeking and design as problem solving, in practice both activities are intertwined. The program is the first approximation of what a building should be; it exists without the benefit of full context. When creative design begins in earnest, the attempt to assemble amorphous spaces collides with the artistic disposition of the designer, the site, and client. As space is crafted with reference to a program, questions and ambiguities emerge. At this stage the design process turns on these issues seeking resolution. Initial respect for the program is essential, but as we discover nuances within the evolving design, we remain prepared to challenge, redefine, and improve program concepts via the tentative conversions of program data into three-dimensional space.

Individuality

In the act of engendering a mindset for seeking and solving problems, it is of some consequence to understand that we all have individual perceptions, experiences, and preferences. As a general rule we seldom meddle with these in any conscious way. These tendencies are an important part of who and what we are as designers (11-5,6). I have always felt that flexibility is essential to quality design, but that the ground for flexibility resides within the person confronted by each choice as a design takes shape. Introspection is part of design; the possibilities for growth stem from what we learn while creating buildings. As such, there is no actively conscious effort to question our motives, but internal change is the result of new knowledge: being flexible and adaptable. If we choose to minimize our options, it is to our long-term detriment.

The Difference

Finally, it is absolutely essential for each and every person involved with design to grasp the fact that our structures make a difference in the lives of those people who use, visit, study, and live within every building. Not enough is said about the effect of our work on the well being of the individual. In actual practice more emphasis is placed on economic issues from the design, client, and construction sides than on dialogue about what people need in their buildings. This is not an indictment: it is simply reality. Threaded throughout this text is an unspo-

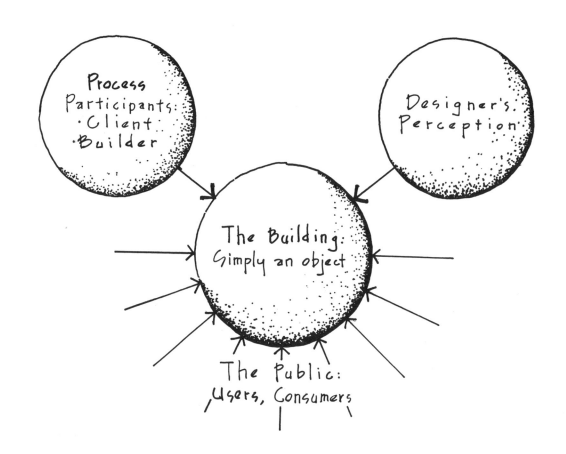

11-7: Design quality diagram—for perceived excellence to be upheld, all parties must agree that they got a quality project

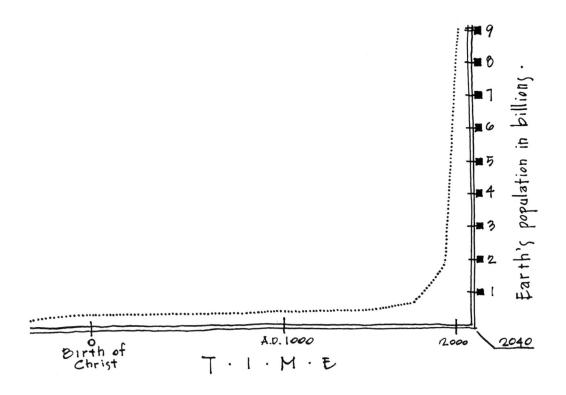

11-8: Historical pattern of human population growth

ken assumption: that we know what quality design is and is not. The thesis of my text rests on the belief that quality process yields quality design. Dana Cuff meets the issue of defining excellence in architecture head on (11-7).

> *The design quality debate is a controversial issue. Rather than take on the philosophical question of whether design quality can ever be absolutely determined, I define design quality as a phenomenological entity perceived by individuals, not as an inherent quality of the object or building. Thus, design quality is dependent upon those who make the judgment of quality. I maintain there are three principal evaluators of any building's quality and these are the consumers or the public at large, the participants in the design process, and the architectural profession....An excellent building is one perceived to be excellent by all three of these groups (Cuff 1991).*

The designer facilitates these groups. The fundamental choices made in everyday practice are grounded in our process and the quality of our communications to and from both the public and related disciplines. Scott Johnson of Johnson Fain Pereira & Associates makes a valuable point.

> *The execution of architecture at the highest level, the most serious level, is*

*no longer a solo performance...It is truly
choreographic. It is an orchestral performance. I see the process more in
terms of a moving target, of identifying
influences that will impact on the design (Frantz 1991).*

The designer becomes a communicator using each
and every available tool to its utmost in pursuit of
excellence. Our work truly does make a difference.
Understanding the influence of our work begs
us to consider issues in need of further study by the
profession. One that immediately comes to mind is
the effect of construction on the environment. In the
past few years we have begun to realize the extraor-
dinary volume of material and energy embodied
within our buildings. The design professions are
like an enormous ship with a huge inertia: its
direction is difficult to change. The environmental
issues connected to architecture and interior design
are a significant part of the warning bell now being
sounded all over the planet. Some confusion still
exists about the issues, but the general consensus is
that nearly six billion people now, expanding to
nine billion by 2010, is a recipe for catastrophe (11-
8). We have to face the idea of limiting or directing
our growth and the hard choices we will need to
make in the not too distant future. We must come to
terms with working cooperatively to address the
issues of energy usage and efficiency, quality of life,
indoor air quality, and planning to achieve sustainability (11-9 through 11). How to do this is a
question designers are beginning to wrestle with
even now. Obtaining clear direction is difficult

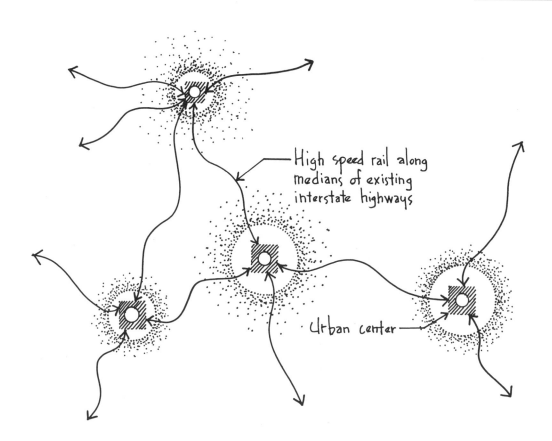

High speed rail along
medians of existing
interstate highways

Urban center

11-9: Sustainability with respect to a large scale transportion scheme

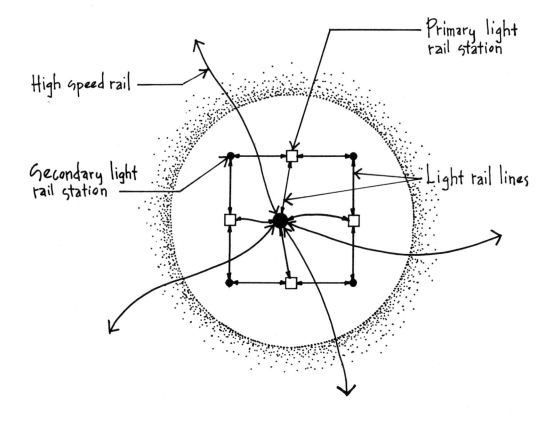

High speed rail

Primary light
rail station

Secondary light
rail station

Light rail lines

11-10: Urban scale transportation scheme

because of the enormous number of variables. Regardless of the complexity, time is surprisingly short, and our focus must be created quickly, then maintained and evolved.

When confronted with the challenge of designing a new building, I almost always experience something close to a rush of adrenaline. There is an excitement inherent in having the opportunity to be creative coupled with enough depth of experience to use an arsenal of techniques in the search for a quality design. The creativity associated with making spaces and buildings does not reside merely in making drawings and models, showing the world how architecture should be done. Making buildings contains within it an enormous and subtle volume of activity needing finesse, patience, and flexibility to prevail in what often becomes an out-and-out struggle to allow the mere survival of a design. The requirement to be creative resides in each and every one of the innumerable situations we find ourselves practicing in. At the outset, we gather information, then transform it into knowledge. The bridge from information to knowledge is where we begin to test and subsequently create the forms that become a building. Some of these activities are interpersonal and communication-dependent, like creating a program by working with a client. Other aspects of the work are highly personal and subjective, such as choosing the inspiration for design vocabulary and how spaces relate to each other within a building. As we achieve what we believe is an understanding of the knowns resident in a project and couple it to form, space, and material, the final step is allowing the design to be tested rigorously on an objective and subjective basis by the client and by external organizations with an interest in the work. When this testing ends, we take the suggestions, demands, and concerns of these parties and respond to them in the design. Our response begins the design process again, but the "grain" is finer, the variables fewer. We work our way through and bring the work back to light for further study and comment. The cycle is akin to being submerged and steadily swimming toward the surface.

Our culture and society shape us, then we shape our buildings. A subtle, long-term feedback loop follows the evolution of our civilization. In essence, we are either reactive or proactive: the choice has consequences that echo beyond our individual lifetimes. To choose to be proactive as a designer forces us into a demanding position. We shoulder a responsibility made of many voices and look to successfully fuse this variety into built form. As the orchestrators of the design process, however, our opinions have the force of skill and experience behind them. We have the opportunity, on innumerable occasions, to be proactive, to place environmental or any other issues that we feel are important on the table. Once in use, a building affects those using it both physically and psychologically. The exact form of these changes may be difficult to quantify, but it is undeniable that our work as architects and interior designers is the spring point for an enormous responsibility. Designers stand in the present, creating both history and the future.

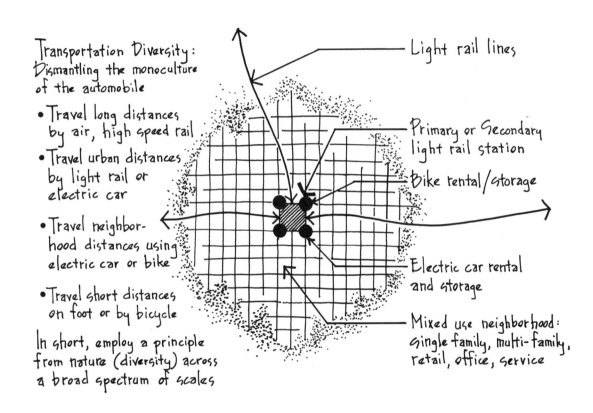

11-11: Transportation diversity and neighborhood scale transportation diagram

PART FOUR

Interviews

Originally, I began conducting interviews with other designers to obtain differing viewpoints and bring my work on this project into sharper focus. I also talked to people working in other disciplines such as graphic design and advertising. Initially, my intent was to use this material to "flesh out" the text. This occurred as I had hoped. I also discovered that many of the conversations were very interesting on their own. As a result, I decided to go after some better known practitioners in the hope of garnering a short look into the special qualities each individual brings to creating buildings and space. Conversely, I also chose to talk at length to architects and interior designers who, although not "famous" as such, had what I felt was an interesting perspective on the business of architecture and interior design.

I feel fortunate in that the sampling of people that follows represents a truly diverse range of possibilities in design practice. Steve Badanes' approach to making buildings is radically different from Scott Johnson's, but the results are of equal quality. Another thing I believe you will notice is that these people love what they do. Passion, commitment, and intensity are the norm rather than the exception. I am honored to add the thoughts of these designers to this text and I believe more than a few gems of wisdom are tucked away in the dialogue that follows.

STEVE BADANES

Jersey Devil, Stockton, New Jersey

Steve Badanes can be found almost anywhere. He is an architectural nomad who moves from place to place, site to site. His firm, Jersey Devil (with partners Jim Adamson and John Ringel), has been engaged in design/build architecture for over 20 years. Steve traces his beginnings to the early 1970's where, after receiving his masters degree from Princeton's school of architecture, he began working with a firm known as Dirt Road. They built a cabin in the Adirondack mountains of upstate New York. The site was miles from anywhere that even began to resemble civilization. More detail is presented in the interview that follows, but in a nutshell, this was Steve's introduction to design/build and he has chosen to follow this path ever since. Jersey Devil's primary source of work is word of mouth. Badanes goes to each site and literally lives there until the work is complete. He is hands-on and the craft of architecture is not a dialogue with paper, but an interaction with materials and power tools that moves from relatively simple drawings (for a building permit) to a finished product ready for occupancy.

Jersey Devil is adamant about achieving fine craftsmanship, respecting each site in terms of context and climate, and bringing a clear notion of concern for the environment to their work. Badanes is currently expanding his understanding of the energy embodied in materials and applying this knowledge to his construction practice and design process. For example, the trees for the Seaside dune walk over, rather than being cut, are harvested from naturally fallen timber in swamps within 100 miles of the building site. Steve also lectures and teaches actively for a part of each year. He brings both his environmental concerns and design/build skills to a variety of colleges nationwide in the belief that there is intrinsic value to both causes. He anticipates taking a group of students to the third world to build shelter and turn his beliefs into action while simultaneously teaching the next generation of designers the value of making buildings with their own hands.

Jersey Devil swims strongly and effectively across the main current of standard architectural practice. If, for whatever reason, you should choose not to take them seriously, have a good close look at some of their work. They appear regularly in a variety of trade publications serving several markets. The results of their craftsmanship are elegant, balanced, and unusual.

Steve Badanes: Hoagie House, 1984

SM: How would you describe your practice?

SB: Old fashioned, I think, would probably be a pretty good description. It's the old way of making buildings one at a time, traveling to the project location, and sometimes living on the site. We actually build the structure and extend the design process out onto the site. So, instead of the architect drawing then someone else building (a design), it's more like a painter or another type of artist who gets feedback from making the object and the design process continues as the structure is being built.

SM: So you, Steve Badanes, are hands-on, in the field?

SB: Personally, yes. There's two of us here, my partner, Jim Adamson and myself. Then we have John Ringel in New Jersey, too, who occasionally works with us. So, the company is Jersey Devil doing everything as a group, including the design. There's a common basis of agreement on what's good and that's the direction in which we go.

SM: How do you get to "what's good"?

SB: Well, I think that since we've been working together for almost 20 years, we have a kind of a common sensibility. It seems like all that stuff has been ironed out years ago and I don't exactly remember how. I think basically the common thread that holds a lot of it together is expressive structure. A solution (employing) energy efficiency and high-quality craftsmanship, a lot of stuff that nobody can really argue with. People are stopping by this project we're doing now, they just do. We're doing a little beach walk over here at Seaside and they're amazed. This is a town full of

high-quality carpenters, but they notice that this thing is particularly well crafted.

SM: So, how did you get started in design/build?

SB: I went to architecture school in the late '60s and early '70s. It was a very interesting time to be in school, for sure. At that time, there were a lot of people doing (design/build). It wasn't a new idea. There were guys up in Vermont, the Prickly Mountain Project. Ant Farm had built some stuff. There were a lot of these counterculture type groups and building was a part of that. Another part was futuristic technology spun off, in part, from space exploration. Another was social responsibility like community design centers and energy efficiency. I think that was the last time in architecture when social responsibility, basic technology, new technology and energy efficiency came together. Since that point, we've had nothing but Post Modern historic allusions or this newer de-constructivist work. They say it reflects the complexity of our society. You know, maybe the response to a complex society might be something simple. We've been really adamant from the very beginning, as soon as we learned about alternative energy technology. The '60s activists became the energy advocates of the '70s. We've just stayed with it, and it looks like we're going to have another shot at it in the '90s. It's coming back really strong. I'm being invited to a lot of these conferences on "green" architecture and climate responsive design. They're looking around for people, and they find out that we've been doing it for 20 years. In the old days, establishment people were a little nervous about the

buildings. The buildings that we did looked a little weird and the solar people didn't like to take credit for us because they were quite nervous about being accepted, especially in the early '80s when Ronald Reagan shut off the tap of federal money. You know, Jimmy Carter was a big sponsor of solar. He put solar collectors on the White House, initiated tax credits, and gave a lot of money to Department of Energy. When Reagan came in, he took the collectors off the White House at our expense, fired all the guys at the Department of Energy, and started pumping money into oil and nuclear. So it was panic in the solar world. The easy times of the '70s, when there had been some government money around, were slipping away. They just looked around and saw guys like us and said, "Well, if this stuff didn't look so weird maybe we could still get some funding."

SM: So, how do you feel about incorporating technology or high technology into your buildings?

SB: Well, there's a place for some of it. Do you remember the Hoagie house? Well, Jim Adamson, my partner has a patent on that roto-lid revolving panel for skylights. There are seven of them in (the house). They're attached to a computer, they track the sun, they're the most intelligent building device probably ever built. Some of the people who've looked at it say, "Yeah, that's pretty much it. That would be top of the line." It was reasonably expensive, but it was basically a prototype. I think there's a place for that, especially on a prototype level, and then there's room for production. But a lot of structures that we have built since then have been pretty low technology. The next house we're doing will probably be finished about 1995, when (your) book comes out, maybe. It will be made out of rammed earth. Nowadays, what I'm starting to get interested in is the energy that's embodied in the materials. They're telling me now that the production of concrete and aluminum together contributes to 20 percent of global warming. So we've been building buildings down in South Florida that don't need any air conditioning, but we're using a lot of concrete and aluminum to do it. We're saving a whole lot of energy, but there's a lot of energy (embodied) in those materials. I don't know if you know this guy in Texas, Pliny Fisk of the Center for Maximum Potential Building Systems (Max Pot). I think he's been up to Ball State a few times. He's been making these buildings out of caliche (covers 11% of the world's surface). It's a clay. He can get a 9,000psi block that's stronger than concrete. We just built a deck out of recycled plastic, for instance. Why not? You use wood, plastic maybe, but it's toxic. Somebody's got to figure a way through the puzzle, but if we're going to get another hundred years in this business, there won't be any raw materials left, we'll have to be recycling. This deck that we're building down here at Seaside is called a walkover. It walks over the dune so that people don't disturb the vegetation that holds the dune in place. It's built out of juniper; a wood which I think more correctly is eastern white cedar. It's fallen trees from the swamps here in Appalachicola which is less than 100 miles away. Then it's milled somewhere between here and there and brought to the site. So the energy embodied in that wood is almost zip compared to all that pressure-treated

pine and everything that it replaces. Plus it smells like a pet shop out there on the site instead of chemically impregnated arsenic. They won't take that pressure-treated wood at the dump, you know?

SM: Yes, it's considered hazardous waste.

SB: You can't burn it. So what are you supposed to do with it? I went one year to the Building Technology Conference in Albuquerque for the Association of Collegiate Schools of Architecture. And we asked the (pressure treated wood) rep what to do with the waste and he said, "Well, you gotta really plan your cuts so that you don't have any waste." A lot of people are getting smart and going back to the (naturally rot resistant) woods. Anyway, we are incredibly interested in materials and technology. Certainly, photovoltaics for generating electricity are pretty high-technology. You can hook them to a little refrigerator in some developing country and you've got (a way to store) vaccine. Typically, it's still the cheapest way to provide electricity for parts of the earth that are off the grid. Now, even with no government subsidies, the people who are in that business have no competition in remote applications. One of the most exciting remote applications is these developing countries where just a little light bulb, and particularly something like refrigeration, makes a difference. So we're interested in high-technology and we're also interested in doing something with simpler materials and recycled materials. But technology has always been a big part of the program. If you look at the houses and other things that we've done, often times you'll find that they're not quite one-liners. There's a strong idea that revolves

around either some kind of material like this corrugated asphalt we did the Airplane House in, or some kind of technology like solar. We are unlike a lot of architects where you'll see a certain style time after time. In our stuff, we tend to jump around. A lot of it has to do with (the fact) that we build all over the country. There's a different region and a different climate for each one, but a lot of it has to do with trying out new materials and ideas.

SM: How would you describe your design process? What happens?

SB: I guess it's probably two parts of the brain at once. You have to start with the program. You have to decide what you're building and talk to the people it's for even if they're just users rather than clients: really listen and solve each problem. This is a service profession. There's no doubt about it. Somebody's paying you to do a job and you do it. So you start with that, but on the other hand there's a part of the brain that you can't control that's always kind of pumping out these light bulb ideas. In my case, there's a lot of that which goes on. There's a little bit of sketching here and there, but I can't sit down at a board and crank something out. That's one reason why I build. I get an idea and then I'm up moving around. The physical pace of building suits me better than the static pace of sitting at a board. Although your mind is active, I find it's a lot more active if I'm out driving in a truck or flying in a plane. And so, I like to leave stuff sit. I like to work myself into a corner and not try to break out, but let it stew. In our case, we are fortunate in having people that aren't in so much of a hurry. You can drop something for a month and

be doing something else. All of a sudden, it'll come through. I think I'm finding a big input for me is traveling; looking around and seeing new things. The more places you go and the more you see how people live, the more raw material you have that somehow is behind this light bulb surge of ideas.

SM: Kind of like cultural fuel?

SB: Yes, that's a good term. It's doing research without really knowing it.

SM: Do you find that the "light bulbs" are spontaneous?

SB: A lot of times they are and sometimes they're fairly crude, too. Then you go into the traditional architectural mode of trying to draw it. Then, once you work on the board, you kind of begin to improvise. This thing we're building now (Fall, 1992); the idea for it came five years ago when we first came for the job interview at Seaside. It's been changed a few times, but really we haven't done a lot of designing. What we're doing while we build is make all those detailed decisions. But the scheme has been around for a long time. The last job we were on (finished before this) was a place in the Keys which we designed and built over a period of about two and a half years. So the initial concept for that was about two years old, too. But as far as taking on a new project, interviewing somebody, coming up with a big concept and following it through, that happens every year or two. We don't overload ourselves. I find it hard to imagine how someone could have a dozen projects going at once and not confuse them. Then, of course, that's what staff is all about. Then you become like a critic. A radical example of a guy who doesn't take this point

of view is Robert Bruno in Lubbock, Texas. He's spent about 12 or 13 years building this one house. That's why you wouldn't know him. The house is steel and he has a crane. He works himself around and welds on it. It's a very abstract sculptural looking building which looks a little hokey when you first see it in photos, but when I saw it in person, it was quite beautiful. Bruno told me the reason why he doesn't hire any help is that he felt like when you get to feel your time is too valuable to do it yourself, then you have to begin to make shortcuts in the design so that someone else can interpret it. And so he felt like if he did it all himself, then he could have incredibly high standards. It shows an amazing amount of patience. I've always thought the model career would not be somebody like in the Skidmore, Owings, and Merrill vein. I don't know who you'd talk about that was highly creative, but Antonio Gaudi did maybe a dozen buildings in his life. And they are all pretty fabulous. I think he had a pretty good career and I would be happy with one like that. At this point, I don't know that we have all that much more to prove. We're just looking for really good opportunities to go forward a little bit. To do that, I think you have to be really selective in what you decide to design and then what you do with it, so it justifies spending all your time for a period of time on one project.

SM: I personally like that idea very much. I think there's a lot of value in that.

SB: People find some economic problems with it. That's a justification for the normal architect to say, "Oh my, I could never do that. I've got to have four or five things going." Even without a

drafter because he grinds through the work so fast, if you just draw it. But if you build, then a job can last quite a bit longer. I think the economics involved in successfully constructing something for profit are a little better than designing it, too.

SM: I agree, I think the economics make decent sense, really.

SB: It trims the design process down. It virtually eliminates working drawings. Working drawings are basically something that you do to tell the contractor how to build. If you're going to be the contractor, then the work is a conversation between you and yourself. You could just as easily have that conversation on a scrap of lumber as you could on seven sheets of blueprint paper.

SM: How do you address codes and life safety and all of that business?

SB: Everybody asks that question because they first see the buildings when I give a presentation. They get pretty excited and it seems like a fairly loose approach. But you can't get a permit for any of this unless you design within the codes and, of course, you can't get it inspected when you build unless you meet the code. We do enough drawings up front to get a permit. When you go for inspection, you fail if the 6" ball goes through the pickets in the railings. Now there have been jobs that were outside the jurisdiction of building codes. We built a house in Baja California, Mexico. If you know that house...

SM: No, I don't. Sorry.

SB: It's a house we did in about 1988. There are no codes, no inspection, so then you set your own standards.

SM: Right. You literally become the code official.

SB: We find the inspectors somewhat helpful in many cases. I don't know what it's going to be like in south Florida now after the hurricane. They're going to be a little overzealous. I don't know if we'll be doing work down there or not. And we did some work up in New Hampshire where there was virtually no inspection involved beyond the septic system.

SM: So, where do your clients come from?

SB: I think some from publication, but very few. A lot is word-of-mouth. It's interesting that everybody says, "How do they find you?" We're always traveling. We live in these Airstream trailers, and there are some interesting stories. This one guy hired a detective to find us and it only took 45 minutes. We have a low profile, but we're in the news fairly frequently, so if you pick up a magazine and use a little effort, you can find us. We don't have any marketing the way a lot of offices do. People seek you out and when they make a significant effort to find you, I think that it would difficult for them later on down the line to feel that they made a mistake. They have a lot more at stake. On the other hand, if you twist their arm, which a lot of architects do, and get them into something before they're ready, then there's always this hesitation, this feeling on their part that they may have been talked into something. We've gone from being considered outlaws and radicals to "artists" who have a waiting list. We're virtually no different. We're getting a little better at what we do, but not that much better. We're still building, moving a little slower, but maybe we take fewer steps with the job. That's the reputation that we have now. We provide a high quality, hand-crafted product which is getting more and more rare in this computer age, mass-produced society. We, essentially, are artisans or artists, especially because of the hands-on stuff. We find that when somebody calls, they want the autographed model. They're not interested in me sending them a set of plans for their local builder. They want to be able to come down there on Saturday and find me. In fact, they're really glad to know that I'm not going to be juggling them with some other client. You know, we're moving out of a lot of this residential work after 20 years of it.

SM: Are you doing more institutional kinds of things?

SB: Not institutional. This is public work that we are doing here (in Seaside) and we've done some Public Art in Seattle.

SM: You say you interviewed in Florida for the beach walk over the dune?

SB: They asked us to come, but we did interview.

SM: But it wasn't like there were four or five other firms sitting in the waiting room?

SB: No. There were four or five of these beach walks and the developer gave us one. You know the story of Seaside, right?

SM: No, I'm sorry, I don't.

SB: Seaside is a community developed by Robert Davis and designed by Andres Duany and Elizabeth Plater-Zyberk from Miami. It's won of a bunch of awards and they've made an effort to bring a lot of big name architects into this little town in Florida. It's something like Columbus, Indiana, but not exactly. Columbus was an existing town which needed schools and public buildings, and Irwin Miller (CEO of Cummins, Incorporated, headquartered in Columbus) said, "I'll pay the fee if you can pull from this list of architects." This is different. Robert set up the town, had the plan, and the architects set up a code for all the buildings. The residential buildings had to have screened porches and certain pitches on the roofs and so on. Within that list of restrictions, you had complete freedom. But the public structures are non-coded. That's why they felt it was a good place for us to fit in. It's interesting for us to do this kind of work because it's one of the first that we've done.

SM: So when you look at a site, what kind of things do you see?

SB: Well, obviously there's a couple of things. One is the terrain. It depends also on the size of the site. Some are 75 acres and some are a quarter acre. Sometimes you've got to fight to squeeze the well far enough away from the septic and deal with the car and where you put it. But what's important, also, is the region and the climate for us because we work in so many different parts of the country. We work in the hot, humid tropics and up in the snow belt, on the west coast and all the way down into Mexico. Each site is completely unique. It's sort of a triad: you have the site and all of its features, the client and his/her program, and the budget. All three of those things constantly input into the design. Another (triad) we always talk about is quality, speed, and cost. There's three things there and you can always only have two. You

can never get all three. You can never get a high-quality building real fast for low cost. The high-quality building is real slow sometimes for low cost, particularly if you're really scrounging materials. But you can get a low-quality building real fast for cheap. Throw enough money at it, sometimes, you can get a high-quality building fast, but it'll be very expensive. But there is no way that you can pull all those three together and basically, the client almost always comes to you wanting all three.

SM: Right, and you have to sit them down and some how tactfully educate them to the fact that maybe that's not the case.

SB: I'm not that tactful. I'm pretty blunt. We've lost a few jobs by telling people, "Listen, this is what we can do it for." We never low-ball anybody. In fact, we often try and scare them off. We're pretty idiosyncratic and strong willed. We know it is a service business, but if we think we're right, we're going to fight with you on it.

SM: So, you build models, right?

SB: Many times, yes; sometimes, no.

SM: What kind of a situation makes you want to build a model?

SB: Well, there's a couple. There's a study model which can be kind of thrown together really fast to clear your head, although it's not usually necessary. A lot of times they're pretty helpful for the client. And even more so, when it comes to construction and subcontractors have to look at it. For what we're doing now, we built a framing model of this complicated wood thing in Seaside. We have it in the shed on the site. We pull it out and we use it to build with. So there's a number of

different models. There's a really kind of scrabbly one put together with the glue gun that's occasionally done, but rarely anymore. More often, it's a presentation model for the client. We've found that there's not much disagreement with the scheme on a big scale. The clients, in many cases, have come (to us) because they're interested in the product that we deliver. They'll accept that and we almost never have them send us back to the drawing board. The place that they like to get involved is when you get inside. And, in our case, we usually don't design the inside until we get there. See, what we'll do is the drawings that you mentioned that I need for the building department. I can do those without any notion of finishes. The building department doesn't care about finishes. The building department cares about structure, egress, and a number of other things, then they'll stamp it for a permit. And really, that's all we need to know. We have to have some idea in our brain about lighting, for instance, but we don't have to lay it out until we're framed up. Then we can go around and clip on some lights, baffle them, and mock it up with the client. And we can say, "What about this lighting scheme?" I'm sure it's better that way than trying to figure it out on the board.

SM: I love it.

SB: That's the way to do it. And many of our buildings are clear span structures. Many times, things will change once it's framed which is often difficult to do with a normal job. There is a change order and that's where, of course, the contractor begins to hammer you.

SM: Right; but in your case its, "Okay, I want

to move a wall." And the answer is, "Fine."

SB: In one case, I remember we changed the house so much that when the electrical inspector came, he said that it didn't even resemble the plan and wanted an as-built drawing. I mean, "It's all right," he said, "but I want an as-built drawing." So I had to do an as-built, but usually they'll let you go. We don't generally know what the (finishes are) and, of course, when you get to that level, you know what you've spent in terms of dollars for the shell, so you can begin to economize if you have to.

SM: Is there any particular approach you take to your clients when you're working on a program with them?

SB: I ask them to do a little homework and write a list of what they like and don't like. I don't ask them to come with magazine clippings which they often do. I don't care about the clippings. I need to know what they like and what they don't like, and how big they like things and so on. I'll try and get them to come up with that list and then if it's not clear enough, I'll ask them a lot of questions about it. Then, I've generally got enough material to be able to do the design. Of course, since it's built so slowly they're able to come out and if something's not quite right, we can change it right then; but it starts with that whole list of stuff.

SM: Do you generally come to your clients with one scheme after you've had the chance to absorb all the programmatic material?

SB: I'm usually somewhat attached to a drawing.

SM: You've got some serious prejudices built up?

SB: Well, not necessarily, but I think I know the way it ought to go. What it means is that we don't usually tinker with it that much or throw it out and do another one. That's hardly ever happened. I remember one particular job; the Silo House. I don't know if you know that one, but the client had recently returned from seven years in Tanzania. They wanted something resembling African huts. And they kept coming in with these little drawings that looked like dumb bells. I kept coming up with curves. I said, "Well, they want round, so I'll do curves." And I did two or three of these curved schemes and they just kept throwing them back at me. Finally, I think I was taking a bus to New York City and I saw these oil tanks. I saw that when they're in a group of more than two, you begin to have a composition. You know, in Indiana, you'll see three of those grain silos with a feeder line across the top and that's basically what the house became. We bought three silos and put this solar collector across the top that connects them and then I felt like I had a fairly strong composition. There was a little resistance, but in the end everybody was happy with it. It was one of the early solar houses that was built in the country around 1975. The house was also partially wood heated. A lot of our early work was an attempt make use of industrial type components: agricultural or industrial materials, manhole risers, bus windows, silos, that kind of thing because it was cheap. We built a couple of buildings out of curved barn rafters because we were fascinated with using something else. When the budgets got a little higher, a lot of that disappeared because that was often an attempt to save money and still do something interesting.

SM: You obviously get out to quite a few different schools. When you get to do that, what do you tell the kids? What do you think is important for them to learn?

SB: I spend a part of every year teaching. And I also do a lot of lecturing. I teach a design/build class. In fact, we're going to start one at the new architecture school at UCSD in La Jolla, California. What we do is two things; we do a little introductory class in the shop where we give them design projects using materials. Basically, they'll get something like a sheet of ¼" plywood, or a couple of sacks of cement, and they'll build an outdoor light fixture. They'll design the pieces, do shop drawings, and actually make them themselves. Then we'll move into working as a group and we'll build a community project. Hopefully, at UCSD we're going to be working in developing countries. They're considering India, Africa, and South America. I have taught at the University of Washington where we've worked in the International District for the Danny Woo community garden. We've also built some stuff on the campus. It often works out to be a course that the students are tremendously changed by. They really like building. Then years later, they call you and they say that they're doing a design/build project and they never would've thought to do it if they hadn't taken the class. So it's pretty important to me to keep doing this kind of thing. It shows students that architecture can be more than a dead end office situation. I just gave a lecture to the Western Florida AIA in Pensacola and people said, "It made me remember what I decided to become an architect for," or, "That was inspirational." Something about what we do strikes a responsive chord both in students and practitioners. In a way, it's an idealized vision of the practice of architecture that everybody thinks they would like to do, if they could do it. Now, it's not very easy to have a family and be able to travel in a little trailer and live on job sites all over the place. It's not practical for everybody. There's something about it that is a role model because I think the other alternatives are not that attractive these days. The big offices take in a lot of institutional work and do it in big teams. In school, they train us to be kind of renaissance people where we can interview somebody, go home, and solve their problem. Then we can go out in the field and have it done, whether we do it ourselves or lay it out and supervise. And, I don't know if they teach you that in school, but at least they teach you the notion of following it all the way through the design. Then in the real world, we know it's not like that.

SM: The work ends up being delegated and separated. I think your observation about building is kind of an instinctive drive. When I was little, it was always something I loved to do. Even now, I'm one of those "Office Architects", you know, and I will after a certain amount of time, crack, and have to build something with my hands. So it's very interesting for me to talk to you and inspirational as well.

SB: Well, I try and tell (the students) that it is possible. Start on a small scale. There are a number of jobs that are too small for an architect and also too small for a contractor: like a little deck. In good times, people can't find anybody to come over to do that kind of work. And they can't get an architect to do it either or can't afford to have an architect do it. A young student, just out of school, will build about seven models and sleep on the site. And in building it, of course, you keep getting passed on to the next neighbor until you're established. I've been teaching my students how to bypass the office routine. I try and teach them that architectural school is pretty much a general education. It's a great problem-solving type of education. They give you a lot of information and you process it through your brain and you come up with solutions. There's not many other kinds of education that are like that. In most cases, you read a book and you write a paper. In our case, we're actually coming up with a product. It's good training for anything. We're trying to instill some sort of sense of social responsibility in them, too. And that's been paying off. We have a lot of students working for non-profits and doing affordable housing and they're busy as hell nowadays even with the recession. And all the guys who were feeding on the glut and excess of the '80s are hurting, cutting back because we've built too much office space. You'll notice our cities' monuments are unleased office space. I think a good rate is considered 70 percent occupancy and you've got guys sleeping in boxes in front of them. I'm spending more and more time in the academic environment building things. We're building in cities and I'm getting a shot at projects that I normally wouldn't get. Jersey Devil has been known for years as custom house builders. Mostly, people call for houses and, for 20 years, we've been

doing pretty high-quality custom houses. We do a really good job at it, but we're interested in doing some other projects as well. It's really hard to do that unless you've done some of it. It's like the architect who does branch banks and keeps hoping for the big residential commission, but no one's going to call him because he hasn't done any houses. What we're trying to do, and what I can do by working with students, even though I don't design it, is get to do these community based projects. Residences are good commissions, especially if you can pay attention to the energy embodied in the materials and the operation of the house. You make some people pretty happy and you get friends for life and the whole experience is fun and, in our case, we build it and spend so much time on it that we generally make sure it's a pretty nice place to live for a couple of years, too. I'm not saying we're not doing that anymore; in fact, we're working on one now, like I said, that has to be done by 1995 in Palm Springs, California.

SM: Is that house underway now?

SB: No. It's not even designed. I've got to get to the site yet.

SM: It's cued up, then?

SB: It's cued up. The owners are not in a particular hurry and it's actually the third building we've built for them.

SM: So, if you could change any thing about the practice of architecture, what would it be?

SB: Well, that's a hard question but, you know, I don't want to be intolerant. I remember seeing Christopher Alexander being very intolerant. He doesn't make many friends.

SM: But he's a great philosopher, isn't he?

SB: My way is not the only way to do architecture. It's a good way to do architecture, but I don't think architects need to build all their buildings. I think they ought to take as much pride in them as if they had built them. That's the issue. I'm not asking them to go out and pick up the hammer, but nowadays, all it takes for an architect to do buildings is to sign a contract. That's why we have so many dogs out there. All the architect does is meet with an owner who wants to put up a crappy building along the strip. They sign a contract, the architect gives the program over to some draftsman who does (the documents), and then bids it to some contractor who subs out all the rest. Meanwhile, the architect is chasing more work and really his total involvement in that structure, in many cases, could be only half an hour. And this is a building that might last 40 or 50 years. It's probably not built to last much longer, and its going to be sucking energy and look like hell at the same time. (The architect's) name doesn't go on it. If we had to put the architects's name on every building, then some of these kind of guys would fade away. There are a lot of things I would change about the profession of architecture. There's a lot of good architects who practice in a traditional way and make good architecture. But when you say, "What would you change," I'll definitely look around and see problems. We can tell that since most buildings are designed by architects because you have to stamp them to get them constructed. There are a lot of bad ones out there. Buildings use *40 percent* of all energy (electricity and natural gas). This doesn't include the energy involved in the manufacture of the materials, transportation of the materials, and construction. The government is boosting nuclear energy which I think represents the death and destruction of us all: oil as well, as featured in the Gulf War. Solar and renewables represent sustenance and survival, so if you want to contribute to the continuation of the species, then you'll design energy-efficient buildings. I think the profession is starting to get interested in it, you know, as we speak. As we're talking here, in 1992, your book will come out in 1994, and in 1993, the AIA Convention is on energy and the environment. I was just in a big symposium that AIA threw a bunch of cash into and videotaped. I think this time they're not going to miss the band wagon. So maybe there won't be too much that needs to change about the practice of architecture by the time this book comes out. I hope that's the case.

SM: There's a lot of inertia and a lot of things that we can't control.

SB: As we speak now, there's a recession going on and architects are feeling a major part of it because the profession is so vulnerable to bad times. However, the people that are doing affordable housing, nonprofit work, are quite busy now.

SM: So what do you see for your future? What do you look to be doing in another 20 years?

SB: Let me see, that would make me 70 years old. It might be hard to be building. I want to try to still be making things. I suspect that this part-year academic thing might become something that I do on a regular basis, particularly if we can get this design/build thing going in the developing coun-

tries. I enjoy working with the students and I've spent 25 years now learning all this. I think it's about time to give some of it back. There are definitely some things that I would like to build and I think some of it would be in the public arena. The scale of the kind of work that we talk about would be best suited to these little parks. The kind of commissions Fay Jones has are really nice. Those, in a way, are almost design/build because the guys that build them are friends of his from Fayetteville and they go to these little towns to do it.

SM: Have you ever thought about associating with a more standard sort of architectural practice in undertaking some larger work?

SB: Well, not necessarily larger, but we associate with them all the time. It depends on what we do. We did a job in the Florida Keys and you needed a licensed architect for the documents. Anything in south Florida must be stamped and we aren't licensed. We used to have a partner that had a license, but we don't anymore. We worked with Taxis Architects in Miami, and they have the computer capability. They also are sort of night owls. Right about now, they'd be kicking in. They'd be really rolling and no one could call them. It's perfect for us to work on the site during the day and come in at night. All of the permit drawings for the Keys job were done on computer. We've worked with a number of architects in local places. I think that's an interesting way to go. I had dinner recently with Malcolm Wells. He says he takes some grief because of the way he does his buildings nowadays. He kind of sketches it out and sends it to a local architect who takes it from there. He said, "I take

a little heat for it, but I paid my dues." He's 66 years old and I figure maybe that's what I might do, but I don't know if they'll turn out so good. In our case now, we're there everyday and the control is an important part of it for us. That's the goal of a lot of architects and I think many of us would be glad to have complete control because we think we know how it ought to be. That's what art is and, again, the lesson of Robert Bruno in Texas. If I start dropping back and delegating more, then I think the quality will definitely go down. I know we still make some incredibly big screw ups in the conceptual stage, but we go out on the site, we start to build them and we go, "Oh my, this is not going to work." We nip it in the bud and change it, mock it up, and do it. I'm in awe of the architects who can turn out really good buildings and not actually build them. They can provide a complete set of plans and have that thing turn out to be a masterpiece without ever having to have the building there under construction for feedback. It happens all the time. I know Frank Lloyd Wright did it. He designed buildings that are just unbelievable and, for some of them, didn't even see the site. Some apprentice of his would go and report on the progress. He would send a set of drawings and somebody would build it. Maybe he never saw the buildings in his life. I know that Auldbrass is a South Carolina plantation that he did. I don't think he ever saw the site and I'm sure he never saw the completed building and it's fabulous. Now, I worked for Eric Lloyd Wright, the grandson of Frank Lloyd Wright, in Malibu, California.

SM: Was this when you were out of school?

SB: No, I did just about three years ago. I got

back from Mexico, things were a little slow and I went up to Malibu, California. It's a beautiful place. I built concrete forms for Eric with Devon Lloyd Wright who is Eric's son. Devon wore the pork pie hat like FLLW. He's big; 6'-5" and a master surfer, so I don't know if he'll become an architect.

SM: That's something. So, where did you go to school?

SB: Well, I went to college at Wesleyan University in Connecticut. I studied art and then I went to architecture school at Princeton. Princeton was a fairly conservative architecture school, but I went from 1968 to 1971, which was not a conservative time in this culture. We built inflatable structures for school events and started a community design center in New Brunswick, New Jersey. We were able to do a lot of alternative architecture and the faculty was glad to let us to do it as long as we didn't burn down the school. The students actually had the power to determine the curriculum. It was a good place to go to school. I actually built my masters thesis. It was a demountable building system for migrant workers. Since there weren't any migrant workers in Princeton, I got to keep it. I took it with us and we used it on the first few jobs. Then I eventually sold it to a guy for a hunting camp. It was designed to fit in the back of a 4' x 8' U-Haul. It was a little panelized structure with a vaulted roof - 12 feet square. It was the kind of thing that architects were working on in the '70s when we felt like industrialized housing might make some progress. And, of course, it has, but it's all been done in Elkhart, Indiana. You know, the mobile

home is the Number 1 selling house and architects have little or nothing to do with it. But twenty years ago, there were architects working with Operation Breakthrough sponsored by the government. There were a lot of architects involved in housing and industrialized building and it was a really good idea. It kind of died off.

SM: So as you look back on your career to date, your practice, and education, are there any people that you feel particularly influence your work or your methodology?

SB: Well, I basically learned every method that I do right now on my first job, which was my only job out of school. I worked for some guys called Dirt Road. That's Barry Simpson and Charlie Hosford. They're graduates of Yale Architecture School and they worked in Vermont. They still work up there and they do design/build. We built a house of Simpson's design. We prefabricated it in Vermont, took it out by truck, and floated it by boat in panels to a site in the Adirondacks which had a 200 pound per square foot roof load because of snow. It was a cable roof house with two panelized box beams and a suspended roof in between. People thought we were crazy to build a saggy roof in snow country. We camped out on the site in my thesis building and built it. I made $3 an hour and loved it. I learned the basics of moving to a remote site and designing and building a custom piece of architecture, particularly in that case where we were in six miles by boat and then an hour by dirt road to a phone. We basically had to have everything. We could go out every couple of weeks and get materials, but we had to have everything together. Even-

tually, I did a job like that myself in 1989. I went to Baja California, Mexico, and put up a house in a place that's really remote. This was before fax machines. I spoke to the client twice the whole job. (Dirt Road) was an offshoot of something called the Prickly Mountain Project which was started by Dave Sellers and Bill Reinecke, two guys who graduated from Yale in the mid-'60s and decided the architect could also be the builder and, in their case, the developer. They borrowed a bunch of money, bought some land in Vermont, and built these amazing houses. Maybe it was before your time, but I'd say those guys were pretty influential. As far as Jersey Devil goes, there were a lot of counterculture groups around in the late '60s, but obviously the primo American version was the Ant Farm. These guys are (my age), but they started a little earlier and got a lot more publicity. They built the Cadillac Ranch and the House of the Century in Texas. Just the idea that these guys could do art, architecture, construction, traveling, lectures, and go into a kind of new technology like inflatables was real influential to us. As far as architecture goes, basically looking at Frank Lloyd Wright, Bruce Goff, and the organic school is helpful although we're not necessarily in that mode. I mean, you can't look at Frank Lloyd Wright and not be inspired, particularly when you see those buildings in person.

ROBERT DORAN

The Architecture Studio, Cincinnati, Ohio

Robert Doran, a principal in The Architecture Studio, practices architecture along with one other partner in Cincinnati, Ohio. He has forged a most unusual career path beginning with two years of technical school and a degree in architectural technology. He began his professional career in Cincinnati and supplemented his nine to five regime with evening design courses at the University of Cincinnati in the mid 1960's. He was not impressed with what he discovered. The academic focus of the time seemed completely at odds with his beliefs about what design was and is. He retreated from formal schooling and studied independently for eight years. During this time, Bob began to nurture his interest in teaching and academia, designed a variety of projects, and moved from Cincinnati to Nashville, Tennessee. Several of his projects in Tennessee were recognized for their design quality and while working for a firm in Tennessee in the late 60's, one of his projects received an award from Progressive Architecture magazine.

He was formally teaching before his departure from Cincinnati and continued his interest in academia at the University of Tennessee in Nashville. At this point, he had qualified for the licensing exam and passed the first time through. The possibility of starting his own practice began to percolate in Bob's mind and he spoke with his employer, Nashville architect Earl Swensson, in this regard. He not only received moral support, but due to the size of the practice in Swensson's office, smaller projects were available that were not suitable for

the scale and overhead associated with a large office. Bob opened his fledgling business with projects ready to go and the good will of his former employer as well.

Bob continued to work in both academia and active practice, but there was one nagging problem: no professional degree. A former employee of his had been accepted to Harvard's GSD and while on vacation in New England, Bob stopped in Cambridge for a visit. With encouragement from his friend, Bob decide to apply to Harvard. Much to his surprise, he was accepted with one of the highest standings ever afforded a GSD student. After receiving his Master of Architecture degree, Bob returned to Ohio where he joined the faculty of the Department of Architecture at Miami University in Oxford, Ohio. During his six year tenure at Miami, Bob acted as the coordinator for Miami's graduate program in architecture. He left Miami in 1985 and began working with KZF, Inc. in Cincinnati as the firm's Director of Design. His years there saw the firm grow from 55 to 180 people. Unfortunately, he discovered that the larger the firm grew, the more separated from design he became. In 1991, he decided to strike out on his own again, and The Architecture Studio was born.

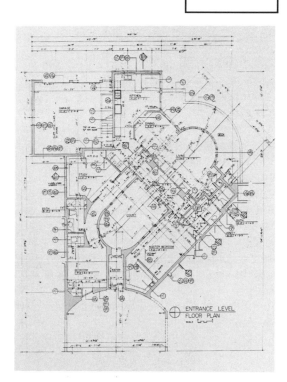

Robert Doran: Condominium plan, Oxford, Ohio

SM: What has been your recent experience consisted of?

BD: I left Miami (of Ohio) in 1985, and went to a relatively large firm as the Director of Design. The firm grew from about 55 to 180 people during the time I was there. We were fortunate and experienced a high degree of success. For the first two or three years, I found myself immersed in all of the firm's projects. But the larger the firm became, the farther away I was from what I wanted to do. I was beginning to do a lot of marketing as well as a lot of staff administration. The learning curve was very positive and I became a member of the firm's Board of Directors. While the experience was a very positive one for me professionally, I became restless as a "hands-on designer." With some help from KZF in June 1991, I decided to open a practice with my colleagues Rob Pfauth and Joe Power. I had known both of them for some time. I met Rob through KZF's collaboration with William Turnbull Associates of San Francisco. Bill Turnbull was doing the master plan for a project along the river front here in Cincinnati and KZF was selected as the local architect. I was to act as the liaison between the local team and Bill's office. Rob Pfouth was working for Bill at the time. As luck had it, KZF needed someone that could manage the project as a project architect and I asked Bill if he had any objections to my approaching Rob about the position. Rob wanted to relocate in the Midwest in order to be closer to his family in Pennsylvania. I said to Bill, "Look, do you have any objections to me offering him a job?" Bill said, "I'd rather have him come with you than anywhere else." In fact, Rob came to Cincinnati and

was here about two and a half years working with KZF. He ended up becoming a partner in The Architecture Studio through that relationship. My relationship with Joe Power began around very different circumstances. Joe had established a firm here in Cincinnati almost three years before we began collaborative discussions. Joe had left a position in a large firm in Cincinnati for much the same reasons as I left KZF. I met Joe through his involvement with the new Design Art Architecture and Planning building, a project at the University of Cincinnati designed by Peter Eisenman in Joint venture with a local firm, Lorenz and Williams, Inc.. The project was selected for exhibition at the Venice Bianale, and has gained much acclaim. The project was developing quite a bit of stress around program, budget, and scheduling issues and Joe was asked by the College Dean Jay Chattergee to manage the project internally for the college. For some time, the Dean had been planning a symposium to celebrate the opening of the new DAAP building, scheduled for Fall '94. The Dean asked some members of the Dean's Advisory Committee to form a committee to plan the symposium. He also asked me if I'd be part of the committee. That's how Joe and I became acquainted. We found a lot of common interests, and to make a long story short, decided that the three of us could experiment with a collaborative design practice. We've tried to make it anything but a standard practice.

SM: What do you mean when you say it's not a standard practice?

BD: I had been in academia for 15 years and had a lot of time to look at the practice of architec-

ture. I taught a lot of design theory and practice courses. I was always looking around at the way people made architecture. First, in the form of process, but also from a practical standpoint. How do you actually make this profession work as a business, but at the same time not loose sight of all your personal values. During my years at Miami University I spent many summers teaching a studio/ theory course traveling through Europe. As you may be aware, Miami University has a foreign study campus in Luxembourg. My time at Miami as well as the years that I spent in private practice have given me a chance to really get to know and work with many interesting people. For instance while I was at KZF, we were hired by a Geneva Architect/ Developer as the local counterpart to his Swiss office. The project was to be the Cincinnati Entertainment Center, a 60-70 million dollar project in the heart of the Cincinnati central business district. I was going to Geneva regularly for about three years. For a time I also found myself going to San Francisco to collaborate with Bill Turnbull and traveling to Geneva every couple of months working with the Pluss Organization.

The exposure I've had to European practice through teaching and my experience with collaborative work with other architects in both the US and Europe helped formulate an idea of how I wanted to practice. It is much more the idea of a European "Atelier" than a standard architectural practice that we are looking for. The idea was to be anything but the normal hierarchical, ego-driven practice. What I had searched for in my practice experience and what I had found while looking at other practices that I admired, was a richness of what came out of the design process in terms of the architectural product as well as a high degree of concern for the "quality of life" for the people creating it. The style of practice we envisioned was much more conducive to a "real" working collaborative environment, not one that spends most of it's time talking about collaboration. This desire for an environment that would flourish through collaboration was what motivated us to establish The Architecture Studio. All three of us had been practicing for a while and we were all a bit gun shy as to how to actually initiate the beginning of this kind of culture that we all know as a very ego driven profession. The question that we continually asked ourselves was, how do you remove the tension created by the ego between designers, or between principles, or between partners so that our practice doesn't become just another professional nightmare? All of us were in different stages of our careers and to no one's surprise our family lives were all remarkably different. We wanted to develop a certain degree of flexibility. For instance, if Joe wanted to take off on Fridays and be with his new daughter, or if I wanted to take off and spend time with my son we could be free to do that. At the time Rob was not married and was extremely involved in his volunteer interests in various community organizations. We realized that circumstance like these could complicate the issues of a normal practice. If we weren't all working exactly at the same time and committing ourselves in exactly the same way, how could we prevent the tension that we had noticed within other firms? We were all at different places in the chronology of our

individual practices. I had developed an extensive network and had already proven my ability to bring work into the office. Rob, on the other hand, being relatively new in the Cincinnati area, had cultivated few business contacts. Joe found that his practice was extensively committed to his involvement with projects at the University of Cincinnati. In the beginning we found that there was quite a noticeable diversity in the way we approached our practices from both a financial as well as a philosophical standpoint. In the beginning, as a period of professional courtship, we created The Architecture Studio as an umbrella organization to supply the support needs of a practice, and let us find a professional fit through our collaboration on projects.

SM: So you in concept practice separately, but can bring everyone together and focus on a specific project to take advantage of the background and variation of expertise?

BD: Yes. We bring in many varied allied professions. We work with various artists, graphic designers, and other consultants in this region as project needs dictate. Our goal has always been to create an environment within which we can bring to fruition many diverse talents. We hope to be in a position to merge all the various talents without allowing personal ego to negatively be part of the equation. We had seen that in many partnerships bound together mainly by profit motive partners are always upset with one other when on the surface it doesn't look like the other partner is working as hard or it seems that one partner spends his time doing all of the fun things while the other does all the work. We didn't want any of that to happen here. So we

have a relatively simple but distinct formula that we use in terms of creating a project participant's remuneration. It removes the ambiguity and most of the problems that you see developing within practices. So far, so good; the system has been up and running for about a year and a half. We've gotten stronger, we've gotten closer, and it seems to be getting better and better. In fact, we had four partners in the beginning. Two have left, not under difficult circumstances, but because of philosophically different directions that they wanted to pursue. I think we found that the way we were working together has allowed that to happen in a way that didn't get nasty but fostered a transition that made a lot of sense. After working together we find that in terms of our individual design processes we're also quite different. I see myself as being a highly interactive person reacting heavily to both client and context. I use a lot of reference materials. I use a lot of things to quicken the dialogue between architect and client. In design schools there is a French term used for this process called "bricolage."

SM: What's that?

BD: The way I've distilled the term is that a bricoleur is a person, for example a builder, who would literally go survey the countryside collecting fragments or images, pieces of buildings, carting them home and storing them out in his field at the back of his house. As he would get involved in a building project, he would again survey his collection and study the project looking at the things he had at his disposal. In a simplistic way, the idea of bricolage allows you to bring fragments, ideas, and issues together into a unified fabric.

SM: So it's much more than objects?

BD: In an intellectual sense, it is the context of a situation that allows it to happen. I'm not one to believe that designers are born as "gifted" individuals. As an academician, I believe that you can teach students to be competent architects. In my opinion, the process of educating happens through exposure to a plethora of architectural theory, analysis of historical and contemporary projects, theoretical studio design experiences, strong but supportive constructive design criticism, and an amazing amount of hard work. A quality architectural education happens only through creating a very special kind of learning environment. Unfortunately, I do not think that these circumstances are in place and established universally. Certainly a threshold of personal commitment and intellect needs to always be present as a foundation for positive student development. Architectural students have to develop a creative personal vision, but this vision can be learned. In much the same way, I feel that almost every project can be successful in terms of its architectural success, but first you must work with your client to define what "success" means. I find personal success in a project is most profound when I have a building that has met my personal criteria and the criteria of my client as well as establishing a sense of a personal bonding with them throughout the process. I want to have personal satisfaction, not just in terms of the architectural reward, but also in terms of the experience. I like the fact that I can wake up in the morning and really like coming to the office. I like the fact that I socialize with my clients and that we have developed a mutual respect for one

another. I try to diffuse as much tension in the design and construction process as possible by allowing them to wholeheartedly get involved, to know everything. Our clients look at all of the design options, they look at everything we've done in the pursuit of the solution to their problem. The way that I try to bring them into the process is different with each project, but the goal is always to allow them to understand what it is that we're trying to solve in each step of the process. I almost find myself returning to an academic mode of thinking with each client, working with them to develop their design goals and objectives. In establishing a dialogue with my client, this educational aspect of predesign is always a declared process: never one that is subversive or veiled in obscure terminology. I find clients quite preceptive to the process.

SM: Is that something that occurs along with or separate from any process or programming that you undertake?

BD: I basically insist on doing what we can refer to as a predesign phase in each project. For me, predesign work is really the majority of the educational time that you spend with a client. It's not only educational time with the client, it's also educational time for me. I spend a lot of time up front doing programming and trying to understand what it is that the client likes, what their needs are, and then help them understand what I like and what I need. I take them on a walk through the "bricolage in my backyard." We talk about contemporary architectural problems that we may encounter and analyze examples of projects from history; anything that we can think of that fits the same set of circum-

stances particular to their project. This walk through the "architectural remnants" is really a way of letting people understand firsthand the kind of criteria that may help bring the problem that they're grappling with to fruition. Again, I find that the process does work pretty well. I use a lot of slides. I use a lot of books. I use a lot of travel sketches. In fact, we've done a lot of traveling with clients.

SM: Do you undertake this process even with building types that you're familiar with where you may have an internalized program?

BD: I have to because it's not only me who is being educated. It's the whole design team, including the client. I think that it is important that a client understands exactly what is going on during the design process and that I understand what is motivating my client. It is the client who is the expert with respect to their needs.

SM: It seems like the more people you get into a room representing your client, the grayer things can become in terms of pulling out major decisions. It's almost like the increasing size of a group diffuses the ability to make decisions. How do you go about trying to reach a consensus?

BD: In fact, we try to limit the number of people who are in these discussions at any one time, although it is important that everyone has a chance to relate their needs and ideas. It is this sense of being involved that allows us to get to the point where we're confronting the really tough design issues.

SM: So you feel that you'd be prepared to present to a larger group?

BD: We're always looking for input. But

again, every organization has their own developed hierarchy. You depend on them to make decisions and set priorities, establishing where they want to make compromises around the financial context of a project: decisions that you and I couldn't make, that we shouldn't make. These decisions are not up to the architect. We put a lot of responsibility on the client. They know up front that they need to be part of the process and that it is very important for them to understand everything that we've done; why you've taken this turn instead of that turn. Then they understand why they're spending their money. They understand why they maybe need to stretch a little bit to find more creative ways to get capital for a project or why they need to walk out into the unknown sometimes. We try to keep an understanding of "value" as clear as possible.

SM: When you meet with a client for the first time, what are your goals?

BD: I guess just to get to know each other personally. I find you really need to develop a mutual trust. It's important to understand who that client or client group is. It's important that we are comfortable with each other because we have this giant leap of faith that is always required. We're always talking about very subjective, and in the beginning, very intangible issues. I have a tendency to spend considerable time with clients testing design issues and ideas. I always try to gain a personal respect for my client, to truly understand where they're coming from. This always helps me to insure my own motivation for a project. In the same way, I want them to know pretty well who I am and where I've been, what kind of background I have

and what experience I've had. I think that a personal relationship makes them feel more comfortable as well. The first meeting is rarely anything about trying to solve their specific design problems. I spend a lot of time listening so a client knows that what they're saying is important and valuable to me. Clients need to understand that I'm not some elitist "expert" coming into the process who is going to tell them what they need and what they should consider as good design. I try to give them the same level of comfort as I need when I go to a physician. I want to know that he is capable of finding out what's wrong with me and solving the problem. At the same time, you don't want him to be someone who acts as though the patient is just another clinical case. You give a couple of your "symptoms" and he will dial it into a computer to find out what the solution is. There has to be a personal involvement, but there also has to be a safety net that's developed so everybody is comfortable.

SM: When you look at a site, what pops into your mind with respect to issues you want to address when you get to design?

BD: Typically, I spend a lot of time looking for prospective sites or going onto a site trying to solve a problem. I really try not to look at a site immediately. I try to understand a lot more about the problem before I try to become too intimate with a site. Like everybody else, my first reaction when I see a site is to start envisioning solutions. One of the things that I try to caution myself with is knowing enough about the problem before I begin designing a solution. When you're thinking about solutions, you're making choices applicable to the context.

SM: Are there things that you always look for at the time?

BD: I guess I'm a contextualist in that sense. I think it depends a lot on just what the nature of the site is. Whether it's an urban, rural, or suburban site. They all have different characteristics and they have different things that we should learn from them. I'm always searching for those fundamental issues that make a site compatible with the goals that we're trying to meet in terms of the problem at hand. The fundamental things like orientation and topography are important but are not the only things that you want a designer to develop a design process from. These issues are important in terms of creating an environment, but while fundamental, they are not the base progenitor of my ideas. I always have a tendency to look for ways to reestablish a strong sense of the "public realm" into the context of the design problem. I'm a people oriented person. I would like to see people becoming less privatized and have more options that offer public interface, more opportunity to establish relationships with others, or at least give them the option to do so. I think that at times it's quite important to be able to go off and be by yourself, but that option is only valuable if you also have the option of having a stronger interaction with others. I think that one of the things that society in many areas of the world has lost is that valued sense of the public realm. Just as personal bias, I'm always looking for ways of creating public space. I think you can see that as a thread throughout all of my design work.

SM: Is there any particular individual or event over the course of your career that has really

effected or influenced your design process?

BD: Too many to single any one out in particular. My father was a really interesting guy. He didn't have any formal design education, but just loved architecture. When I was a kid we would frequent places where he felt comfortable. He went out of his way to point out the places and buildings that, in an architectural sense, made him feel engaged with life. Subliminally, I've always had this need to find myself in similar types of places; the places that make me "feel engaged." Most of the places that I respond to are places which encourage a high degree of social interaction. A kind of see and be seen relationship: places where you can experience spontaneous interaction, the sidewalk cafes, or Saturday morning coffee shops, those kinds of places. I think those times with my father manifest themselves deeply, but subliminally into my psyche. I was constantly discouraged throughout my early education in architecture as well as my early professional experience because I didn't see a lot of support for my inner concern about the demise of the public realm. When I arrived at Harvard, it was a completely different situation. The issues that I always championed in a subliminal sense seemed to find support. In an intellectual sense, my exposure to Harvard faculty members such as Fred Koetter, Colin Rowe, Michael Dennis, Gerhard Kallman, and Jerge Silvetti helped me to legitimize my work. In a matter of months, I was being introduced to a completely different focus in architectural theory, information that intuitively I had connected with, but didn't know existed. It was like coming home having never been there before.

SM: So was that experience pivotal in your focus?

BD: Absolutely. As I told you earlier, I was a student at Harvard for only three semesters. You certainly don't answer all of your questions within that time span. I left the GSD and spent the next six or seven years teaching. I focused that time on synthesizing all of my new found information. I have been very fortunate. I had a lot of good practical background before I went to graduate school. I knew how to build. I had a lot of rewards in the profession. I entered graduate school and was bombarded with things that legitimized, in fact codified all of my previous feelings about architecture. In reality, I left Harvard feeling intellectually exhausted. I had all of this new information which I still hadn't been able to manifest into a personal design philosophy. Coming from school and going directly into an academic scenario, I found myself in a somewhat protected environment where I could develop and test my emerging ideals. I worked to solidify them over the next five or six years. I was supported by the academic richness I found while teaching at Miami University, the polemic points of view of the faculty, the ever-changing students, and the focused student desk crits. Often, I found that I didn't know exactly how I felt about an issue until I was confronted by needing to discuss it with one of my students. Then as I was saying it, I found myself thinking, "Did I really say that? Where did that come from?" It was that kind of exchange over the next five or six years that really allowed me to develop a commitment to my personal ideas of architecture. I would say that for me teaching was

quite pivotal, allowing my philosophy to emerge and solidify.

SM: Planting a mental seed?

BD: In the beginning, then nurturing that seed and allowing it to blossom. I really didn't know what the seed was in the beginning.

SM: Lets assume that you've attained some mastery of the profession. How do you feel about that notion?

BD: For me it's always new. It's always fresh. If I've learned anything because of my background, it's that you never really know it all. I guess the first ten years of my career I read everything I could possibly find because I always felt a little bit illegitimate. I was reading, analyzing, diagramming, and thinking. In the beginning, it was my substitute for formal training. Then, after what seemed like a lifetime, I arrived at the GSD which was almost completely overwhelming. For me, the important thing was that I learned that I had to continue to read and examine and test myself, and I still do that. I have this book fetish and I travel constantly. I've been really lucky to be able to do that. In the last couple of years I've made three trips to the Ukraine. I have a couple of volunteer projects there which have allowed me access to a whole new culture.

SM: Are there any theories or principles that you apply consistently in your work now?

BD: Well, again I think that this sort of revitalization of the public realm is something that is consistently there and it should happen at almost every scale. For me, at least philosophically, I think Americans have become much too privatized. We spend to much time in our cars and too much time in front of the television. Reality of experience is amplified through conversation. There is too little spontaneity in our lives. We live vicariously. I'm not the kind of person who wants to live vicariously. I want to get out and experience it myself. I like interacting with people. I think as an architect I should help create an opportunity for that by establishing a context for it. I think a lot of our problems could be solved if we had a bit more dialogue, a bit more of human interaction, a bit more listening. I find myself, subliminally at least, searching for those opportunities in almost every project. I don't believe that there's a difference between urban design, architecture, and interior design. I think that they're all the same type of problem, you're just looking at them at different scales. I have had some experience in urban design work over the years, both academically and in practice, and I approach an urban design problem the same way I approach an architecture or interior design problem. The process doesn't change. The method for gathering information and establishing a client dialogue may have to be different because of the scale of the problem.

SM: When you're actually sitting down to design what is the typical medium that you use? What do you work with?

BD: I typically use either pencil or ink on yellow trace. But these are products of the process, not the process itself.

SM: Do you build models?

BD: We do a lot of model building in our office.

SM: Do you personally build models?

BD: I personally build very crude models. I'm not a great draftsman and I have a tendency to do more soft drawings than I do hard-line drawings. I like to work with people who can do finely crafted drawings and models because I admire the quality of the work, but unfortunately I don't particularly have those skills. I do a lot of three dimensional sketching, more to test ideas than anything else. I rarely do presentation drawings. I don't think that they're necessarily valuable to me during the design process, but they do help communicate the design ideas with our clients. Our computer also helps with this in a very direct way. For me, drawing is a designer's way of establishing a dialogue with yourself about a project, a dialogue through the medium of pencil and sketch paper. I've never had a bad idea *ever,* until I draw it, then recognize it's shortcomings. Your mind's eye pictures everything in wonderful proportion, the best coloration, everything looks terrific. It is not until you draw an idea that you realize the truth of what you've conceived, and then you begin the tedious task of refinement.

SM: Are you implemented with a CADD system?

BD: Yes. We have ARCHICAD which is a three dimensional as well as two dimensionally based CADD program.

SM: Do you personally use CADD?

BD: I'm learning. I haven't immersed myself into it very deeply, but I hope to soon.

SM: I've made, and continue to make, an unrelenting quest into "design" issues with little reference to the day to day context of practice. How do you see the business aspect of our work fused to the desire for quality design?

BD: In reality, you've got to stay in business to be an architect. I'm not independently wealthy. I find myself, at times, wishing I would win the lottery, but in reality we've got to make financial ends meet. We've got to deal with reality, raising a family, getting them educated, just being able to afford the opportunity to get away and relax. If it weren't for the disgracefully low salaries paid to faculty in architecture schools in this country, I might still be teaching. To answer your question, yes, I have had to spend a lot of time understanding the business of architecture. It is not because I wanted to be practicing strictly for financial gain, but like everyone else I have a family and life-style to support. If we're not making positive cash flow and staying open for business, we're not going to have an opportunity to do any work. In a business sense, one thing that I find important in this discussion is that we find it invaluable to have really close contact with our client so that we don't have to design things twice. I've never had to completely redesign a project. Many projects in our profession have to designed and redesigned. I rarely miss design and construction budgets. I don't have the building estimate 20, 30, 40% off. I attribute that to several things. I have a strong practical background. I was a partner in a small construction firm at one time. I learned early to understand the reality of what things cost. I always keep testing that. I'm a strong believer in value engineering and I constantly use a VE process when designing our projects. I don't always do that personally. In some instances, I think it's difficult for the design architect to esti-

mate the cost of a project. You get too invested. So I bring in another person. It may be my partner or, whenever I can, I ask a contractor to give me feedback early on. I also try to make sure that from the very beginning clients understand what things are going to cost. I've seen a lot of projects where if you don't literally explain to a client the complete extent of what he has to spend, it's easy for them to misconstrue things. "Oh, I thought that was going to include your fees," or "Gee, I thought the cost of permits was included in that," or "You mean you weren't talking furnishings as well?" I make sure that all along people understand not only what bricks and mortar are going to cost, but what Furniture, Fixtures, and Equipment is going to cost, what fees are going to cost, and what permits are going to cost. This condominium project in Oxford is a good example (we refer to a Progressive Architecture article). I sat down with the clients, who were acting, for the first time, as their own developers and had serious discussions with them and tried to explain all of the soft cost ramifications of a development like this. I needed to show them that they were going to have a lot of expenses that weren't necessarily going to show up on the construction estimate. You do those things for self protection. Everybody can love your design, but the first thing that goes when the budget gets tight and clients feel the need to make those difficult financial commitments is the "architecture." The subtleties of architectural detailing is largely maintained through the VE process because we've maintained a comprehensive understanding of project costs and have maintained a good close relationship with our client. Another example of this is a project at Wright Patterson Air Force Base that I designed while at KZF. It's a complex building, wonderfully built. We made it through the Federal Government's blind value engineering process with the architectural character intact because of our management of the economics of the project.

SM: "Blind value engineering," what is that?

BD: If you work with the federal government's Corps of Engineers, throughout a project you send them your documents at different levels of completion, they in turn send them off to someone anonymous to you, and this third party evaluates the project as related to possible ways to reduce cost. They send you back a list of all the things, in their opinion, that you can do to cut money from the project. Our project went through that process, the list was returned, and the owner said, "It meets the budget, we love the building, and we're not going to accept these value engineering statements out of context." That only happened because we had led the client through the process and they understood where and why they were spending their money. It would have easily been the opposite of that if they weren't tuned in.

SM: Do you typically generate multiple schemes?

BD: No, never. I generate, perhaps, multiple approaches in the beginning, but I try to protect as much of the design budget as possible. I don't like to exhaust a design budget examining options that I don't necessarily believe help to solve a problem. We do a lot of experimentation. We do it along with the client; I don't do a series of studies, pick one and present the one I want. I'll bring our client in early, show them what the studies are, show them why this is good or bad before we take it too far, so that they can buy in early. If you look at an architectural fee, it's a relatively small amount of money. If you work in a collaborative way, as we do, you can burn up a lot of hours quickly. At the beginning of a project, we'll spend 25% of our architectural budget instead of maybe 15 or 20% doing schematic design because we allow it to evolve in greater detail. Hopefully, we've been able to experience a strong predesign process, paid for as a separate phase of the contract, to help educate ourselves and our client; before we get deeply into the design budget. We like to do our preliminary strategies by means of predesign diagrammatic feasibility studies. Again, if you can eliminate as many of the variables as possible before you get into the schematic design phase of a project, it allows you to have more time to spend developing the architecture.

SM: I interviewed Bart Prince for this project and one of his "gifts" is that he can see something and tell you exactly how big it is. He apparently has the facility to literally design a building in his imagination and have the scale and grasp of it in hand. When he has it figured out, he sits down and draws the building in its entirety. How do you approach design from the aspect of space and scale?

BD: I think the idea of being able to mentally visualize things in scale is something I've gotten through experience; just having seen a lot of buildings and places. You can intuitively understand scale. I don't think that it comes easily for everyone. Architecture has the ability to manipulate your frame of scale or reference. We're trying to alter your sense of reality in a way. St. Peter's, in Rome, is probably the best example of that historically. I don't know if you've been to Rome, but as you approach St. Peters, you cross the Arno, turn toward the site, and start relating yourself to St. Peter's in the distance. As you finally approach the Piazza, you can't imagine why it's taken you so long to get there. It's because the scale of the facade is layered in such a way that it's giving you multiple scale readings which are constantly changing relative to your proximity. It keeps shifting scale in relationship to you as the viewer. It's really amazing the way the facade is able to affect you in a psychological sense in terms of its representative scale. There are many buildings and natural landmarks that can affect you this way. Historically, successful Baroque and Renaissance architectural gardens, for example, have had the ability to make things look larger or smaller than they really are in terms of your perception, completely manipulating your personal frame of reference. By the time a designer reaches the level of being able to manipulate architecture this way, you've left all of the "one liners" behind. You're able to create a more rich, a more dense architecture. In my opinion, this only comes from experience. I don't think that you are born with it or acquire it because you have studied volumes of books or photographs. You've got to go to places and see them, feel them, understand them, and analyze them. You begin to understand why things happen, by feeling your own internal responses, watching others react. In my opinion, you see so many designers developing projects that never quite

reach the level of success as the historical archetypes that they have used as "role models." They were lifting off the surface and not intrinsically understanding what made those buildings work. I think that is why so much of second and third generation Modern architecture failed. It's why Post Modern architecture ended up being so maligned. The idea of Post Modern architecture is not shallow or anti-modern. I believe that designers who practiced from a rich sense of experience understood what Post Modernism was about. Many designers who did caricatures of the world's monuments or classic elements of architecture ultimately dealt a real blow to the values of Post Modern philosophy. All the people who superficially copied the buildings of Le Corbusier didn't share his understanding of classicism. They couldn't figure out that when all was said and done they couldn't make it work.

SM: That's interesting. There's a generation of architects, I guess born in the late 1800's, who nurtured modernism over the course of their careers, then brought it into fruition in the 20's, 30's, and 40's, and reached the height of their careers in the 40's and 50's, and then started to taper off.

BD: I spend a lot of time studying and teaching from that point of view. I think I would classify myself as a "pre-modernist" with latent Early-Modern Humanistic tendencies. For me, modern architecture developed from the central thematic idea of returning to the essence of why things are done and not just decorating in an eclectic sense. For example, Charles Renee Macintosh was early modernist, but in a humanistic sense. There

are a lot of good architects and designers that in my opinion have lost their connection with the people that they serve. It is easy to believe that after studying the edicts of Philip Johnson and others from the 30's many architects and designers see Modernism as being completely separate from classicism. I totally disagree with that. I think modernism developed to a point where it split into two factions. There was what I would call the "humanistic modernist" and then the "industrial modernist." I think that what happened may have been very politically motivated. It had to do with World War I and the creation of the manifestos that established the beginning of Naziism and Fascism. Under persecution and forced isolation, many of the intellectually motivated designers began to leave their homelands.

The political climate produced in the work of the great architects such as Le Corbusier, Van Der Rohe, and Gropius a distinctively reactionary architecture. Many of these architects fleeing their homelands came to the United States and found an audience. As teachers and practitioners they blossomed and prospered. They affected the global sense of architectural thinking through the International Style. For me, Post Modernism in its most positive sense was really the idea of evolving from within Modernism, a reconnection with the beginning of Modernism. There are many creative designers who are still very strong proponents of these ideals. I think these are the people who eventually will end up carrying the day.

SM: I almost wonder if we're still in transition. It's interesting to link architecture back to the

evolution of our culture and technology. Some of my reading recently has dealt in the emergence of the global marketplace. I believe we're at a juncture and it's changing the way we practice. There is evidence of that now in our own work on the computer, in the ability for you to travel to the Ukraine and work on projects. That whole thread starts to reach out and connect across the planet. I think that's great but then we're challenged to ask ourselves what then is good architecture and how do we take the way we practice and make it work in the Ukraine or make it work in Hong Kong?

BD: I personally refute this idea of a universal architecture in the sense of an "international style." Architecture can not be developed anywhere without respect for specific context. We've been working with a group of Ukrainian architects to try to help them understand professional privatization; to create independent professional practices. They wanted to develop a more individualized housing industry and wanted to rethink their way of dealing with their critical housing shortage. They came to Cincinnati to look at American housing types and recreate them in the Ukraine. We spent a lot of time trying to get them to understand that not everything that has happened here in the last 50 years in housing was correct. We said that in fact, a lot of the manifestation of suburbia basically fed right into the demise of the postwar nuclear family; something that we had noticed alive and well and had valued when gaining insight into their culture. What we suggested they do was understand how housing needs have changed for them and to understand both the good and bad of the last 50, 60, 70 years of

American housing and transplant within the Ukraine only what makes sense for their specific circumstances.

SM: In your experience what was the most striking difference between school and practice?

BD: I'm more of a believer in the kind of holistic idea of an architect. I think architects need to be grounded in aesthetics, sociology, and psychology. I also think they need to understand economics and construction technology. I don't think you can create good architecture unless you understand all of these issues. I think schools, for the most part, pigeonhole their students as being design types, technical types, or economic types. You can't help but have that reinforced when people evaluate you quickly and advise you to take certain kinds of classes or give you stronger desk crits in this or that because of what their early assumption of you might or might have been. I think the education of an architect is very difficult. Primary and secondary education in this country doesn't prepare you well for what is required to be an architect. There are those who have been very lucky because they come from an environment that promotes holistic thinking. Some students almost accidentally find the school that is right for them, others do not. There are, luckily, a lot of schools that, because of the personality of the faculty, have a very broad liberal arts background. I think most architects ought to be trained first in a strong liberal arts program. You've got to have a broad understanding of what makes the world tick and what makes human beings tick. All too often, you come out of high school pretty naive, pretty unworldly. You run into a foreign curriculum

and quickly faculty makes a value assessment as to where you should be in architecture. If you haven't been one of those people who have had the right background, you can easily end up being pigeonholed. Design happens throughout the process, not just in the early stages of the development of a project. The original organization of a building is important, but I'd say equally important is how you detail the building construction; the window sills, the door jambs; all the nuances that effect people in a tangible sense. The plan diagram, the organization of a building spatially and formally, obviously effects how people relate to a building, but this happens in a very subliminal way. The thing that often falls apart in architecture is the end result; how you detail a building. If you look at many of the declared "design projects" that we see published, the ideas often becomes quite thin without the benefit of a perfectly composed photograph.

SM: How do you prepare for an interview presentation?

BD: We try to do as much work as possible before we go to an interview so as to understand who the client is. We talk more about what the particular design problem is than what we've done before. If I can, I like to include pertinent design information for a client's project in the request for proposal as part of my proposal submittal. It gives prospective clients an idea of who we are and what kind of work we've done in preparation for their project. I would prefer to go to an interview without slides and presentation boards. If anything, when you have enough advance information, you may discuss a few early sketches relating to their particular problem.

Most of the time I don't like to use that approach: I haven't had time to develop the predesign issues I spoke of earlier, but at times it can be very successful. I worry about getting too presumptuous early on about the solution to the problem. A lot of times, clients will ask you to do some sketches before the interview. If I'm forced to do that, I normally keep those things in a generic form and try to show opportunities for studying the problem and not the solutions.

SM: What kind of advice would you give to a student of architecture?

BD: It depends on where they are in their career. Ideally, if it's somebody graduating from high school who wants to be an architect, I'd tell them first to get plugged into a strong liberal arts program, take a few architectural appreciation courses, and then in graduate school enroll in a professional architecture program. I think for somebody who is already in a school, I'd try to evaluate what that school has to offer, every school has different strengths and weaknesses, and parallel his goals with the program's strengths. In any case, I'd like to tell them to travel as much as possible, to sketch and photograph as much as possible, experience as many divergent courses within the architectural curriculum as they possibly can, and meet as many people with different opinions as possible. I also think that people have to understand that the strongest design students are almost encouraged not to become good technologists. I think that's a fallacy. In my opinion, good designers are the ones who understand how to build. Some of today's designers who I admire, Tom Mayne, Bill Turnbull,

Warren Schwartz, and Hans Hollein are designers who think as much about the building process as they think about the final architecture. They realize that an understanding of materials and construction is what is really going to make it happen. If you don't understand how buildings are assembled and if you can't successfully detail an assembly to be manifest in a proportional sense, a structural sense, and a technical sense, you have missed a valuable opportunity. We have all seen what happens when a designer doesn't understand these basics and he can't figure out why his building doesn't look the way he thought it was going to look. If you look at Frank Lloyd Wright's work, as he matured, he came to understand this phenomenon completely. His early work in terms of materials and construction literally fell apart. The more he evolved as an architect, the more he examined his early work, and learned from its problems. I think as a professional you should consider yourself as always being in school. The problem is that many architects don't see that. They go to school for five or six years and practice for 30 or 40 years what they learned in the first five or six years. The problem is that most young designers who are at the cutting edge in terms of their ideas haven't experience enough to mature as architects in the holistic sense. It's a difficult struggle. Designers in mid-career need to be continually investigating the theory of architecture and the aesthetic design process as well as continuing the development of their understanding of technology. If you look at Louis Kahn, he probably did his first important building when he was 50. There is good reason for that.

SM: What do you see for your future? What are your goals?

BD: I think we would just like to be involved in the most interesting projects possible. Be involved in projects that keep us challenged; keep feeding ourselves intellectually and keep our level of energy peaked.

SM: Is there any particular building type that you've always wanted to do?

BD: I don't think building types have anything to do with it. I think really good architects can do any building. There are a lot of esoteric things that you learn about doing special kinds of buildings. There are things you need to know about those nuances of the client and their needs, but again I think in a collaborative sense, you can get that by working with others. A really good architect can bring other people into the design process that can give you that esoteric necessity in terms of a literal functional program. You can create a building that meets the esoteric necessity of the client and is good architecture in the broad sense. That is why my colleagues and I believe in developing a strong collaborative effort for our projects. Some of the most disappointing projects happen when a client hires a specialist firm: a hospital architect or a nursing home architect for instance, and what evolves is a regurgitation of that firm's previous buildings. This approach doesn't generally solve any of the contextual or public realm issues relevant to the specialized building type but only focuses on the preconceived functional problem. I think architecture needs to solve basic functions, but there is so much more to be accomplished.

SCOTT JOHNSON

Johnson Fain & Pereira Associates, Los Angeles, California

Scott Johnson is the design partner of Johnson Fain & Pereira Associates in Los Angeles, California. He has maintained a commitment to design excellence initiated by William Pereira, the firm's founder. His background, prior to his arrival in Los Angeles, is most interesting. He received his Master of Architecture from Harvard in 1975 and began working with Skidmore Owings & Merrill in Los Angeles, then subsequently in San Francisco. In 1978, he left Skidmore to join Philip Johnson's firm in New York City. He worked closely with Philip Johnson for five years and, over the course of his tenure in New York, realized that he would have to move on to fully realize his potential as a designer and architect. The question became, "Where?"

Serendipity came to answer in the form of a friend of Scott's from Harvard. Bill Fain had joined Pereira Associates as an urban planner some time before. William Pereira offered Scott the position of Chief Designer and Partner. After long reflection and additional consultation with Bill Fain, Scott took the position and left New York for the west coast. Managing the transition from Pereira Associates to Johnson Fain Pereira was challenging, difficult, and even risky. Regardless, the transition was accomplished and currently the firm prospers under the leadership of Scott Johnson and William Fain. Many remarkable buildings have emerged from Scott's hand since 1983. A complete listing would be impossible here, but a few deserve mention: Rincon Center, San Francisco, Fox Plaza, Los Angeles, and the Opus One Winery, Napa Valley, for the Mondavi/Rothschild joint venture.

Scott Johnson is loosely following a thread of artistic inquiry. This journey follows his evolution as an individual and artist. Perhaps the majority of practitioners simply respond to client demands, tight schedules, and tighter fees, but within the struggle to survive lives the need to actively seek answers to the questions confronting us as we finish the twentieth century. I had the pleasure, in early 1993, to listen to Scott present a portion of his work from 1983 through 1993. I found a transition evident in his designs. The early buildings were strongly sculptural objects on the land or within the city. In the intervening ten years, the focus of his design effort has begun to meld the building

with the environment, context, and site. The early buildings were intellectual objects placed on the land; his newer work achieves an integration of the structure with the concerns of site, ecology, and client needs. I have a strong bias toward his newer work, particularly the Opus One Winery previously mentioned: I readily admit this is consistent with my philosophy. It is with great pleasure that I present a designer approaching the zenith of his skills speaking to the complexity of creating buildings as the twentieth century closes, and a new millennium begins.

Scott Johnson: Sketch study of Rincon Center

SM: In reading through the summary of your work that you sent through the beginning of 1991, I noticed that there seems to be a general thread of artistic inquiry. Would you elaborate on that a little bit?

SJ: Well, doing architecture is in some relative proportion (half and half, 40/60, or 60/40) both a set of intentions and a set of discoveries. To some degree, you have strong intentions and you try to manifest those in design. You are doing things and then standing back looking at what you've done and realizing what your intentions are to the extent that design is, aesthetically speaking, a self discovery process. It is for me, personally, and for our office, as I mobilize the design effort here. A Japanese magazine was interested in publishing our work and since there was a language problem, I said, "To simplify translation, I'll just sit down, write this out, and tell you what I see." What you see (in the narrative), is either one generation of work or maybe three little micro-generations of work in the office. And, yes, there is definitely a thread or lineage of work there. I moved here in '83 from Philip Johnson's office in New York. I'm now here just about nine years, so in very simplistic terms the work seems to follow three-year cycles. It's overlapping and continuous, but you discover and you make more, and you discover and you make more. I guess this is an aesthetic position that one might define in somewhat moralistic terms as well, but I don't see a stylistic analog to morality in architecture. I don't believe that there is any longer the kind of matching relationship between an architectural language and a stylistic language of appropriateness. I think appropriateness

in the '90s or '80s is so fundamentally different than it once used to be. In my opinion, there's no metaphor-of-the-moment to say Ionic is right for the ladies tea house and Doric is right for the banker's club any more than that kind of compartmental thinking is relevant. I don't believe in that kind of thing and I feel that because we're in an age of information, we have an ability to absorb periods, stylistic languages, and enormously different architectonic views of the universe, some of which in our current time, span only a few years, live and die - hardly get to breathe - and some, if we go back far enough, lasted for centuries. As one reads books, so one can read architecture. There's an ability to use that knowledge and bring it forward. There isn't on my part and the part of the office, any interest whatsoever in imitation at any level. There's no interest actually in derivation, but there's always an interest in cues. For example, if one has to do a building in Los Angeles that's by the freeway, and the nature of the planning constraints on the project create the need for it to be low and flat, one might go through history and just look for long, low, flat things. We go through our library of architecture and see what buildings have solved those problems. You might have a building with a scalar problem, where proportionally it's not what you might want it to be. Then you might go to a series of periods that had massing problems or compositional problems irrespective of the narrative content of those architectures and learn from those periods and then use the abstract idea in terms of your modern architecture. So, if any of that makes sense, that's how and that's only how history is used relative to design ideas here.

SM: You talked about the idea of micro-generations of design process and, obviously, we have a pretty big time gap between January 1991 when your narrative was written, and now the end of 1992. What has been significant to you from a design perspective in the intervening two years?

SJ: We are definitely in a revisionist period. Now, I can get personal with you and tell you why I am in such a period, or I can be generic about it and tell you why the industry is. Most of those things are obvious. I am 41 and my partner is a couple of years older than I, so we look for a fairly good size practice so we can be free to do a range of project types. I like to think we're still on the young side, so I think it's normal that we're maturing and there is transition inherent to us. Change in the industry in general is brought on, very much, just by the economy. The fact is that the entrepreneur developer has presently gone away and, therefore, the nature of the work is totally different. The scale of the work is totally different. The promise of designing the speculative program has gone away. So, it's a very healthy time, a very calisthenic time. It's a hard time, but any time you're questioning yourself and what you're doing, it's going to be hard. I think it's interesting because I have always been interested in a range of projects and I guess I'm old enough, now that I've just told you I'm young, to feel that specialization has its limitations and that design is still an entity. It's a commodity in itself that can be applied to a broad range of things. It's almost sort of the Italian view of design historically. It's a continuum that is called *design* and it can be applied constructively and be valuable for a range of things. Well, I believe this runs up a little bit against the economic grain. I don't believe I have to specialize in health care facilities or schools. I believe that design, in the best sense, can handle many of those things and, as we all know, projects of scale are essentially a team effort or a choreographic effort, so the relative specialties can be put together to make those things work at an operational level. I've been trying constantly since I've been here in Los Angeles to broaden our range of projects. The economy just bounced us right into that. We have some single-family houses, a couple large multifamily housing projects, many mixed-use projects, and some office buildings, but we don't have a lot (of office buildings) as we once did. It's now a broad range because the nature of the markets have both reduced and then opened up. So we are going through our design transitions from within. The larger economy is also mirroring that.

SM: So, how do you view your design process now?

SJ: Well, in terms of our process, we have a research component in the office. The process really starts with research and that can either be with a capital "R" or a small "r", depending upon how you look at it. But it's to define the user, the location, time frame, and so on. It's something that can happen even before or parallel to programming when you're trying to assess the knowns and interpret those knowns. That's all design in a way; we're going to try to make this into logical steps. The advantage of doing that is, in a sense, you are beginning to meditate on what you're about to do. You get to editorialize the knowns. You're, in fact, making choices at every turn. Research is not an undifferentiated scientific thing in the case of architecture and urban design. It's actually a choosing and selecting of certain directions and eliminating others, so that by the time you have your program, you have a data base. You're already inclined to a set of value ideas or value attitudes. And with that, you then begin, more or less, to start the process of drawing, sketching, modeling, or whatever. We are extremely three-dimensional here. We are, I would have to say, probably described as being formalist in a sense, but in projects of scale, that process can take quite a long time. There's a number of projects that my partner and I collaborate on which begin as urban design projects. I'm speaking now of the larger ones. My partner is an urban designer and planner as well as an architect. On the larger projects, he will begin to understand the entitlements involved, the political infrastructure which will affect what we do, and then begin to assess all of that. Also, he's very interested in the history and morphology of cities. Then he'll work through the circulation, the road systems, the open space overlay, the various land uses, the zoning, a whole series of things, trying to get to where he and I can talk about site plan and building feasibility. I'll be involved, and I'll start to work with him and study building within that matrix of a whole set of issues; only one of which frankly is incipient architecture. Then, as we further move through the process and beyond the master plan, I will be involved more fully, designing the buildings. He'll be less involved, so in a sense, we hold two ends of a baton. He and I are a spectrum: a continuous kind of activity that on each extremity is different but is connected.

SM: Strategic scale and tactical scale, perhaps?

SJ: Exactly. Of course, you know, if you do a house in suburbia where there's no definition, no design review, and virtually no entitlements, we have a project with very few planning implications. In that case, it's more purely architecture and I'll be more involved, of course, in the design. But frankly, the more thorny projects, the projects that are urbanistic tend to have serious components of both. We are urbanistic people. We both were educated and lived and worked in cities that are very urban, mostly on the east coast, and then moved here. Los Angeles has become, in the last two decades, a very urban city, notwithstanding its original suburban styling. It has the ethnicity, the information, the densities; it has all the things that cities have, so in ways, it's very enjoyable to work here. It's very timely to be in Los Angeles with urbanistic preferences, because that's where the city's at now.

SM: Is your office doing any work in the Pacific Rim?

SJ: Yes, we have quite a large project in Guam, in the Northern Marianas Islands. In fact, it's a new town and about two percent of the island mass. It's 1300 acres, and involves more or less 3000 housing units in a variety of types, a village center with urban amenities and elements, a resort hotel, and several club houses which are recreationally organized for full 24-hour uses because it's essentially a town and we are in the first phase of construction. We have several people over there on the island now and we coordinate the design through our office here in Los Angeles.

SM: How do you approach translating working in a new culture into a design? Does that permeate everything from the urban plan all the way down to the architecture?

SJ: It does, but I would say we don't attempt to necessarily ape the language of the place. It's interesting that frequently the dynamics of dealing with Asia is: Asians come to America in general and southern California in particular to get their creative consultants. They come here because there are aspects of the western landscape and life style in which they are interested and they don't necessarily want you to do Japanese architecture, for example. They certainly have many Japanese architects who are better at that. Now, that may be right or wrong in concept, relative to what they want, but we do not attempt to do anything but bring our view to the place, interpret that location and then do it in our way. We do grasp their formal language, try to understand the grain of the place, the climatology, the geography, the native tradition and then deal with that in our own way.

SM: So, I don't know whether I'm getting this quite right or not, but it sounds like a contextual response, but shaded to western expectations.

SJ: It's not literally derivative. In the case of Guam, to sort of simplify it; there is not a sophisticated labor force there. The climate is extraordinarily difficult at best - typhoons, heat, humidity, all of that. There is also an Hispanic tradition, the Chamorran, and the native Marianans were Spanish (colonies) for about 400 years. We've evolved a language in this particular case which is visually and constructively heavy. It's built out of masonry units and plastered over. It has heavy tile roofs because in fact that makes sense given the climate and the 160-mile an hour typhoon winds. It can be placed by people from all over Asia who are brought there to work for a year or two or three on the job site. I think someone said there were about 18 languages spoken by the workers on site, so it needs to be things that are translatable and achievable. We didn't design a cybernetic piece of death-tech architecture because we could never achieve it there. The thing has to be buildable and translatable. That's what I'm saying, I'm saying we didn't go to Guam and say, "Hey, there's a style of architecture, let's do that style."

SM: From my point of view right now, where I'm at in my career and understanding of the profession, as limited as that may be, my view of architecture seems to indicate that there are some pretty tremendous changes on the horizon in terms of the influence of, for example, environment and ecology, would you tend to agree with that?

SJ: Yes, there's no question about that. I believe in the end that architecture has physicality; it has flesh. It has to be about the making of architecture. There will always be a truth to that fact and many practitioners feel that, in the end, architecture is about architecture. But the reality of that is that architecture, particularly right now and in the last couple of years which you point to, has to subsume many other things. And it's my belief that it has to be accessible as well because with very few exceptions, architecture is a public act of art making. It's there, people see it, use it, it's going to be there for a long time, usually. Everyone shares it. There are a few people who live in it. But there are many people who experience it. (Architecture) marks the landscape and the only way to deal with that in a rapidly democratizing world is to share it, to explain it, to entitle it. It has to have a degree of accessibility to people beyond a few tiny practitioners or a few tiny users. It has a mission that has to be larger than that. Environmental is one part of it. And the environmental part of it may be in California, Title 24, limiting energy consumption. It might be passive solar, wetlands displacement, or sustainable forestry. It might be any number of those things that are environmental, but it might be a bunch of other things too. It might be designing something within a community framework in which there's a community board, design review, city council, block/neighborhood groups, whatever, in which consensus has to be built around a thing that is ultimately architecture and built itself. So, if we thought about it over time, we could probably list a whole series of things which I believe will continue greatly to open up architecture. Concern for the environmental is one of them. Community and neighborhood issues are another. There's a political overlay, and there's obviously a traffic and an access overlay. There's a whole series of things which are public and have to overlay most architecture unless, of course, you've got a single house on a hill far away and it need not be part of anyone else's program per se.

SM: Planning question: when you look at the condition of American cities, the flight of people to the suburbs and all that sort of business, do you feel that between yourself and Bill Fain, for example, that there's a way to go back into the cities and address infrastructure and zoning and fitting the act of architecture into that so that we make cities livable for people again?

SJ: Well, that's the hard question. I want to talk about it because it's the thing I want to literally do. We're talking about city making, for the moment, in a more political light. The success or failure of your answer probably hinges on something that's not architectural fundamentally. It's something political and it is the following: how can you create a political system or lets call it something different, a system of consensus making, which voting and elections are about, that gets politicians who have a lot to do with the question you're asking to be long-term viewed, rather than focused on the short-term? You know, decisions are made incrementally and that's fine, but how can we get them to look for long-term goals? It's very hard. In my opinion, and I'm sitting in Los Angeles where, in a way, I can make this case stronger than maybe other cities, there is a piece of LA everywhere. How can we get politicians sufficiently informed and energized about the possibility of urban living to initiate an act that might take years beyond their political lives? They're only going to run half a lap and then others are going to have to run beyond that rather than sell off for immediate gain, immediate visibility, reelection, whatever the issue is. So, that's the whole political thing. And that relies on having gifted and informed leaders and probably, at a practical level, relies on the profession of architecture and planning to educate the public so that the public becomes part of the political dialogue. It's been a long haul, but in Los Angeles we have a mayoral election coming up and you can ask the mayoral candidates something you couldn't ask them ten years ago, particularly in the wake of the April civil disturbances in LA which were globally televised and watched. You could say what's your plan for open space, let's hear about what you intend to do with traffic, what's the master plan idea, what about land uses and recreation, what about the isolation of south-central LA versus the suburban areas, what's your game plan? What's your master plan? And they have to have an answer for that. Now, ten years ago they wouldn't know how to spell it.

SM: You sound a little bit like an activist. I like it.

SJ: Takes time, you've got to stay with it.

SM: Persistence always wins. Who or what would you say in largest measure has influenced your approach to design?

SJ: I have a few people that, as individuals, have influenced me. And then there's the whole stream of what I want to call anonymous architecture which constantly informs me and inspires me. You know, I don't know if I want to get off into this because this is an enormous topic, but it's very interesting. It has to do with hero-making in America and you might be talking about Mickey Mouse, or Liberace, or other icons. Things are expected of them: they have to begin to respond to a set of expectations. In a way, that can be good or bad. A brilliant artist is a brilliant artist and he'll use that as steam in his engine to get more work and then continue to invent within that. You know, when we look back 100 years from now, or someone looks back, despite all the media gloss of the last 10 years, the ones that'll last are not the ones that had the most publicity, but the ones that innovated within their opportunities. You know, you're "famous for being famous" kind of thing? There's also a process that you as an architect or designer understand. You "read" cities; you read buildings the way people read books or movies. There's a process of just reading the city that you drive through or walk through. You begin, I believe, to appreciate a whole level of anonymous innovations within a city to which you can probably never give credit. It might be an improvement made by a highway engineer in the way that a median is planted and broken through a city that makes the street a real boulevard. It might be a planning idea that was encoded in the master plan that has to do with ground level retail and setbacks at a courthouse site. You know, it might be a building that's just a little odd yet wonderful in its way, but you can't find out who did it. So I think (for me) there's both sides of being influenced by architecture and I'm very interested and keen in the anonymous side of things. The less anonymous side you know: I worked with Philip Johnson for a long time and he is, even today, a very energetic peripatetic invasive reader. He's interested in everything, and more in architecture. I think while we approach design differently, the energy affected me at a time when I was very affectable. I also have known Frank Gehry for a number of years since I first met him in the '70s when I was teaching at Southern California Institute of Architecture. He was quite a lot less known and certainly less busy than he is today. At that time, everything he was trying was enormously uphill and I can't imagine a person who's more iconic or known today across the globe for architecture. His persistence should be an inspiration to

every young architect.

SM: What do you think makes you an excellent designer?

SJ: Probably, if I have a strong point relative to design, it is that I acknowledge the void rather than the object. I don't mean that physically. I mean that what I try to do is kind of let the unseen hand guide. I don't mean that in a spiritual sense, or in a religious sense. I mean that in any situation out of which architecture will grow, there are a set of natural things that will occur and evolve. In a sense, I believe you can create important ideas. One can say, I think somewhat speciously, "Oh, architecture is about having a bunch of attitudes, and about making things and doing them your way and getting them built your way." One can describe that but I would describe architecture more as allowing the forces to come out and play and very carefully and somewhat humbly removing those forces which don't build on an overall purpose. It's an issue of letting forces happen, and slowly and carefully pulling away things until you have strength in the center. That's different than saying, "Oh look, I've got an idea. I did a round white thing 14 months ago, I need another round white thing, but now I think it should be an oval white thing." It's a different attitude about placing yourself either in the middle or placing yourself at the edge. In some ways, it sounds more like a Latin or an Asian idea than maybe a Western European idea/sequel to the Sun King. But I see it as a tool of power in a consensual environment where you have to make architecture happen.

SM: Are there any particular theories or principals that you apply as you work?

SJ: That's hard because our range is large. I look for a kind of clarity as a key to the accessibility that I was talking about: doing architecture within a democratizing world. I think one of the things I'm interested in getting more refined is a kind of minimalism as a method, as a device of clarity. You know, projects as different as I sent to you like the winery (Opus One) and a large project like LA Center. Each of those have a kind of iconic clarity, a minimalism. I'm continuing to pare and minimize that and make the move smaller grained and more subtle, but there is a center to that. There is a readability in the idea. One is clearly a simple platonic hemicycle or half-circle (that's the winery). The other is a series of rotations around an octagon which attempts to create mobility or diffusion or multiplicity which is my interpretation of the urban site in which it falls. So I'm trying to reduce it down to a readable idea so that one doesn't have to have narrative or literary information or training to be able to understand it. One can understand it right from the eye to the brain, bypassing the training and all that. I would say that's the propensity; that's the theory. It's not the theory like I went and studied it and decided to do it. It seems to be where I and we are going here.

SM: What's the principal medium you use when you design?

SJ: Well, I'm kind of an old hat. I use a Pentel Fineline on trace. I color a lot with either water color or pencils, chalks or oil sticks, whatever. But the office is highly computerized. I would be dishonest to say that it wasn't. We do 3-dimensional rotation, color and materials representation, photo digitized screening, and all that and occasionally even a video from CADD programs. We have quite a young office as far as age goes and we found that the younger folks are extremely quick at adapting to new programs and computer technology. Now, I'm almost too old to roll over, personally.

SM: Trust me, you're not. I'd literally never touched a computer until two years ago and I'm doing it. If I can do it, anybody can.

SJ: Yes, maybe I'll crack at some point. I'll keep that in mind. Maybe there's hope for me. But, you know, I'm quite busy during the day and as a technique, (drawing) is easy. I do draw a lot. I've drawn for a long time and it's generally easier for me in the kind of thing I have to get across to just sit down and draw it, draw it, and draw it. Then I have someone go away for a few days or a few hours and lay it out doing either a three-D program or a flat two-D program, and then come back to me and that lets me sort of do overlay after overlay. As soon as we're able, we always build three-D models. We work in wood models a lot. We work in cardboard or paper where we can tear them apart and put them back together.

SM: Do you typically go after multiple schemes when you're working on something?

SJ: Yes, I do actually. I do as a method of dialogue and of drawing out a client to kind of understand them better. In reality, someone usually comes to you and within a matter of days or weeks or months you're designing for them. There is a tremendous amount you don't know or can't know. To actually position two or maybe three very early ideas, I don't mean when we're way down the line and we're detailing the architecture, is a way of drawing them out, involving them. And, I think, also beginning to understand the whole set of perceptions they have that you'll have to deal with next week or next month or next year. So, I like doing that. I don't show things that I don't think have validity in a certain context. I don't do it for its own sake, but I think its part of the exchange.

SM: How will you prepare for a presentation?

SJ: Well, it depends on what kind of presentation it is. I like presentations generally to be as simple and productive as possible because in the end, I think it's about relationships. I think the best work is usually reflective of the best relationship. So I put a lot on that. Who's doing it? Who's going to be there? Who's in it from our side? How we handle it verbally. I think we usually figure out what the narrative is, which is to say, "What are the things we want to talk about?" Then we put together the visuals that are required for that. In some cases, something that happens in Los Angeles, and I would say more than that, in Hollywood, is that the movie industry is all based on storyboard. Scripts are sold or not sold based on storyboard ideas. It's not a bad metaphor for some projects where you're dealing with lay people to construct a storyboard.

SM: A graphic storyboard?

SJ: Yes. At the very least, a narrative storyboard and, depending upon where you are in the process, a graphic storyboard to describe the place and get into the site: talk about the parts to sketch or visualize, as you will, the various elements and how they interrelate. If you've seen a storyboard, it's a series of phrases, not unlike a comic book. There are

frames that progress and it puts the client into a medium that they are frequently used to dealing with. The level of communication is sometimes higher. And it breaks down the idea, you know, "What's under the tarp?" Pull the tarp away and there's chicken *cordon bleu* or there's an alabaster model in the middle. There may be a point that's what you get to, but certainly in the incipient phases something that's much more familiar to them sometimes works. It demystifies.

SM: In your experience with large projects, how great is the separation between what you originally envisioned and the final built product?

SJ: I don't see it in those terms. In fact, my evolving understanding about the idea is that it's a moving target. It's not as if at some point early on, I conceptualized the whole piece. I do it in layers. By the time I comprehend those very refined small detailed layers, the building is virtually what it is. So, in a sense, I'm a moving target as the building is evolving and I've found, quite frankly, that we have worked in very complex environments and very choreographic environments when many people are inputting to the process. I don't share the Faustian opinion of many architects that you might give up so much, sell it all away and its a shadow of its former self. Now, I don't see the process in those terms. I see the process in sort of identifying the, I mean there are exceptions to this but, in general, I see the process as identifying the players, the people involved, the place, and through that you gain your power and you create the thing or things that deal with their views. I think it's a passe early Modernist fable to say the architect imagines the thing and then he has to take

it and sell it through the process. The public realm doesn't work that way now. It would never be successful even if it succeeded in the process.

SM: So, its something that's not, in your mind, crystallized say after schematics, and then somehow the architect carries this magic football all the way through the process and scores a "touchdown" at the end if he gets it built the way he originally saw it?

SJ: No, although by the end of schematics you're relatively far down the way, but hopefully you've done programming and you've determined who the clients are. (The architect) has communicated, yes, something that's visual and quite defined, but as I said, it would be archaic now to say you sit down in part of your studio; you design the thing and then you see it survive the entire building process. No, you internalize the process, you take the process on, you understand the process, you manipulate, you exercise the process, you challenge the process, and your architecture comes out of a proactive, frontal dealing with that process, and that's what the architecture is.

STAN LAEGREID

The Callison Partnership, Seattle, Washington

Stan Laegreid currently practices architecture in Seattle, Washington, with The Callison Partnership. I first met Stan in 1992 while he worked on the Indianapolis Nordstrom store for the Circle Centre Mall. He received his undergraduate degree from the University of Washington and then went on to UCLA for graduate school. While he was at UCLA, he worked for Charles Moore and was involved with competitions underway at the time. Moore's office made an indelible impact on Stan's apprehension of the profession. Moore's office reflected a strong interest in engaging the client and the promotion of the design process as a product of the client's own dreams and individuality. Ultimately, Stan decided to return to Seattle and joined the Callison Partnership as a designer. He had heard of Callison's team approach to design and found that this approach, in tandem with a large firm producing varied projects, appeared to be an excellent opportunity both in terms of his personal philosophy and the type of work he would be responsible for.

Early in his career at Callison, a hotel he was project designer for received a regional AIA award. Since that time, he has designed many projects including several Nordstrom stores and his work has been published numerous times. Stan's approach is strongly contextual and emphasizes a high level of interaction with his clients. He acknowledges the effect of Charles Moore on his basic approach with a tendency to look first at the site and overall building on the site. Ever aware of context,

he prowls urban sites seeking ideas for projects when they occur in cities. He has also been involved recently with some international work. The design team literally went to the client for intense charrettes of short duration. This complete focus has yielded rewarding progress on diverse projects in a short period of time. This charrette process is participatory and dovetails neatly with Stan's enjoyment of a team approach to creating buildings.

Stan believes that designers and the design

process tell a story. Sometimes the narrative seems simple from the design side of the table, but the reality is that successful communication with lay people is often difficult. The challenge faced by every practitioner is first, deriving a quality solution, then describing a concept in a way that gives the client a grasp of how the architecture supports their interests and dreams. If these criteria are met, the possibility of quality design emerging from imagination into physical reality is high indeed.

Stan Laegreid: Detail of initial design study for a mixed use project near Seattle, Washington

SM: Who are your design influences?

SL: Two artists that I find constantly prod me when I see their work are Stanley Kubrick and Michaelangelo. They both tell a powerful story and have a tormented command of space, especially the sequencing of their spaces. They also display a shifting of perspective that I find both disturbing and invigorating. Most notably, I am impressed with their sense of choreography, of travel through somewhere to somewhere else. For me these two individuals have much in common although they probably aren't used in the same breath very often.

SM: No, definitely not, but they are both great artists in their own way. I was just reading earlier today that in the renaissance, the majority of architects were visual artists: painters. Obviously, Michaelangelo would fall into that category. How do you tie Kubrick's work in films to the act of painting?

SL: Michaelangelo's paintings pulse with activity and tension which, I think in part, is a product of his medium, the fresco. The fresco forced him to work quickly and sometimes spontaneously. I think there is a curious link between that kind of medium and cinematography. They both approach their composition with structure and intent, but are subject to perishable conditions. The final crafting of their mediums often captures the anticipation and vitality of the process. Architectural design, though sometimes hectic, is very often stripped of the immediacy of its process. To the degree Michaelangelo could express that I admire him and maybe it is due to his painterly experience.

SM: Do you employ a conscious design pro-cess or series of principles as you work?

SL: No, not at all.

SM: When you sit down to design what kind of a mind set do you create?

SL: I like to draw quickly. As soon as I have the project, I like to start generating ideas; I like to go through a purging of ideas. I often times end up with these drawings that I work over and over and over on one sheet and it will just become black with ink. In those shadows somewhere are the memory of pieces that then I start to overlay and assemble. I take the pieces that I thought were working in certain areas and some of the things that I like, the things I felt strongly about, then start building on those. The base sheet is covered with lots of ink and is pretty indecipherable. I start extracting my impulses that were playing out as I was being uninhibited. It isn't an effort of doing a whole series of drawings so much. It's just laboriously grinding ink into the sheet and letting things build up.

SM: Do you visualize the spaces that you create?

SL: I do as I go. I very rarely do going into it. I try not to have strong preconceptions. I don't even have a strong image going into it often times. From Charles Moore's office, I learned that he tends to work on the site and roof plan a lot in the early stages. I find that I tend to think that way. Also, I wouldn't say I design a site plan and a roof plan per se, but I tend to think of it first in plan, and then go quickly into perspective sketches where I think more spatially. Typically, elevations develop further down the road. Unless the elevation is critical; unless its largely a compositional study. For ex-ample, the Circle Centre Nordstrom is primarily just an elevation study. Giving proper respect to all the urban, sidewalk, and context issues, you can go into elevation fairly quickly. But looking at larger architectural challenges, I generally think more in plan view and the roof plan too. When I say roof plan, by implication then, spaces are started to be described by the roofs. Underneath the roof, some of the primary spaces start to take shape and have some kind of evocative quality by virtue of what you are describing in the roof, complimentary buildings, rooms, and spaces; whatever starts to spin off from that.

SM: Where do you find inspiration?

SL: You mean in a broad sense or as I actually sit down?

SM: As you work.

SL: I try to draw my inspiration from the site and all its history, its manipulations, and the personalities involved; their hopes and expectations. Then what I try to do again is really get as much ink on the sheet as possible, and start drawing lines and thinking of the more formal issues: what views you might have as you approach, entry sequences, primary spaces created indoor and outdoor, relationships in context. Anyway, a lot of the traditional architectural design concerns; absorbing those and representing them with heavier and heavier line weight on drawings. What I find is that I am developing considerations or prioritizing considerations. I find that the line weight starts to do that for me. Just the act of overdrawing lines for emphasis creates certain forms and gestures. It becomes some what of a formal exercise: you know there is a story that's starting to develop. I guess the design starts to take on its own life by virtue of the exercise of just working the drawing. Once some stronger gestures take shape, and let's say there is somewhat of a concept, I respond more towards the context and let that start to suggest what kind of form and shape (the spaces) might take, and whether they take a consciously formal or informal quality. There is also tremendous strength in a project's formal qualities, and to me, at a very fundamental level, I try to be as clear and simple and articulate about compositional devices early on and use that as a starting point.

SM: When you meet with a client, do you find that you go through a process of programming, either formal or informal?

SL: Very rarely. Most of the work I do is commercial, and as you well know, the programming requirements are usually fairly well defined by industry standards and the clients prior experience with similar types of projects. The architectural issues are usually related to context and what ever other parameters get involved. So as a matter of the kind of practice I do, there is little programmatic development other than in terms of mixed use type projects: what the intention is for the interaction of the particular uses. Generally in a commercial project, the client has definitive ideas of what the program will be in terms of different uses, functional relationships, and where they go on the site. If I work with a client that does not have a strong program (this is where I differ quite a bit, I would guess, from the profession) I listen to the client and let them air all their interests, concerns, biases, or whatever. I prod gently and have some casual conversations. Not so much directly about what their interests are in terms of the project, but provide them a vehicle for them to talk about the project in other terms.

SM: So you get a feel for the person?

SL: Yes. You know, if they like to talk about movies, it would be interesting to have them describe their project in terms of what kind of movie it would be. I find it more interesting. I don't know if its more effective, and I don't know if I'd encourage other people to do it, but I just find it a lot more fascinating to seek parallel expressions; metaphors that are more accessible to the client, ones that will free them. I tend to think that a lot of clients are uncomfortable trying to describe "architecture".

SM: Yes, because they don't understand architecture in graphic terms.

SL: And they are probably intimidated by the fact that they really can't articulate (their intent), not realizing many architects can't either. So I tend to like to digress in the conversations that tell me a little bit more about the person in other mediums: where they've traveled, where they like to eat, do they like to commute or do they not like to commute, what that might lead to. It tells you a little bit about their attitudes even towards cities. I'm kind of drawing straws here as examples, but those are the kinds of conversations I find valuable. This isn't a very labored process. This is more informal and probably shorter. With commercial work, I tend to listen very little. Although I listen to what the client thinks is important, I don't put a lot of value on a lot of research or programming in the beginning. My preference is just to get things out in front of them.

I'd rather go draw for awhile and get back to them tomorrow or preferably draw with them or in front of them to get a quick response. At the very early stages, I use sketch perspectives that describe the spatial characteristics so it becomes less of an academic exercise. I think also plans by themselves tend to be dispassionate. I would rather get the client excited and involved, triggering their excitement early on. The only way I feel I can do that is not to sit and talk about where the service goes and how many elevators they need, but to get some sketches in front of them and say, "You can try this or you can try that. The reason I am showing you this is for A, B, and C." That's the way I work and I've found it relatively successful.

SM: So your style then is interactive,

SL: Hopefully, highly interactive.

SM: Highly interactive with lots of client meetings, visual materials with the accompanying explanation to draw them out, get reaction, and begin to focus the design in a direction that's constructive?

SL: That's right. I think I should probably qualify all this because my experience is not through any deliberate career decision, but from my own skills and interests, and the way both employers and clients have responded. My particular niche is, at times, almost a marketing role in the sense that I get involved with clients at an early stage to get them excited about the project, eliciting their involvement early on, especially with clients who may or may not have an interest in talking to us. There is a definite marketing component to this. It's just a function of the fact that I've been doing commercial

architecture for twelve years or so. I am sure that factors into part of the reason I am the way I am as I approach the design process though. I don't consciously go out and think of the design process as a marketing effort, I think you have to be realistic enough in your own self appraisal to recognize that as an architect in the commercial sector, or a designer in the commercial sector, that (marketing) is a significant part of your role.

SM: In your experience in school, and then afterwards in the practice environment, was there a point in time where you felt that your design approach came together?

SL: I'm trying to think of when that would be. I know we just went through some exercises in Bangkok and then Santiago. We basically go and find out about the project, visit the site, then we lock ourselves up in a conference room for three or four days and intermittently work with the clients and start to basically design the project before their eyes, and after a week, come away with something that they are excited about and have participated in. They have the feeling that in a week we've done about two months worth of work by their traditional standards. There's no epiphany in this kind of drawing experience. I've seen this as more of a deliberate effort. It's something that has materialized over time that's been rewarding and most effective. The idea of going to some other location, immersing yourself in the project, not being distracted with phones, and after having a brief introduction to the project saying, "I think we can start, just give us a day or two to draw like crazy, we'll get back to you and get your reaction." Later, they look

at the work and say, "Oh, this works great, but this doesn't work or this is what we really meant and in this country we really can't do that." (We've worked at getting a) design that's very responsive to their needs through being able to maintain the energy and excitement that as an architect you like to see in the project. You know you've fundamentally got into a position where it works and you feel good about the design direction.

SM: Is the charrette in that form an approach to programming?

SL: I guess that in summary you could say that.

SM: But it's not couched in a lot of jargon or methodology. It's sit down, roll up our sleeves and let's get crackin.

SL: I really detest the position of architecture being problem solving, but from a client's point of view, you are problem solving. I like to think of the process as breathing life into the project. You're just not wrapping the skin around the plan that functionally attends to their concerns. Hopefully you've clarified a concept and embellished that idea architecturally to the point where you've animated the project and it can tell its own story. That's what I call a success.

SM: The realism of the profession right now fragments responsibilities and "cubby holes" the professions. I personally appreciate the attitude that you take which is obviously constructive, meant to do good work, and good design in spite of the fact that those things are probably thwarted to a certain extent by the existing (practice) environment.

SL: I don't want to over emphasize the amount

of client involvement because we don't necessarily have a tremendous amount of client involvement (over the life of a project), but we do in the very early stages. I think the important thing is to get emotional participation on their part so they've contributed and help create the project.

SM: They get some ownership.

SL: Right. I don't think it has to have everyone's complete commitment and involvement through the whole process. I think its very critical in the early stages to get reactions and elicit the client's response and involvement to get that "buy-in". You don't always get that opportunity either. Sometimes you just design things and you're in front of a board of directors and all they do is thumbs up or thumbs down.

SM: What kinds of things do you look for in a site?

SL: It's interesting because there's a fundamentally binary decision right at the beginning. You either decide you're going to work with a site or you're going to make a strong statement in contrast. The site is one of the critical points of departure for the design effort. Ninety percent of the time it is my nature to be sympathetic to the context and site. To that extent, I guess I look at the site two different ways. One is a sequence of events or spaces. How do you approach when you first see the site? What is the primary approach? What is the secondary approach? What does that tell you about entry and circulation within the building itself? Secondly, in terms of the architectural expression, what cues do you look for as to how the building responds to its context, either in the form of fitting in or providing contrast? How do you position the building in its context? In the case of the project we are familiar with (Nordstrom at Circle Centre), there are some very clear cues there in terms of massing, vertical and horizontal expressions, articulation, and detailing. I also can't overstate the importance of the detailing. I don't get too many projects built, but when I do I like to make sure they have attention at the detail level. I think this is an area where (Alvar) Aalto was sensitive to the level where you touch the building. It takes on a whole different meaning than mass and form. I think that one of the things I've extracted from my Aalto studies (is this sensitivity). It's something I heartily subscribe to.

SM: When do you start to think about details in a building?

SL: Sometimes very early. I like to think as many of the pieces at once as possible. I often find the details (inspiring). A good example, the lanterns we were developing (for the Indianapolis Nordstrom) ended up with an octagonal shape. We noticed a number of octagonal lanterns used in (Indianapolis buildings). Also, I know that making round lanterns is a premium as far as expense goes. Therefore, we ended up with an octagonal shape versus a cylindrical shape. That octagonal shape then started to occur in some of the floor patterns within the stone as well as the plan of the escalator court which is the main atrium space within the store. We've found a simple lantern design to be the generator of forms that to be repeated throughout the store. The point being that inspirations, cues, or starting points can come from all different scales and levels of the design process. It's always fun, even at a site plan level, once you start working on sketches to digress into a particular detail because it might bounce back on you on some of the larger scale issues (later).

SM: In reference to design, do you feel that there is an experience that had great value to you in reference to your education?

SL: One particular experience?

SM: Yes.

SL: You know, I wish I could say there has, but there really hasn't. The signpost for me has been a lot of work. I think I started off with some basic drawing skills that are natural for me, but to be able to translate that into design and deal with the full range of issues, both conceptual and practical, has been a fifteen year education. I can't say that I've come to any particular client and said, "Oh I've got it!" I will say that there was a time working down in Los Angeles for Charles Moore's office that I got to a point where I wanted to make my own mistakes. I wanted to see if I could do it or not. I felt like I had some talent and some ability, but it was always either supported, credited, or couched by very respected senior designers. I was flattered if ideas I had drawn and suggested were incorporated into designs, but I never knew if I had the editorial wherewithal to decide when things were appropriate, and when they weren't, and how to embellish and put things in perspective. It was very important for me to try it myself. Part of the reason I went to Callison was I was not so much interested in a firm that had an atelier design reputation: I was interested in a firm that was doing enough work and would give me enough responsibility that I would be able to sink or swim of my own accord. That really doesn't answer your question directly.

SM: The digression has value though. I find that my experience has been steady evolution, but I'm at a point now that I feel as if I'm about to "break through the ice." I guess my question is motivated by curiosity as to whether other people have had that sort of experience or not. At any rate, it doesn't validate or invalidate either approach or experience.

SL: I've never gotten to the point where I feel like it's all come together and it's all there. I don't know if there ever will be. But by the same token, I don't think I lack the confidence to not keep charging ahead and feel good about what I'm doing. But also not having the feeling that you've reached a certain level does act as motivation to keep pushing me too.

SM: It's interesting. You have an inherent flexibility about your work that to me seems like a valuable trait. I think it supports a creative approach to design and it gives you the opportunity to treat the situations that we get into, both with your clients and sites where the buildings are being contemplated, to take that flexible approach and use it to best advantage.

SL: I might make a couple of comments here. One, very early on, working at Callison, I worked on a hotel project which won a regional AIA award. In that sense, I guess there's a point of gratification because it was one of (my) very first projects. It should've been a point where I felt like I'd arrived, but I never had that feeling at all. In fact, I felt like the project was one of missed opportunities, and I was looking forward to the next one. In hindsight, I really never put much weight or importance on it.

I'm not trying to be modest here, I'm just trying to say that kind of recognition isn't where the satisfaction is.

SM: Actually, though it's a philosophical point, it's not unusual in eastern philosophy to find writings that reference the pleasure of doing work as opposed to the gratification of reaching a goal because once you reach the goal, you immediately reset and begin to work again.

SL: At a very fundamental level, I'm "ungoal" oriented. I'm much more direction oriented. I don't ever intend to get there in other words. I don't want this to be too heady here. The other point I was going to make is that I don't have a strong manifest still. I tend to be very environmental, and responsive to the people, context, and surroundings of what I'm dealing with. I also don't have a real strong agenda myself. Some architects have a strong agenda, and they use architecture as a medium to express that agenda. I'm envious at times of people who have that clarity of vision, but the excitement (for me) comes from the blank piece of paper, starting to absorb some of the input, and then to start scribbling like crazy to see what emerges out of it. That's what gets me excited. Because of that I can get just as excited about doing a historically sympathetic building in downtown Indianapolis (Nordstrom) that's in the historic district, and turn about face and do a building that would be quite inconsistent with that. Although I think there are schools of thought that would say that I lack conviction by virtue of (my) range of expressions, and no clear agenda that ties these works together, it doesn't bother me. I think the challenge is to let the building be a function of the inspirations around it, that particular set of circumstances. Then your job is to somehow breath life into it, make it something that it wasn't or that wouldn't be.

SM: If you were to go and speak to a group of students about architecture and seek to give them advice, what would you say? What do they need to know to succeed?

SL: I think its important to find out what excites them and be able to find a medium to express themselves in, both visually and verbally. Over the course of time, they'll learn the architectural nuts and bolts of the profession, and be able to translate that into buildings. But number one, they have to be able to get excited about something. I use the example of movies because, personally, I use movies as a parallel comparison. If they have an interest in film or cinema, then from an architectural point of view start to draw and learn how to articulate what they're drawing and where they're going. They may use whatever familiar forms they know, that is, movies or otherwise. Over the course of time, let their ability to express in built form evolve naturally. Don't feel like you have to rush it.

SM: Would you be prone to give working professionals similar advice?

SL: I'm not sure a lot of technical people are inspired by that kind of motivation, but for the people who are giving the building form and life, it's a test you can apply to your grave.

SM: It tells a story. The other great thing about it is, again making reference to lay people, the fact that its difficult to take someone who is unfamiliar with architecture, sit them down with a plan and then get comprehension as you present the document. It just doesn't happen 96% of the time. So in perspective, no matter how loose, (the presentation is) going to work better and tell a better story because of the sequence. We are so visually oriented anyway. There is no way that (storyboard presentations) couldn't be vastly more successful.

SL: You control the presentation, too. You control the approach, the whole sequence. If you show an elevation, people see it and make a judgement before you have time to explain. You put an elevation up and get a reaction, positive or negative. Once you start to tell a story, then you have more control in terms of their attention. You're avoiding the trap of an instant reaction to one image. Once they've made that association, there is nothing you can do to talk them out of it. I think its fascinating: that's what motivates me, although there is a tactical side, too, that I think has some merit.

SM: How did you get connected into Charles Moore's office?

SL: He was instructing at UCLA at the time as well as his partners John Ruble and Buzz Yudell. They were doing competitions, so I got involved with that office as many students did.

SM: Have you been satisfied with your experience at Callison, do you feel like there is anything more that you want to do?

SL: I have been quite satisfied. It hasn't been without its frustrations. Commercial work has its own inherent limitations. But by the same token, it's a fast paced effort and one that has gotten me involved with a large range of people and places. I've enjoyed that. Architecturally, I've been given

plenty of latitude, and I'm quite satisfied by the number of opportunities and responsibilities I've been given. It's hard to imagine too many other places where I would have been given that. There are plenty of other things I would like to explore. As you might guess, making movies is really what I'd like to do. Other than that I think, it would be fun to do some very small buildings, some kind of compulsively crafted buildings, especially wood frame houses.

SM: I share a fascination with houses as well.

SL: I would love to just lavish over a house, maybe even build it myself. I also think it would be fun to develop some smaller projects in the City, small mixed use projects on my own or with a team of varied disciplined individuals. The idea of collaborating with a group of nontraditionally trained architectural people, but with strong viewpoints and expressions is appealing. At any rate, there are things out there that over the course of time I'd like to explore.

GAIL M. McCLEESE

DesignWorks, Houston, Texas

Gail McCleese loves her work. It shows in her attention to detail and a broad base of repeat clientele. Her focus in the design profession is hotel and resort interior design. She will literally work inward from the building shell and study every aspect of the design right down to the tables, silverware, and staff uniforms. I know, I have watched her carefully study uniform options for a restaurant after a twelve hour day and patiently explain to a food and beverage director why one choice better integrated with the design vocabulary than another.

Gail recently started her own practice and has not really missed a beat. Sometimes she seems annoyed to have to deal with the management and marketing side of the business. I believe she would much rather work at creating elegant, exciting spaces for her clients than suffer through billings and spreadsheets. Such is the nature of autonomy, however. Her education and background have a strong practical emphasis, both of which are reflected in her work. She has an abiding concern for creating both beautiful spaces and using materials that will stand up to the day-to-day beating they will receive at the hands of hotel staff and guests.

Interior design is a demanding field. To practice and survive is one thing while to practice and prosper is another. Gail has a broad range of projects and an international client base including work in England, the Caribbean, South America, and the United States. Gail likes to "stretch the envelope" especially with clients who know her work and return expressly for her creative flair. She

is careful in new locales however, even with clients she knows. Her focus continues to be grounded in the context of the facility, new or old, and the culture that will use the finished product. She carefully studies the environment for a new design and sets a conceptual ceiling to fit the solution within: she decides how much the envelope may be stretched then settles in to fit concepts to functionality while working to understanding the client.

In the near future, Gail hopes to expand her repertoire from interiors into product design and marketing. Customized pieces occasionally become part of a design in progress. She is finding that these special items may have applications beyond where they were originally conceived. This work keeps Gail very busy, but she was able to take time to chat about her design process, beliefs, and approach in what follows.

Gail M. McCleese: Storage ladder sketch

SM: What do you feel is the most important part of getting a design started?

GM: It varies, depending on the project. Basically it's function, the style appropriate to the client's needs, and the target market.

SM: In the Indianapolis restaurant we worked on, did the client address the issue of style or was that more in your court?

GM: Defining the concept was in my court, which reflects the style. The client set the marketing profile and had some ideas for concept. They expressed wanting to keep the fine dining atmosphere because the restaurant has a reputation known for engagement occasions, due to its beautiful view. Also, business people use the restaurant at lunch. It needed to express romance at night yet continue to function during the day for the business patron. The space had to serve both purposes. I think design concept should entice your marketing clientele and the style enhance the building context and region. It should relate to the type of food being served, and have something to do with the established general surroundings. I proposed a "stellar" concept due to the existing space (revolving restaurant), the name (Eagle's Nest), and desired romantic atmosphere. I presented this idea to the client and pointed out how we could solve existing functional problems. The concept and solutions worked well for the romantic and functional aspects, and for the needs of the staff in terms of service.

SM: Does your approach tend to vary from project to project?

GM: Yes, but there are certain criteria you have to acknowledge and design towards. Most importantly, the space must function. Secondly, you must recognize the locale/geography as not to over-design so that the space has substance and longevity. It should respect its surroundings and be aesthetically pleasing. I think aesthetics enters in third.

SM: What do you do when you actually sit down to do the design?

GM: I list the criteria and concerns I heard from my client and then I study the space to find problem areas. I ask a lot of questions. I approach the problems and solve them with proper space planning and other elements of good design. I go to my resources and study them for unique solutions. I examine what I'm trying to achieve and ask myself if I've achieved it. I define a style and form a color palette using elements from aspects of my daily surroundings, experiences, and travels.

SM: Do you ever get stumped?

GM: Yes, all the time. Restaurant design is a specialty in itself. You can be more daring, but if you don't know your client well, it's hard to present something more innovative. Innovation can cause uncertainties. However, there are those times when I have that innate feeling that it's right!

SM: Does the quality of your relationship with the client allow you to stretch the creative side?

GM: Yes. If I know the reason they came to me is because of my creativity, I feel more comfortable. The more time you spend with a client, the more you know exactly what they like, what they want to achieve, why they picked me as a designer. I find in my relationship with my clients, I'm focusing on a specific concept and adhering to it in defining creative elements and spaces.

SM: It almost sounds like there is a driving concept; something that you use to focus your design effort.

GM: Ever since I started designing, I have developed concepts and used elements to organize the design. I always tie elements together. I try not to overdo it, of course, but enough so that the average patron realizes it on a subconscious level. Those little subtleties pull it all together.

SM: How much would you say you learned about design in school?

GM: A lot. School enhanced the innate sense I already had about design and made it logical. I went to the Art Institute of Houston. They focus on design functionality in relation to the arts and architecture. It's a well rounded school concentrating not only on the arts, but also on the technical requirements of design. The quality of the school you attend is very important. The reason I chose this school was because I was trained by professionals currently working in the field. I think that working with professionals active in the business has helped me to get a real head start. New materials, new ways of construction, new issues throughout the whole design process are always introduced, so I think it's important to be in contact and continually learning. Proper schooling is very important, and hopefully it will help direct a designer towards the type of design they want to specialize in: hospitality, health care, corporate, residential, and so on.

SM: Do you feel that there is a strong tendency in interior design to specialize in those areas?

GM: Definitely. My forte is in restaurant and

hotel interiors. That's what I prefer to design. Everyone has their own niche. I think a designer should concentrate on that niche and develop their qualities and proficiencies. Specializing helps strengthen the designer's talents and ultimately improves the quality of their design. If I was approached to design a health care project, I would have to start at the beginning of the design process and study the elements that are environmentally and legally required for that field. I wouldn't feel comfortable with a health care project unless I was allowed time to study the issues involved for those applications. Therefore, I feel it's really important to select a designer based on their expertise.

SM: How often do you sit down with a client and work out a program? Does that happen very much?

GM: A level of programming is necessary unless you have that comfort level with the client to be assured that the existing problems and design issues are being recognized and communicated. For a new client, it is very beneficial and necessary.

SM: So basically one of the things I'm getting out of what you've just been talking about in the last few minutes almost sounds like the program is embedded already in your expertise.

GM: Somewhat. With restaurant renovations, it's almost a series of givens because it is a renovation and any problems should be recognized. In a large commercial project, being a renovation or not, you have to program because of the extent of the project, the expanse of personalities, and flow that must occur between the personnel and their departments. Every project is different; some clients are

very knowledgeable of the issues and some rely on the designer to guide them through the programming process. If the client is comfortable with the designer, they usually don't let their personal preferences dictate the solutions.

SM: They trust you?

GM: Hopefully, that's one reason why they've selected me.

SM: Where do you find inspiration?

GM: I find inspiration in everyday life. I just look at my surroundings; study and observe. I find details and elements in magazines that inspire me. I pull photographs of published projects and furniture styles for ideas of curve, angle, scale, and form. I find color inspiration in fashion design, nature, even television commercials.

SM: Do you get a chance to go to your completed projects much after the fact?

GM: Most of them, yes. Sometimes budget does not allow for the whole design team to visit the project site. On a hotel guest room and suite renovation for Hyatt Regency in Lexington, Kentucky, I have not been able to see the finished product yet, just photographs. It's hard to imagine, without seeing and feeling the space, if our *total* design intent was successful. It's definitely an advantage to experience the spaces and learn from your accomplishments and mistakes.

SM: Say you go to meet with a brand new client. Is there any special approach or mind set that you take into that meeting? What do you have in mind goal wise to walk away with?

GM: Good knowledge of what they're trying to achieve for the project and the client's objectives.

I try to understand the client's personality and get to know them better; define how I'll need to work with them. Basically the design criteria, problems, overall scope, the big picture. That's what I try to accomplish.

SM: Is there any time that you're working on a scheme and you have a feeling like, "Yeah, I've got it!"

GM: Oh, yes. You know exactly, too, when you don't. I do at least. I look at it and say, "There's something missing." Sometimes you can't pin it down, and the best thing to do is just walk away, come back in a couple hours or the next day, and look at it again. I'm always asking for different opinions and I'm always explaining my choices and reasoning to other designers to see if they've followed my logic; to see if they can point out anything else that I may have missed. It's interesting to talk to other designers about your work. If something is close, a fine line, maybe they can help you pinpoint the missing elements. It's helpful to have their opinion: not be so protective about your design, because it's there to benefit all. Some designers don't like to share ideas, but to me its very helpful to get constructive criticism and broaden the base of opinion.

SM: Usually, do you create more than one scheme?

GM: Usually I do. For the Eagle's Nest (a restaurant we both worked on in Indianapolis), I didn't. This one I knew we'd hit it because it was right on target. I felt the concept was accurate and I thought it would work. I felt strongly about it. If I don't have that feeling, I may create two concepts

because I can't really pinpoint the client's needs or preference. I think that (my clients) like that as well because then you're getting them involved in the design process. You can learn a lot about your client's needs by having two schemes. If they want fine dining, you can pull an image together with two different types of atmosphere and discuss the conceptual differences. It's especially important to give new clients a couple of different schemes so they can observe your decision making process. Also, some clients don't really understand what you're trying to achieve unless you *show* them.

SM: Do you feel that you can elaborate at all on how to understand your client better, how to read them, how to get a handle on what they're thinking?

GM: I think listening helps a lot, asking questions, and showing the client different options. I did this recently with a hotel client with whom I've renovated three hotels. Now I know exactly what he likes and expects even though the style of hotel may be different. I design for that style of hotel, but I know what color schemes he would prefer. I choose what I know he will like within that context; like a corporate hotel compared to a resort. I've done both styles for him. You can still design different types of properties for the same client if you know what they like and what level of design they expect. I think that's just related to time, listening, educating, and presenting options. I learned that this client prefers "cool" colors by showing him options. He prefers traditional, but in his resort hotels accepted a more transitional style. It takes a little bit of prying into their psychology, identifying their personal goals, hobbies, style, etc., so you can perceive their

character. If they're not willing to give you this type of information, you're going to play a big guessing game. There are times when, even though you think you know them, you haven't hit it right. It may just be an off day. So really it's listening, communicating, and knowing their personal preferences.

SM: Are there any people who are designers, in whatever discipline, that your particularly admire?

GM: I don't really focus a lot on (interior) designers. I admire a lot of architects. Their architecture reflects the type of design they like. I admire Frank Lloyd Wright, that's typical. How could you not? I like contemporary architects like Richard Meier and controversial architects like Frank Gehry. I can't say I have a favorite. I always appreciate something in almost any design, even if I don't like the whole solution. I wouldn't expect anybody to look at my designs and say they're perfect. There is always something you don't prefer or would do differently.

SM: You don't have any particular heroes?

GM: No, I really don't. I like a lot of *styles* of design and I think that's important. As a personal preference, I like contemporary design. I'm definitely not a "Laura Ashley" style (designer), and if a client requests that particular vocabulary, I will tell them that I can't do it. That's one style I would not enjoy creating. I would advise the client to find someone who is comfortable with that style because that's what is important. You have to like what you're doing. It shows in your work. Colleagues and clients know what you like, and it shows in your design. I think that's probably the reason I do a lot

of Hyatt work. They are an innovative hotel chain and allow me to be innovative. Therefore, the relationship is successful. You become a fanatic about design. You live this career, you really do. I think you have to because you are observing all the time.

SM: That's an interesting point. I'm glad we got to that. When you're designing, how much would you say you use your imagination and make an effort to mentally get into a space?

GM: I do a lot of visualization. I've always incorporated that in the design process. I don't know how you could be successful without it. Yesterday, we were talking about adding that sun motif to the glass table tops (in the Eagle's Nest restaurant). That idea was developed subconsciously. I woke up one morning, figured a way we could do it, and ended up saving the client some money! That's part of good design. I think visualization is necessary if you're going to succeed in carrying out a thematic concept. We really tied elements together, and that's what's fun about the design process. I can see what the space is going to look like now, although it will look slightly different, I'm sure we won't be disappointed.

SM: When you make a presentation, besides the verbal part, which is obviously very important, what do you consider essential? Based on what I've seen so far, the interiors end seems to differ somewhat from an architectural presentation. I'd like to get into that a little bit.

GM: Any little thing helps. I pull out magazine articles. I show (my client) a picture of a room with a similar atmosphere. I'll point out the elements that we're trying to achieve. Anything visual will help because you don't always know whom you're presenting to. Anything you can show them three dimensionally; paint chips, pieces of metal, chair samples, fabric samples, actual finish samples, and so on. Drawings and color renderings help to explain color contrast and texture.

SM: Do you ever build models?

GM: Not for small interior spaces. It really depends on the scale of the space. It would be appropriate for a full scale renovation. For example, an atrium space where the model is justified because it's the best tool to communicate your ideas for such a large scale. Otherwise, you have to use the tools necessary to convey your ideas balanced against what you're anticipated profit on the project will be.

SM: Let's chat a little bit about something that's curious to me. In interior design, the materials are specified with contact names. You have relationships established with representatives and suppliers. These people directly supply material to a project. It's different in my experience because I typically will talk to representatives and they will make the pitch for their product, provide outline specifications and so on. We'll review that and consider it for the project. At that point, it's an open field. They're in the ring with four other manufacturers of a product that's equivalent. Then it's bid and the project is built. In this case, you have a preexisting relationship. I wanted to know more about how that worked.

GM: Most firms have interiors and architectural libraries. I meet manufacturer's representatives whenever time permits. I feel it's very impor-

tant to review new products to stay on the "cutting edge" of design products. I owe that to myself and my clients. There are manufacturer's representatives for fabric, furniture, finishes, and so on. I build relationships with all of them based on quality of their product, their service to me (delivery of samples, pricing, etc.), and the service of the product to my client (availability, delivery time, durability). The local manufacturer's representatives realize that even though I've specified them, the general contractor will bid to their local "rep." If my rep is documented, they can receive some commission for their service. The general contractor's responsibility is to purchase and install the *specified* product with no substitutions unless approved by designer and client.

SM: Let's move from a generality to a little more specific situation. You have identified a wall fabric that you want to use. At that point, you contact the rep. Then does the rep provide you with pricing information?

GM: Yes. I call them up and specify the amount of yardage required and ask for pricing and availability. If the pricing is over my budgeted amount, I ask them to work with me. A lot of times we can bring the cost down by altering the ground weight or number of print screens required. The custom process is time consuming, so I weigh the options of utilizing less of the expensive material and more of another fabric or reselect altogether

SM: What kind of advice would you give to somebody who is in school studying design right now?

GM: Don't look into this field to get rich

quick. It's a creative job and you have to compare it to being an artist: sometimes feast, sometimes famine. The salary levels don't compare with the responsibility you hold. We manage large projects and the responsibility that a designer holds is nothing compared to the level of pay. If you want to succeed, it's a lot of hard work. You work long hours. It's a tough job and *you* have to be satisfied with the results. That's where I get my fulfillment: when my work is done. When I can go into the space and see it in use and that it serves its purpose. That's when I can really say I love my job. It's a tough field and very competitive. It's not as glamorous as everybody makes it sound, but it is fun and I chose it because I knew I'd get fulfillment out of being creative everyday. You're drafting, picking fabrics and finishes, talking with reps, architects, general contractors, and clients. You have to deal with so many different levels and types of people and do many different things all day long. That's what's fulfilling to me.

SM: You can't beat the variety, can you?

GM: No, no. That's why I chose it.

DANIEL A. NEEB

Entasis Design, Indianapolis, Indiana

Dan Neeb is in transition: he is asking hard questions of himself and seeking answers both personal and philosophical. This is not an easy task. This internal dialogue stems from a career many would describe as successful, but is tempered by the belief that growth comes from stretching the limits and assumptions which come to guide us out of habit.

Dan is a talented designer and articulate in his observations and concerns. We first met in school, spending many an evening questioning traditional wisdom into the wee hours of the morning and beyond. In those times we began to forge the paradigms that would come to shape our futures. Dan graduated from Ball State University in 1981 and made his way to Savannah, Georgia. He worked for several years as a designer for a small firm before moving to Atlanta and signing on with a design-build office. He steadily expanded his knowledge and improved his craft, advancing to studio head at Carlson Associates. He saw many of his projects brought to fruition, yet still felt that his path perhaps lay elsewhere. Early in 1990, he contacted a firm he had worked for in Indianapolis in years past and found that their practice had expanded to the point that they were in need of someone to guide the design output of the office. Given this opportunity, Dan returned to Indianapolis and has been practicing there since. To the present, he has done work for international clients and is currently seeking the Rome prize to pursue research on urban amphitheaters.

His work largely consists of projects for developers and corporate clients. The taste, budget, and time available for each solution vary dramatically. Dan has risen to a challenge that sometimes seems daunting, if not impossible. Extracting quality design in these circumstances is often extremely difficult, yet he continues to study the problem and offer insight into a scenario which many of us know all too well.

In addition, although this practice environment is often grueling, Dan continues to evolve his approach to design process and position himself in the market to attract a wider variety of projects. In time, I am sure he will succeed. For the moment, enjoy this snapshot of a professional who has been kind enough to take time from a hectic journey to share his philosophy and experience.

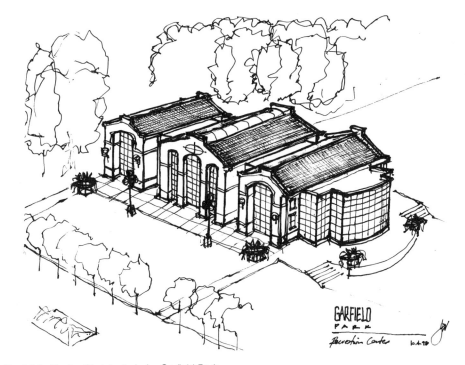

Daniel A. Neeb: Sketch study for Garfield Park

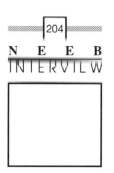

SM: How would you describe your practice, your experience to date?

DN: We live and die by design charrette. Typically, the clients that I've been involved with are classically late in coming forward with their proposed projects, whether it be in terms of construction time or financing or whatever. So inevitably we find ourselves in a position of having all this information and then having a matter of days to weeks, if that, to distill it and come up with some sort of a design solution. Once that solution preliminarily is penned off, your opportunities to reexamine that solution becomes distinctly limited. Whether for budget reasons or owner infatuation with the first thing that you show or your own infatuation with it or whatever, the opportunities to re-examine or refine it in a more architectonic way become more limited. I also find what I would consider to be the most art oriented solutions generally the least possible to pull off.

SM: You feel that you don't have enough time?

DN: No, I'm not sure that that's it. I think you could have a real strong prime concept, but I rarely find the appreciation of what could be on the client side of the table. That may just be a result of the kind of clients that I've typically dealt with. I haven't found the patron who believes that architecture has an art role. It's been more the patron who believes that architecture encloses and envelopes a space for a use and not much more than that.

SM: So quality of life issues are not considered?

DN: Beyond the basics, probably not. Cer-

tainly not intellectual quality issues. My clients would probably laugh me out of the room if I came in and gave some sort of philosophical discussion of the architectural merits of a particular design. I've almost given up doing that because I don't think its within my means any more to inspire (or baffle) people. I figure if I come to the table with a solution that I can live with, I can probably find a way to coerce them into accepting it. Having made that statement, I know too that I limit myself because of knowing my audience or making a guess at knowing my audience.

SM: Do you deal with developer clients typically?

DN: Primarily, or single users who are doing "build to suit" things, generally on a smaller scale. The trouble is that by the time they get to the position where they realize that they need to build, the process is so forced that the time to examine multiple sites or options is generally very limited. You find also that a lot of our clientele is brought to us through their relationship with contractors, not necessarily through their relationship with us. Generally, what will happen is I'll be sitting in the office and somebody will call and say I'm so and so contractor and I have a guy here in my office who wants to build this building. We've had experience with you guys before. We'd like you to give our client a proposal for the building. Generally it's visual first, followed by a financial sort of proposal. So we do a lot of stuff at risk, if you will. That's just the nature of the thing. It's almost like every job in certain ways is its own miniature competition. It just depends on who all is in it as to what the

competition parameters really comprise.

SM: A little earlier you talked about the idea of "knowing your enemy." When you put yourself in the shoes of your clients, what do you think their world view is?

DN: I think that their world view is generic. The image that they choose to convey is first seen in terms of their marketing or product and second, in terms of the shell that encloses it; particularly with the single user. From the developer standpoint, because of the financial climate over the last eight or nine years, the approach is based more on what their competition is or isn't doing as opposed to what kind of a path they as individuals should take. You don't see people in development going out on a limb with a building design, from the amount of square feet per floor to the materials that are used in the skin. They all do their proforma work, etc. on a sort of similar basis and they all seem to believe that they understand what the banks will or won't be willing to commit to. So you come up with a general formula or range that you know is going to be acceptable.

SM: And that starts to shape the architecture then?

DN: Absolutely. The perception that a curve is more expensive than a corner; the perception that a lot of glass is more expensive, either initially or long term, than solid walls; the perception about the conventional properties of components of the building like length to width ratio for lease depths and so on. All of that comes into play. I've never dealt with a singular corporate entity that has solely been concerned about the facility and not as much on its financial impact. One of these days, maybe I'll have that experience. But to this point it's been from the other side of the game: a marketing oriented perspective in terms of dollars per square foot.

SM: How do you characterize the difference between your design experience in school and your design experience now?

DN: The things that schools miss are the governmental restrictions: zoning regulations and building codes are barely touched on, if at all. That part is a missing component of the educational system. Also, once you get a conceptual solution, people tell you that you will have an elongated period of time to massage and further develop this thing into a highly detailed series of components which may be one-off (custom) or off the shelf. I don't find that we have that time. I find that I do a parti, a series of concept sketches, and a rendering and I'm committed. I had better be happy with it at that point or I'm lost from an architectural perspective. That's why I no longer feel that it's my responsibility or that I have the time to some how philosophically enrich my clients. I prefer to take a practical, highly logical approach, so I'm talking their language, not mine. If I'm happy with it, that's a secondary consideration in terms of my presentation to them. The thing that is stressed over and over (in our practice) is that you should be prepared to walk in with multiple solutions to a singular problem. The thing that has always scared me is that I get one that's real good, then I do two others just to satisfy our internal posturing. The problem is: are you a good gambler. Can you walk into the presentation and make sure that concept "C", the one you

really want, is the one that gets sold or do you go in and sweat it out knowing that "A" or "B" is a potential reality which you couldn't live with. There are a lot of people who would believe if you can't live with it, then you shouldn't present it. I don't know in our practice if we have enough time to really get three equal quality solutions to the same problem. To me, it's like asking Picasso to paint the same painting three times with different colors and see which one the museum really likes. Maybe you like one with a tan background or do you really think it should be black. I don't know how to answer that question.

SM: As you look back over your practice is there a particular project that was pivotal for you, that was particularly exciting, and started to inform what you thought architecture is in the real world, as you made the transition from academic environment to actual practice?

DN: I think there were two projects, a series of projects first, and then one particular project after that. When I first got out of school, I was working in Savannah, Georgia. We did a number of retail stores in a mall that was being expanded. All of them were for local merchants. They were in the same general vicinity of one another. It was a great experience for me because I got into color, texture, and all of the various interior furnishings and build-outs that you can do. Each one of the stores had to be different because not only did those people expect it, but their products were radically different as well. So it was almost like designing a subdivision of homes where each one of them had to have their own kind of unique thing. They were generally

inexpensive in terms of total dollar cost per project. They all happened and opened almost simultaneously. The other project was a five story office building that I did in Atlanta that was right across the parking lot from our offices. Seeing it every day, whether I wanted to or not, walking in and out of the office. That really brought home the real impact that a building has on a lot of different areas, not only on the people who build it, but in the readaptation of an environment, and what the implications of it are long term. That was really one of the first major buildings that I've been involved with that was so close by. A lot of other ones that I've done have been in remote locations, so my contact with them was once every two months or something like that in a Construction Administration role. I watched this one grow and change daily from a hole to something that was completely skinned over. I think that those projects were critical to the way I look at things now. They represent two spectrums. One is a highly customized kind of "jewel box" type of mentality (retail) where you don't have to worry about leaks and all that because the roof and structure are already there. All you're doing is placing detailed infill. The office building was very much a study in how the structure can be used as ornament; how the site design issues of fitting a five story building in a very narrow site, the parking deck, and all sorts of other things get put together. Overall, a much bigger scale of thinking. The level of detail in that project was at best equivalent to the retail stuff but was so much larger in scale that it's hard to compare the two.

SM: Who would you describe as your design

influences, if you're willing to admit to any?

DN: I'm going to admit to a few of them. I think that Frank Lloyd Wright's design approach has been something that I've gravitated towards with limited success. I think the other architects that I have a tendency to follow are people who are doing work which is probably similar in programmatic content to what I'm trying to do. Pelli is one that comes to mind along with the Ralph Johnson's and Kohn Pederson Fox's of the world. There are a few of those out there. Historically, I'm drawn to two areas. One is the structuralist type while the other side is the classical in which I'll place Wright, because I believe his work is tremendously indebted to the classics even though it attempted to be projected to the public as something which was radically new. I think it was a different approach to ornamentalism than found in the classics. It's rooted in that level of organization: biaxial symmetry, integration of an ornamental pattern throughout certain areas and typically disbursed vertically through the sections. There is a relationship between the classical tradition and the Wrightian position in how those two merge together. So those are the two camps that I'm interested in. The new stuff: there aren't many people that I really have much of an interest in. Of the ones that are being published now, my focus on has been on Tadao Ando because of his relationship to the structuralist group that I mentioned and probably Fay Jones for his relationship to Wrightian principles, or a guy like Santiago Calatrava who is also in that structuralist area.

SM: What is it about that work that attracts you?

DN: From the structuralist side I think it is the ability to really use a limited palette of materials in a highly refined way. Ando's work particularly jumps out and bites me that way. The quality of materials and execution that he gets is just staggering especially when you're used to seeing lousy concrete floors. His buildings are more like concrete cabinet work. It just boggles my mind. I guess the classical approach is more of an interest in how people are able to take the design relationships that classicism espouses and translate them into modern vernacular. The notion that the entire building can be distilled into the proportions of the column base to me is a real interesting notion. Whether you are able do it or not is a whole other issue as a viewer of that architecture. Given enough study, could you distill the idea down to a little 2" x 2" box and say, "Yeah, right here's the theory of the whole place contained in one entity." I'm interested in that too, so the work of the Fay Joneses and others fits into that. But for the de-constructivists, post-moderns, etc. that stuff is too fashionable for me to take seriously. I just don't believe that it has the time relationship that we expect quality architecture to have. I believe it is very datable. The techniques that I see in the execution of those buildings, from a materials standpoint, are close to lackadaisical, if not laughable. It's a stage set. I just don't see the relevance of it in today's society other than perhaps an expression of its relative rootlessness. I guess both the camps which I'm interested in philosophically and technically have the ability to transcend the vagaries of the age. Those folks are out there working very, very hard to rationalize an approach

to materials, an approach to the design effort, that to me, because of its seriousness, has merit. I'm sure that there are people who could quote passages from Derrida and try to make me feel that their approach was equivalently serious but I just don't see it.

SM: Derrida, who's that?

DN: He's a linguist and philosopher who originally came up with de-constructionism in literature. Where all this foolishness started, from the world of academia, architecture may be translated as some series of signs or signals. Its interpreters make the intellectual jump and say it must be a language. Therefore, we can take that language, de-construct it, and come up with new forms that people are supposed to be able to understand or creatively "reread." I have trouble understanding the literature side of it, let alone how it fits with buildings and the environment as a whole. I'm not convinced that what they are doing has any intent to *be* architecture. The very notion of de-construction implies that they're trying to somehow take away from the materiality of what it is that we do. It's like trying to cut into your own corpse to see the results of the autopsy. I just don't know if that approach has any kind of benefit to those of us who are practicing today. I don't see the benefit of the philosophy. I want to. I'd be more than happy to pay attention to it if someone could demonstrate (its meaning) to me, but I see its application as kind of talking myself out of a job.

SM: In architecture and design in general, how do you try to separate fashion from some kind of true direction?

DN: I think there are people who have taken

varied approaches at it and have almost succeeded, depending on how you want to think about it. One of the people that I use as a model for that is Richard Meier. Here is someone who started his career in the mid 60's and has produced essentially one style of building in a very limited palette of materials for a long period of time. If you and I were clients and we said, "Well, we want a corporate edifice. I kind of like Meier's stuff." You know exactly what you're going to get. You know that the solution will be "uniquely yours", but if put in a line along with 50 other of his projects, you would probably be able to successfully question which one was yours, theirs, or his. I admire his consistency. I think there it takes a lot of nerve to take that approach, but he's done it. He's pulled it off to the tune of some amazingly large commissions. There is a validity to it. (Tadao) Ando is another example of the same kind of thing. You go to him, and it's pretty safe to expect that you're going to get a concrete building that will be highly machined and articulated, modernist in character, with minimal ornament. So it's a predictable thing. Now, when you look at people like Stern, Venturi, or Gehry, I don't know what to think about their work. It's somehow inconsistently consistent. I don't think that those three as a group are as fashionable now as they appear to have been when they initially came forward. They still have an element of fashion in their work.

If you put down all of Sterns projects next to each other, you might have a very different impression of his approach to practice than you would were you to examine mine in the same way. There's the point where I come into all this, purposeful to a certain extent, probably driven by education. I'm not sure that I want to have a constant approach. I think that each client is unique enough that they merit a non-repetitive solution. I try to make it a point either to focus in each project on a different palette of materials or on a different style, depending on the context, colors, and all that. I pick (an approach) and fight that series of battles with the intent to produce something which looks like it belongs. A lot of the work that I've been involved with lately has been in very contextual surroundings or has been an addition to something that's already there.

SM: You choose to respond contextually?

DN: Yes, absolutely. Typically, my response is an attempt to integrate, not to contrast. I have the feeling that contrast has its merit, but it takes a big leap of faith to be able to do that, to have your client buy it, and feel that it's really successful. In the process I described earlier, it's really hard to do that in a very short period of time and feel like you did the right thing. It'll last for a long time and if you screw it up the first time, it's a lost cause. All you can do is drive past it every day and grimace. I don't see that as an acceptable set of circumstances.

SM: This may be kind of like asking a tennis player how to describe his serve, but when you sit down to work now, what goes on? How would you describe your process?

DN: In the last few years, I've not been confronted by a problem which really pushed my limits of conceptual thinking. There are certain kinds of projects which are so loaded with historical information or other things that they really demand that you to come up with a philosophical approach to them first, then a solution. I think with the work that I've been involved with, the philosophical solution is a closely held matter. If people choose to probe into that and talk about it, that's fine. But that's not where I start.

SM: Is there inherent philosophy?

DN: I think there is. It becomes a study in the achievement of a means to an end. Can you make the pieces that form the fabric of the building economical enough that you can do other things with what people see. If you can do that, can you then impart some style to it which either responds to the context that it is in or is something from an image standpoint which somehow describes the client's world view. Every client comes to the table with some sort of image of themselves as an organization, as an individual, as a product; whether it is the highly machined nature of a technical product that drives the way a building looks or how they think that their building needs to respond to their employees. There is a whole psychology that is unique to each job that seems to take over. One of these things gets real strong in the beginning. It's a gut feeling thing.

SM: That's intuitive on your part?

DN: I think so, I really do. In the early stages, I try to ask a lot of questions to see if my initial guess is right. If you can find that intuitive link early, the process of moving a design forward from trash paper sketches to building is a hell of a lot easier to realize than it is if you're fighting that baseline proposition from the beginning. I know people who have done that and come close to pulling it off successfully, but it looks like it was a fight and it

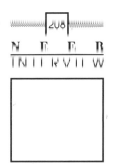

wears you out. I don't know that you could do it for every project. You'd wipe yourself out.

SM: Have you ever walked away from a client? Have they ever asked you to do something that you just could not do?

DN: I've never been in a position where I could say no to them. I've been in a lot of positions where I've walked back into my office and slammed the door and bitched a lot. But to me, the challenge is accepting the fact that I don't like what they're asking me to do. How can I still give it some level of quality that I can live with? That's not always the easiest thing, but there is a certain amount of self knowledge that tells you not every project has to be a high blood pressure event. Some are, but one adage which I was taught is: pick your battles and win them. You pick two or three things on a job that you think are absolutely the most important concepts or ideas and you fight like a cat for them with the willingness to back off on any number of other things in a project to maintain those two or three big ideas. If you can do that, then you could probably be generally happy with your final result. I think my experience in design-build lends that even more credence. There are a lot of ways that you can manipulate the structure, the specification of certain items, and so on. That's several cents per square foot which means that you can get that fanciful screen wall in front of the building or that wild mechanical screen that you thought was the greatest thing since sliced white bread. So that's kind of the approach that I have used over the years.

SM: Sounds pretty subtle. How do you convince a client that these things are of value?

DN: The only way to do it successfully is to make sure in the beginning that the client is committed to spending a real amount of money as opposed to some other processes that I've seen. Some client's ultimate goal is to start at one place but then to really whittle it down $5 or $6 a square foot to something that they can really live with. But they start out with something that they think they can get you excited about. Then it becomes a process of cutting away until you're at the point where you just want to throw up hands and say, "screw it!" That's not acceptable from my viewpoint. I'd rather have them tell me right up front, "Hey, look, we only have $40 a foot. This is what you've got to work in." Then its your job along with working with the contractor to find a way to make it buildable. And you better hope that inside that money you've got enough contingency and you've got a good enough knowledge of the site and the other constraints that you're going to encounter that you might actually make it. People forget that these things are really sort of research and development projects from the beginning. Theoretically, if you take the position that I have where you don't work with the same palette of materials consistently, or the same kind of design approach consistently, then it really is a one-off product. People in Detroit spend millions on prototypes and clay modeling and all this other stuff. Well, I don't have the chance to do that. You hope you got it right the first time and really sort of keep massaging it as you go. My employers have asked me a lot, "Are we done with such and such a project yet?" We're not done until three months after somebody's already had the keys. If it's gonna break, it's gonna break

early. You can't just do the design and documents and sort of walk away because that's not what prototype design is all about. It's hard to rationalize the prototypical approach when you're inside an organization which views itself as a production house. Ultimately, my work has not pushed technical or design limits by any stretch of the imagination. My work to this point has not demanded high levels of craftsmanship. We're not talking about leaded glass and fine iron work and furniture and all these other things which historically have made other's reputations. I just haven't had the opportunity to deal with people who went looking for that. Who knows, maybe down the road. It hasn't happened yet.

SM: When you work now, what is your primary method of evolving a design?

DN: I do a lot of my work on 8 1/2 x 11 paper. Primarily because I still have this notion that image, however hazy it is, is still the thing that separates architecture from building. I'm also a believer in a "big bang" theory of architecture where I'll mull a problem around for a while under reasonably controlled conditions and all of a sudden it coalesces into an image, a mental picture that I then put on paper. Then I work backwards from that image and back into the building if you will, into the innards of it. Where the elevators go, how do you put the bathrooms in, etc. Architects in the past were viewed as being manipulators of materials to form a visual image. If you look at old documents, they don't go into how you attach a stone skin to a steel frame. They poche'd it all and said, "Look, this is the image that I want." How you, Mr. Craftsman, choose to produce that is your own business. So they described a basic set of materials, joint pattern and decoration schemes and away they went. Now its different obviously, at least in North America. I still have a tendency to do that old fashioned thing where I believe that the visual part of it is still the thing that makes it or breaks it.

SM: So that's your first step?

DN: Yes.

SM: Are you sketching in three dimensions?

DN: I favor axonometrics and I'm getting better now at perspective. Two point typically. I want to stand at a corner of the property and have some sort of a visual impression of how the thing's going to sit on the site and present itself to the public. Then I sort of work from the big picture down. Again, I can do that because the building types that I focus on typically have been consistent. If somebody would come up to me and present me with a problem like the Holocaust Museum that I did for my thesis, my approach would probably be much different because of the highly charged content of the program. Commercial buildings are commercial buildings.

SM: It's like what we talked about before, the embedded program as opposed to a truly unique, one of a kind design.

DN: Right, typically my clients will own a building for a period of time until its complete, maybe a couple of months afterwards, and their intent is to sell it, make money, and do the next one. They don't have a long term use interest in it. There are very few clients that I've dealt with who actually inhabit the buildings that we've designed for them.

There are some, but not many.

SM: You don't get much feedback from your users after the fact then.

DN: Only if it was on budget, if there were construction difficulties, or if there was something radically flawed in the way that we approached it in the beginning that we just plain missed. Fortunately, I can't recall one where the last thing has been an issue. But I'm sure there might be one down the road.

SM: There's always that chance, isn't there? I like the logic that Stan Laegreid used. He was talking about designing at Callison and he said something to the effect of, "They trusted me and given me enough rope to hang myself. I haven't done so yet."

DN: Absolutely. I hang on that same rope, every day. I've always viewed it as something where, with each project, I'm able to garner a little more rope. I'm able to hang a little longer or tie the knot more loosely, if you will. But that hangman's noose is definitely there all the time.

SM: Do you sometimes get stuck in your design process?

DN: Absolutely.

SM: What do you do to escape?

DN: I try to make an environmental change. I'll take a couple of days and go some place just to get away from the environment where I'm working. If I can go to the beach, I'll go to the beach. If I can go to the woods, I'll go to the woods. Just something to separate myself from the day to day grind that goes on and try to come up with a strong idea that I can feel comfortable with. Fortunately, that hasn't

happened too often either, but it has happened sometimes.

SM: Do you engage in a lot of visualization when you design?

DN: In what way?

SM: Actually take your imagination and make a picture in your mind.

DN: Yes. I try to carry that through the whole documentation process. I view the way that this thing comes together as seeing the basic form of it; that image issue that I talked about initially, then continuing to just sort of walk around the building getting closer and closer to the facade to develop a level of detail to appreciate at a small scale as well as at a large scale. When you're doing the construction documents, it goes a few steps further than that because you internalize. To me, it's just a continuous walking around process. Once the basic image is established and that's been accepted by the powers that be, then I just continue to develop it that way. I think I've been fortunate up to now in that I've never had a project where we've accepted it one way and kept on with it and all of a sudden I've walked in and said, "This ain't it." That hasn't happened yet. I don't know what I'd do if it would.

SM: Do you build models?

DN: Only for presentation purposes. Generally, the drawings or sketches that I show the clients are closer to renderings. Again, the work that we've dealt with over the years has not been massing intensive like a high rise building would be where you view it from a distance and have a whole series of issues that go into the visualization of it. My work has been smaller scale overall.

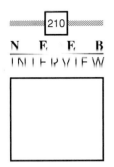

SM: Sounds as if you were in a context where massing issues were at a certain level and size of importance, the model would pop up.

DN: Yes, and this is the place where I think the computer is going to have the most impact in what we are doing. Even though it's sort of a television oriented medium, with what's happening now with holographic projection and all that, there will be a time where the design effort that we do can be spatially projected. Better than models even. Model photographs are great, but most of my clients aren't really ready to spend 30 grand on a model that's really gonna show them what they need to see.

SM: But if you can set them up with a virtual reality rig...

DN: If that's the mode that we choose to practice in, that might be okay. On the other hand, I have an aversion to the whole computer issue because I think it takes away something from the artistic side of it. Some how it becomes too homogenous. Sort of McDonald's come to architecture which I find kind of bothersome. Maybe I'm looking at it from a too simplistic point of view, but there's something about that whole idea that I'm not really thrilled about.

SM: If you were talking to a kid in school studying architecture, what kind of advice would you give her?

DN: Be prepared to have your best work put in the drawer and never visualized further than you could take it without someone else's money. Recognize that no matter what school tells you, you are not the primary player in the process. You are a part of it, but you are not the primary player. The person with the money is the primary player. Period. Until you're in a position to do that, like John Portman, be prepared to have to rationalize varying levels of compromise. Last, I guess, is don't be afraid to develop a well reasoned approach and point of view that allows you to have a philosophical base prior to the time that you approach any project. Whatever that philosophical base is, is fine. There will be people who will gravitate to that and there will be others who will never gravitate towards it. But at least you know you are working in a direction that feels comfortable to you from a mental as well as a realizable standpoint.

SM: How do you see your future? What's next?

DN: We talked about the Rome Prize possibility. My expectation is in one of two areas. Either I'm going to come back from that experience, provided I can make it happen, to my own practice with a couple of people I know and trust. Or, I'm going to gravitate towards a firm whose body of work I appreciate and attempt to get on there in some position of design responsibility. I believe design is where my talents lie. I know I can administrate and do all the other things that are necessary to produce buildings. But I still think that design is the place where I belong. So we'll see. I do feel after a few years of doing this that I was very fortunate in making the choice that I did when I thought that I should try to be an architect. It's proven to be as much fun as I thought it was going to be, and as challenging. Every day is something different. I am really doing my own version of research and development and the products...some of them have been realized, not all of them, but some of them. I can't sit here and say that I have some grand overreaching philosophy that is or should be noticeable by the rest of the world. I'm not looking to publish a philosophical treatise that says architecture is this and nothing else. I just don't see my position in the whole scheme of things that way.

EUNICE NOELL

Eunice Noell & Associates, Portland, Oregon

Eunice Noell grew up in Bend, Oregon. As a child, she watched her father build houses and later, assisted him in their construction. This experience struck a chord within her that she chose to follow and expand upon. She took her Interior Architecture degree from the University of Oregon in 1966 and began working with George Schwarz, a well known interior designer in the Portland area. After three years, she decided that her own business was the next logical step and set up her office in Portland. Her son was born five months after she began her practice and, in the beginning, it was not unusual for the baby to be in the office with her. She was balancing her career and child rearing long before it became an American cultural icon.

She boasts a broad knowledge of design concepts specifically applicable to user and environmentally oriented interior design. She currently specializes in work for the elderly applying an intricate knowledge of daylighting principles at both an architectural and physiological level. She prefers a team environment with the opportunity to participate in the design process from the outset of a project. This has important advantages related to her design goals. First, to accomplish the daylighting aspect of her work, the design of a building's skin must be approached in a particular way. The result is that as an interior designer, she transcends the notion of "interiors" and presents form giving ideas to the architectural component of the team. Her experience has shown that ego sometimes tramples concepts she originally identified as essential. Conversely, in more cooperative ventures, her goals have been met and the results to her satisfaction.

Her practice has spanned quite a range of projects over the last 20 years, but recently she found a point of synthesis in her concern for the environment and design for the aging. Her environmental beliefs permeate and guide her design process. Simultaneously, the special needs of the elderly are often short changed by traditional design rules of thumb. A homogenous approach to design is refuted by Eunice's research: older people have a higher sensitivity to airborne toxins and thus, achieving good indoor air quality becomes an axiomatic goal of all her designs. Also, the visual acuity of the aged is significantly lower and as a result, they have special needs with respect to light levels, both for general vision and physiological responses related to health. Note also, these notions are applicable to all people, regardless of age. The principles Ms. Noell applies in her designs are timeless and have the intrinsic value of quality applied with care, experience, and genuine concern for the user.

Eunice Noell: The Athena Chair

SM: How would you identify your approach to design process? What do you look to accomplish at the beginning of a project?

EN: I try to address the needs of the client and also the needs of the building occupant. I can remember, early on, doing work with Kaiser Permanente and thinking, "Oh, we've got doctors, nurses, housekeeping, and administration, but we have no one representing the patient." So I would always try to put myself in that role just so that everyone who was going to be served by that building was represented.

SM: So you would role play?

EN: Yes. In fact, one time I was designing a beauty salon and actually went through the whole beautification treatment. I told them to give me their standard "Do" and it was very interesting. You get to the shampoo bowl, they tip your head back and all of a sudden you're looking up through this egg crate ceiling. If you're standing it looks just fine, but as they tip you back you're looking at the most God awful mess of ducts and cobwebs. So by putting myself, as I say, "Running myself through the car wash", I really got to experience what someone else typically experiences at a salon. You have to put yourself through that as much as you can. If someone isn't there to represent all of the uses, then I will try to put myself in their position.

SM: That's interesting. Are there any theories or principles that you consciously apply in your work?

EN: The main things that I look for are the human qualities and the spiritual qualities, and also making the building shelter, but not a barrier. I see

the interconnectedness of many things and if we focus on the built environment as being the goal in itself rather than the built environment supporting human activity and human health and human needs, then I think we've focused on the wrong thing. Let's take, for example, the buildings that were constructed in the 80's where there was so much surface decoration with less emphasis on how this building needs to serve the users. I think that was kind of a sad time. Being an environmentalist, too, I see this work and think, "What meaning does this have in the long run?" It's like the race to see who can have the most glitzy materials or whatever. Many of the buildings from the 80's left me feeling hollow.

SM: Speaking of the environment, how do you look to practice so that you include your environmental philosophy in your design process?

EN: There are two different aspects for me. The first would be energy and the second would be materials. Relative to energy, I try to work with architects to get as much natural lighting into the design as possible because I think that's one of the interconnectedness aspects that is so important. We, as human beings, have evolved under this natural daylight cycle. The more we can bring that cycle within our buildings, the less energy we are going to have to use for electric lights. Also, the building occupant will be healthier. In fact, under environmental illnesses I deem air quality to be one, light deprivation to be second, and then what I call acoustical or sound overload as the third. All of these impact our health. I am specifying more and more natural materials: cork floors, linoleum, and wallpaper using cotton fabrics and natural materials. It's

actually worked out better because the fire marshal here in Portland (Oregon) would much rather have natural materials used than the synthetics because of fewer toxic fumes in a fire. Right now, I am specializing in designs for the elderly and on one high rise retirement center, before we ever started to design the building, I worked with the fire marshal to employ natural materials on the walls and made certain that all foam rubber was encapsulated in a fire blocker. As a result, I would not have to use any wire glass in the building and we could have open hallways as long as we had the doors on automatic closers. So to get rid of the wired glass was a major accomplishment when I'm trying to make a space look residential. The fire marshal supported this position. What I try to do is use woods that are indigenous to our area and plentiful. I don't do what I call "minimalist type design." I try to make certain that the people are comfortable and that I don't do a contrived environment. I try to practice what I call "timeless design" so that the minute something is out of vogue you don't go in there tearing everything out and replacing it with some "what's happening now" type motif.

SM: What does that vocabulary begin to look like?

EN: It goes back to what I would call Transitional Design. Not traditional so much, and given the Portland area is a little bit on the conservative side. That is what would be right for this region. Let's say we were talking about Arizona. It's a place that would have a totally different look.

SM: I am curious about the design criteria you employee for the elderly. Please explain.

EN: As we age, we become more dependent on our environment due to frailty and reduced mobility. The environment should act as a "nonstop support system," rather than one more obstacle to overcome. Going back to the issue of lighting, the light level that we need to synchronize our circadian rhythm (day/night cycle, sleep/wake cycle) is about ten times greater (200 to 400 footcandles) than the ambient light levels needed for older adult's general vision (20 to 30 footcandles). Sleep disorders affect 50% of the older population, primarily due to light deprivation. In order to get this light level up so that people can have this exposure and, set their body clock essentially, I try to use indirect natural light. A light shelf will take the natural light and bounce it off the ceiling, then distribute it back into the room. By doing that, it makes the light level of the whole room higher rather than just having the light coming in the windows streaming down, hitting the floor right in front by the window, producing glare which is a problem for the elderly. What we want to do is have a higher ambient light level. Sometimes high clerestory windows where the light bounces off the ceiling and the upper part of the wall into the space will work, but I try to not have any strong daylight patterns hitting the floors because when you do that, if you have a mullion or some visual division, it will create a light and dark spot on the floor that the elderly may misinterpret as a step just because of the change in value. Right now, I have a research proposal with two of the doctors at the medical school to Mitsubishi on light studies for the elderly that would address everything from light shelves to the more high tech solutions like the Himawari which is a light collecting device that distributes sunlight through fiber optic cables. Another concern is the need for ultraviolet. Window glass often blocks ultraviolet light. What I am trying to do is get some ultraviolet in the space because ultraviolet on the skin synthesizes vitamin D_3 and we need that to absorb calcium. There is a new window glass that PPG has that transmits 89% of the ultraviolet. They have donated some of their glass for our use on one of the buildings so that we can see how much effect it is going to have in raising the vitamin D_3 component of the elderly residents. We already have the light shelves going in on the skilled nursing floor. We have both assisted living, independent living, and skilled nursing here all in the same building. Assisted living is really the growth industry right now in senior housing.

SM: What was the time frame and the situational context in your life when you really became concerned about environmental issues?

EN: I've always said that I was more Indian in my heart than I was in my blood. I am one sixteenth Santee Sioux, so I've always felt this connectedness with nature. Growing up, I used to ride horseback and swim in the river on weekends. I had a very high quality of nature experiences when I was a teenager. I had that richness in the very beginning. When I went to school, there weren't many synthetic materials. Then vinyl wall covering started to come into use along with more and more synthetics. We were thinking it was the greatest, but when you're touching, feeling, and smelling the material you're thinking, "This isn't really that great." Until I started reading about the impacts of environmental illnesses, I don't think I started focusing on it nearly as strongly (from a practice standpoint), but I used to recycle when it wasn't popular. I would have to drive clear across town. I've come from the kind of feeling that I didn't want what I was doing, either personally or professionally, to leave a legacy of damage on the earth.

SM: In your experience, what was the biggest difference between designing in school and being faced with the real world.?

EN: I just felt that the real world had a lot more opportunity. My schooling was really quite difficult. We had a head professor that should have retired about ten years before. I always questioned whether she gave me such a bad time because she figured I had to be tougher to survive and so she was going to be the drill sergeant or if that was truly the way she felt. But she passed away before I got to ask her that question. She certainly made me stronger and built my perseverance. I had to develop a harder "skin," but I always tried to keep a warm receptive inner core so that I could treat other people well and serve them well. I genuinely like people and I think that's why I want to do my very best. I take it very personally if something doesn't meet someone's needs. I try very hard to serve everyone that is going to be utilizing the space.

SM: When you meet with a client for the first time, what are your goals?

EN: I first try to listen to them as to what they are saying. I also try to listen to what they aren't saying. Often, I phrase some of my questions almost indirectly to get to the information I need, and many times I'm not meeting just with one single person.

It's a matter of drawing many different things out from all of these people. Sometimes within a committee you have diverse opinions so you have to be somewhat of a psychologist as well as a designer in order to get the information to go forward. From the first meeting, I try to glean as much from what the possibilities are, what the restrictions might be, and the needs that have to be addressed so that I can mentally start processing all of this information.

SM: How much does visualization or imagination play out in your designs?

EN: I would say it's played a large part. Since I do interior work there is either a new building that is about to be designed or an existing space to make better or different than it is currently. I try to familiarize myself with what the structure is planned to do and all the requirements. Then I can mentally process that for sometimes two to four days before I actually sit down and work on it. Many times, I study project information in the evening then try not to come to any kind of conclusion. Then come morning, which is my best time, the answer just comes to me. So that is kind of the process that I use. If I know the dimensions of a space, I can feel what it is like to be in that space. Then in my mind I can play all these different scenarios about the lighting, the acoustics, and so on. Then it's a matter of using graphic illustration to convey what I have in my mind to the client so that they can understand my intent. I use perspective drawings to illustrate volumes and light so that people can place themselves in the space.

SM: What is your principle design medium?

EN: Generally, plans and elevations, perspectives and assembling of materials and colors.

SM: Do you typically work with pen on paper or use CADD?

EN: I have people who do CADD drafting for me, but I don't use it as a design tool. If I would take time to learn it, I'm certain that I would use it as a creative tool, but right now I haven't taken the time to do that. Most of the time it's just pencil and paper.

SM: Do you build models?

EN: Only when I'm trying to model day lighting. For the most part, the finesse that I try to get I can't do in a model because the textures are always out of scale.

SM: How do you know when a design is successful?

EN: I guess we never really know until it's built, then we find out from the users that we really have been able to meet their needs. I'm probably my own worst critic because there are times when the client is totally pleased and going on about it, but I'm still privately saying, "Oh, this thing happened and I didn't foresee it or this could have been better than what it is." I do my own post occupancy evaluation by talking with the people and then making my own opinions. I try to go on and not repeat a mistake or what I would deem a missed opportunity.

SM: When you look at a new space for the first time, what's at issue in your mind? What kinds of things do you look for?

EN: Typically, I study the scale: how does the space feel? What is the orientation? What is adjacent? What is the sequence of experience? Do we have direct light coming in or not? I think that so many times the space itself it going to have a certain pull, a kind of unique direction.

SM: Is there any difference in your approach to, on the one hand, a space that exists versus a new space?

EN: Oh, yes. If the new space is about to be created, then I feel like we need to go for everything that we can. When I've got an existing space, certain limitations are set up in advance. Part of the job is knowing what your limitations are: trying to be as creative as you can in and amongst those. In a way, it's a different kind of challenge and relative to my clients, they just assume a new space is going to be great. In an old space, they generally know how bad it is, so when you do a renovation and it comes out looking really good, you're actually more of a hero because they knew what it was like before. There are times when I'm working with an architectural team that some of my concerns aren't heard or don't get implemented. There are times that I'm brought back in afterwards to make it right whether the lighting isn't adequate or whatever. That's a difficult kind of problem for me because I'm patching up my own work. It wasn't that I didn't try, it was just a result of the process. Those are the jobs that are hardest on me.

SM: When we talk about working on a team, do you feel that you get sufficient opportunity to participate in the design process of a new building?

EN: It just depends on who the architect is and how they see their role. There are some architects that ask me to participate from the beginning, the very first meeting with the client. Others try to bring you in to "color it up at the end." To me, to get the best project possible, I think of the architect as more of a conductor in an orchestra in which they also play an instrument. When the conductor comes in, everyone is there at the same time, everyone is hearing the same thing, and they all work in concert. Then, at times, each section of "instruments" gets to do a solo, but then they also go back and play together. To get the best project in this complex world where you have to know so much about so many things, I think it is important for the architect to know when to bring in consultants and to trust them to do segments of the work. Only when these consultants are hearing everything can they really give meaningful input to the total project.

SM: Do you typically generate more than one scheme?

EN: Yes. In fact, that's what I like to do. Sometimes I'll generate three to four schemes. I admit I'll have my favorite, but I try not to let anyone know what that is. I try to give them enough variety so that the other ones I do end up helping to sell the one I like. I don't try to use them against each other. If you give them three or four so they know that they have a choice then it stimulates them to play out the different schemes in their mind and then make a selection. When people have a choice they are much more committed to what they have selected.

SM: How do you prepare for a presentation?

EN: I mainly do a couple of perspective drawings showing the relative scale of the space to people and furnishings. Then it's getting the variety of materials, color choices, and talking to them about how these can be organized within the space. Again, people so many times tend not to read plans well. That is why it is so important to include the materials rendered on the perspective drawing and have it in

color illustrating the textures enough so that they get a feeling of the space. They can understand the perspective and real materials. I try to get as much information convened through that as possible. When I do a materials board, I will have everything organized just as though it were the floor or the wall, the trim, just as you would see it in actual physical arrangement in proportion to how much of it you're going to see within the space. I don't want anything to be out of proportion even on the presentation board.

SM: In your mind, what do you think makes an excellent designer?

EN: One who listens well and also has a creative imagination. I think you have to let your mind soar, let your heart soar. I call it "free float." That's where the best ideas come: people who are trying to genuinely solve the problem and not a photo shoot for a magazine. Good design projects are hard to photograph because you can't really get the essence of how they feel and function from the pictures alone.

SM: I would agree very strongly that you don't get a feel for what physical reality is from photographs.

EN: I jokingly say that we, as designers, are visually addicted. So then in having that addiction we deny our other senses. You know, the senses of touch, hearing, and smell. Sometimes the photograph will begin to indicate that if you know what you're looking at.

SM: I think that denial stems from a fear of the overwhelming complexity of trying to deal with all the senses.

EN: I always say it's better to deal with it on paper than to try to fix it after it's built.

SM: Do you run into dead ends when you're working, and what do you try to do to get out?

EN: Sure I do. I think anyone who is honest does. I just leave it alone for a while. I generally have enough going on at one time that I just switch my energies to some other project. When I get to what I would call the subconscious that's when things start working out. I realize that maybe, if you have to push on something too hard, it's not right. When I'm reaching a dead end, I'm thinking through what I'm trying to force that isn't natural. Am I the problem? Am I creating my own problems or is there something in conflict here? Sometimes I need to go back to the client and tell them that you can't have it both ways. Just getting some mental distance from it helps, then I can go back and start picking it up again.

SM: How do you respond to the duality of architecture, the practical versus the art?

EN: I am very much aware of both, but I would like to offer this idea for your consideration as well: if we include what I call the health of the building occupant, then we may have three major criteria that effects design. This seems clear to me from the reading that I've been doing lately on the health effects of the built environment. With the crisis that we have relative to health care in our country in terms of cost and need, it seems to me that we need to place a higher emphasis on design as it relates to the welfare of the building occupant. It doesn't get addressed because we have focused our technology on buildings in a narrow way. When you compare the way we live now to how we lived

before the industrial revolution, we are inside buildings so much of the time that the building becomes a life support system. Poor life support (unhealthy buildings) cause higher health care costs long term. We need to focus on balancing health, practicality, and art. To me, to be a true art form, a building really should enhance human health because that is what it should do. If the need for a healthy interior environment is denied, then I feel that those people should go practice sculpture.

SM: Indeed. What kind of advice would you give to a student?

EN: I would say strive to be as well rounded as possible. Understand what is happening; especially socioeconomics relative to the people that you are serving. In this country, understanding the different cultural and ethnic groups is also going to be very important as we become more mixed. Learn different materials and how they're joined. To me, joinery of the different materials is germane to quality design. Avoid asking the impossible by drawing something then hoping somebody can figure out how to build it. Details are some of the fun of a project.

SM: How do you see your future?

EN: Maybe we need to talk a little bit about my background in order to understand my intent for the future. My practice for the last 20 years has been a full range of everything from attorney's offices, daycare centers, resorts, restaurants, you name it. I started looking ahead at what facilities were being provided for the elderly, and realized that what we need to do is address those facilities with the same degree of creativity, care, and love that we apply to

a new resort or restaurant. I figured I had my fun and it was time to let younger designers go in and do the more "glamorous" projects. I would start tackling the tough and maybe less attractive problems. So I have devoted myself now to design just for the elderly. I'm designing furniture and accessories that allow people greater independence and safety as well as designing spaces for them to use. I'm actually designing a demonstration project of infill housing here in Portland which is typical row house style. Row houses aren't typically accessible to the elderly and handicapped because all of the living spaces are on the second floor. I am trying to show how you can take the same land space, provide living space on the first floor, and utilize daylighting design as well as natural materials. This kind of work remains exciting for me. I always said that I didn't want to be the grand old dame of interior design in Portland, Oregon. I always want to have a challenge and I want to continue learning and developing myself. Older adults need assistance, but they also deserve dignity and continuity within their neighborhoods. I don't really see retirement centers as the solution. I see aging in place or staying in your own neighborhood as the solution. That's where I find my two passions, one for the environment and serving the elderly as having similar problems and similar solutions. Elderly people can't drive as much or many times are visually impaired, so they rely more on public transportation; having their homes close to convenience centers where they can walk to meet their needs is an advantage, enhances their independence. To me, by focusing on the elderly, I can also fulfill my commitment to the environment.

BART PRINCE

Bart Prince Architect, Albuquerque, New Mexico

Bart Prince, as you will see, has always had building in his blood. Born June 24, 1947, in Albuquerque, New Mexico, he grew up fascinated with building. Not just the artistic or heroic side of design drew him in, but an abiding interest in how buildings are put together. He knows the basics, and this knowledge is applied without fail in all his work. His mature work, at right, has a distinctive quality that brings clients directly to his door with one request: build for me a Bart Prince design. The genesis for each solution is solely in the province of Mr. Prince's fertile imagination, the client's needs, and the site.

When I asked him about how he sits down to design, he drew an analogy to having a child, saying that his associates could tell when "it was coming." The designs grow in his mind. Then, when complete, he sits down at the drawing table and lays out the solution. This skill is clearly indicative of the lifetime he has devoted to evolving his mastery of the design process. He was afforded a unique opportunity while still in high school: working for a local home builder. While this might seem mundane, consider the learning opportunity for a young mind. Bart began to sow the seeds of his unique approach to design while still in his teens. Even then, the designs hint at future possibilities, "yet the differences remain subtle ones, and the results are still distant from his mature work." (Mead 1991) He knew that he would become an architect, and after graduating from high school, studied architecture in the five year program at

Arizona State University, Tempe. While in school, fate intervened when Bruce Goff came to lecture. Goff gave his lecture and toured the school, seeming at every turn to find a certain student's work riveted his attention. The student was Bart Prince. That day, in the fall of 1968, Bart met his mentor and future friend. (Mead 1991) Bart received his degree in 1970 after already having worked in Bruce

Goff's office during the summer of 1969. He continued working with Goff intermittently from 1969 onward. In 1972, he returned to Albuquerque to stay. He worked for a local architect, gained some local notoriety for a spec office building of his design, and started his own practice in 1973. He passed his licensing exam in 1974 and has been crafting unique solutions for his clients ever since.

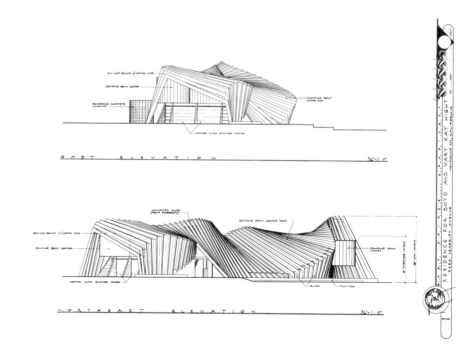

Bart Prince: Northeast Elevation of the Hight Residence, Mendocino, California

SM: Do you take a particular approach to design when you are given a building project?

BP: My process is the same from project to project. I always start out with an initial meeting with the clients where we are just talking in general kinds of terms and take a look at the site. Then I always ask them after this meeting, when they've gone back and they've got some time to themselves, to make a list of things that they like and don't like. It can be in no particular order. Sometimes it's talking about materials, sometimes just strictly functional things and at that point that's all we talk about: strictly things that come into their minds. Sometimes it's a wish list. Things they don't think they could ever even afford, but if they had their choice they would include. That's how I start out. I was telling them up in Aspen at this exhibit that's up there now. We had a thing last night, or the night before, in conjunction with the International Design Conference. They were asking me about process and about philosophy, space, and materials. I said I have never talked about any of those things with a client. I never had a client that was interested in discussing things like that and it isn't necessary really for the most part. They don't care about any of that. They know that you have ideas and that you are trying to achieve something, but that's not really something to talk about. That's something you do. They really are concerned, or they wouldn't have hired me in the first place. My clients are interested in something that is beyond just what they ordinarily see. But they still are concerned about their functional requirements, their budget, and some of

them do have feelings about materials while others don't. Some people absolutely just have got no thought at all about what it should be, and so its wide open.

SM: Do you find that after 20 some years of practice, when you reach back and reflect, say to a time when you were much younger, that your approach to design today is any different?

BP: I don't really think it is. I just think I'm probably more conscious of the process. Of course you learn; you're always learning. It's not that there hasn't been additional knowledge and improvement maybe on how you do things. But in terms of the process, it's still exactly the same process I have always used. Most of my design process takes place in my head. There is not that much that is paper oriented at that very early stage. I don't sketch, I don't build models and take them apart and stuff like that. I don't do anything like that. I'm interested in that list of things from the clients. With some clients, there is more than one very early easy going meeting where we're just talking which is giving me more of a feel about them. Then, eventually when I start working on something, I'm really thinking about it and I very thoroughly work a scheme out in my head before I ever start anything on paper.

SM: Do you find that it's always been easy for you to use your imagination and to use visualization when you design?

BP: I think so, I think that's something...I am able to do. I've found out really early I was able to do that when I was very young. I could imagine something accurately. A lot of times people think of something that sounds like it would be really

exciting in their mind, and then when they start to put it on paper, the more they draw the worse it gets and the further away from that idea it gets. But I learned before I even knew what it was that I could imagine something. I could think it out. I could have it three dimensionally in my head and then when I transferred it to paper or to some other means to show to somebody else, I wasn't going to loose the idea in the process.

SM: So there is a certain inherent mental accuracy then. That's really amazing. I don't want to talk about me too much here but one of the things I've always struggled with is having a vivid imagination and difficulty getting the scale right. To hear you talk about that kind of control to me is fascinating. Do you feel your skill is intuitive?

BP: I always remember one incident. I was in the second grade and a teacher held up a book in front of the class and she said, "What's the size of this book?" I said, "7 1/2" x 10"," and that's exactly what it was. She held up something else and I said whatever it was. Anyway, object after object, they were just flat, two dimensional things, and I always remembered it because she made such a big thing out of it, then she even sent a note home later with my report card about it. That went on to other things. For instance, I learned early on that I could draw to scale, and so in early drawings like in my schematic or preliminary drawings, I decide what scale it's going to be. Once I start I can keep on at that scale. I'm talking free hand... I don't know whether it is an inherent quality. It's nothing I learned in any conscious sense, I mean no one ever sat me down and taught me to do it. I'm not saying that I might not have learned it, but I don't know how you would explain what I was telling you about in the second grade.

SM: Is there any particular kind of play you engaged in as a child, like Wright having played with Froebel Blocks, claiming that was the foundation for his mastery of three dimensional space. Is there anything like that in your background?

BP: Yes, and it often involved things that I made myself. I did play with wood blocks and things like Tinker Toys and Lincoln Logs and Erector Sets. Things that were manufactured...I played with them a lot. It wasn't just a toy that I played with a little bit and set aside. I began making my own fairly early using cardboard and sticks and the like...that was very early. I would construct things and work with various kinds of materials. In some cases they were toys, in some cases they were just things that I made up myself.

SM: So, you've always been a builder?

BP: Yes. Really very early. My parents told me (they didn't tell me until later) they worried because there was nobody in the family doing this: we had no relatives even as far back as you could go who were involved in architecture or construction. I would come straight home from school, usually with a stack of drawings that I had done in study hall and home room, then go immediately to the garage and start working on something instead of going out to play or do something else. This is what I really wanted to do.

SM: You loved it even as a child.

BP: I couldn't wait. Torture to me would be going out to play baseball or something. If you really wanted me to be happy, leave me alone. The other thing that I did from very early on was watch buildings being built; I mean really study. I could sit for three hours, until the sun went down, and watch people working on buildings. So there is some kind of innate fascination. I don't know why. Today I don't know where that came from, but when I watch the children of the guys that work with me, you see how early on they begin to exhibit very specific traits that couldn't possibly be learned. There is something to be said for this, these qualities that are really innate.

SM: That's very interesting. So where do you find inspiration when you design?

BP: I guess everything that you come in contact with. Music has always been inspirational. I read and I try to keep up with things that are going on generally, so I'm just talking now about things that are generally "in the air". Things that are going on are inspiring. When I'm talking about a specific project, then it has more to do with things that might come out of the site, and things that come to mind regarding a client. They are more that kind of thing... I've got two projects right now, for instance, that both started at about the same time. Two completely different clients and completely different sites. Both of these designs came out unlike anything I'd ever done. I don't know where these designs were lurking either. But I never had clients like these or sites like these, so when you put that combination together and when your design approach is one that is very responsive to the client and to the site; as opposed to bringing with you a whole bunch of preconceptions and sort of having a kit of

things that you are going to pull parts out of, which I don't have, then you end up getting this. I'm as surprised as they are. I never had that input before.

SM: That follows. I've had people argue both systems. The unique approach which I, like you, personally prefer and the kit of parts that says, "Well if you're going to have a signature, then you have to have a kit".

BP: You know who wrote something by their handwriting, but what they say with it will be different every single time they sit down to write. So in effect, the thing that differentiates your own work or your personality or how you work is the "handwriting", but what you actually do with it is different each time and yet have it still be recognized. We easily recognize the work of Frank Lloyd Wright because we are so used to seeing it. We know his work. But when he was doing it, the people at the time thought each building looked so much different than the others. Now its hard for us to see how they could have thought that, but at the time they did.

SM: Are there any rituals you go through when you sit down to design? Does it hit you in the middle of the night or do you come in at 7:30 in the morning and have the sun coming up, a vase of flowers next to you and Mozart playing or something like that?

BP: No, there's nothing like that. It's one of those things where its almost like giving birth. I can feel it getting closer and closer. I can tell that its going to be time and I know the guys that work here sometimes joke about being able to tell when its getting closer because eventually I just come in, sit

down, roll out a piece of paper, and start working. It might be on a weekend or it might be in the middle of a busy day. But when it's ready, it's ready, and it doesn't matter what's going on around me. I don't have to have quiet, I don't have to have music, I could work in the middle of a shopping mall if I had a table. I don't need any tools or anything either.

SM: Do you prepare multiple schemes or does the thing just seem to evolve, you lay it out, and take it to the client?

BP: No, I don't prepare multiple schemes. I wait until I have come up with what I consider to be what ought to be done. I'm very aware there is never any one solution because even when I'm going through that process I can see several directions I can go, I could develop one very thoroughly and another one very thoroughly and have them be very different from each other, but that just confuses a client. I have found that the best thing to do is to follow the thing that I see is the best solution, given all the things we're talking about, and that's the one I show them.

SM: Do you feel that there are any things that are essential to quality design?

BP: Well, for my way of thinking, the kinds of things that interest me most, I think, have a sense of imagination and mystery about them that I always consider essential to something that's really going to hold up. When you say quality design, you can always differentiate. I was looking at a house in Aspen the other night where they were giving a dinner party for me. It wasn't my cup of tea at all, but it was really well done, given what it was. These people were acting almost embarrassed to have me

come out there. But it's a three million dollar place. I forget who did it, but somebody whose name you would probably recognize. It looks like a bunch of old farm buildings on the outside, kind of thrown together. But you know, it was very carefully detailed and all that. Then, when you went inside, it was just about what you expected, except the spaces are quite large. Everything was very carefully and beautifully done. So in a sense, I would say there is a quality to that. You could certainly tell there was an architect, or somebody with an idea behind it. It wasn't particularly imaginative: I guess you eventually get into these subjective questions. I can appreciate something like that just because I know the work that was involved. Einstein said our age is characterized by "perfection of means, but confusion of aims," and here was a place that was just beautifully done, but you wondered *why* they did it.

SM: To kind of piggyback along a little bit along that idea, I am reading a book now called *The Interior Dimension* and the second chapter argues that you can essentially separate the veneer or the overlay of form from function. When I first read that I thought, this is the silliest thing I ever heard and then when I thought about it some more and studied some of the illustrations and the points that they were making, I thought, "Well, OK, I can accept this," and then this morning I was reflecting on it and I thought, you can't separate the person and the intent from the act of connecting form to final use. It seems you could buy that to a certain extent, but ultimately the form is connected to the function at least in some measure.

BP: I can see where a book like that would come about because when I talk at some of these schools and see some of the students, they are really being taught that there is just no connection at all. Structure is just sort of an irritating thing that somebody else has to deal with. They go in, and its all smoke and mirrors in a sense. Whatever you think of to put up. If you can't afford stone, somebody can paint it just as well as the real thing. Actually, I've seen examples where that is pretty well true of some of the things they can do now. It's all just like Disneyland in a sense. Its just facade. It reminds me of those old western towns where you see the guy riding down the street and if you looked on the other side, props hold up the facades. There's nothing behind it. It seems a lot of what you see in interiors is really just that. Its interesting because sometimes you can go into a place where you see something that's really quite beautifully done and has nothing to do with the building that its in, yet its an interesting space in itself. It just somehow doesn't seem real. It doesn't have the quality that you feel when you go into something like a Wright building or a building that's got that wholeness to it.

SM: Talking about separation and fragmentation, there's a book by Robert Gutman called *Architectural Practice, A Critical View.* Basically he argues that in the last 50 years, the business of building has been fragmented from engineering/architecture into about nine separate things.

BP: One of the things that has brought this about is some of these very huge buildings that we build and then buildings like shopping malls where one week it can be a Haagen Dazs and the next week its a McDonalds. The next week its some kind of other restaurant or whatever. Its interior stuff, and it really is just changing the inside of a huge building; tenant improvements they call it. You take a non-specialized space and turn it into something.

SM: Who would you cite as design influences? When you were younger and as you practiced, who were the people that really knocked you out?

BP: Well, right away, at a very early age, Frank Lloyd Wright. I don't know, I must have been 7 or 8 and saw some things that were just fantastic. For one thing, it was imaginative, they seemed to be buildings that were beautiful and unusual, yet they were done by an American architect (which I thought was great). It wasn't everything coming from Europe. That was something that really got me early on. Then, there are a lot of them. Antonio Gaudi and Gustav Eiffel. Engineers have always interested me. Really creative engineers. People building structures that are strictly functional are some of the most beautiful things I think we've built. These things that are involved in space travel and satellites and things like that are really incredible constructions. Most people would say they are strictly functional in terms of their aesthetics.

SM: Yes, but they have an inherent beauty about them too.

BP: I think that's part of what brings it about. The things that are there are there just because they're necessary. Its not sort of a labored thing, like when you talk about interiors where you can tell they've just kind of layered and layered and layered. All thin stuff just on top of one another.

SM: When we chatted previously, you mentioned working with Bruce Goff. Would you also cite him as an influence as well?

BP: Yes, if I'd went on with that there would be Bruce Goff, Lloyd Wright, Frank Lloyd Wright's oldest son was quite a fine architect, but just kind of overlooked these days. Meeting Goff was very interesting because, one, here was somebody who knew Frank Lloyd Wright. He'd never worked with him, but they were friends. So one of the initial fascinating things there was just talking to somebody who knew a lot more about this person that I had been so interested in. Then, of course, I was very much interested to see that Goff was able to go his own way. He was very much taken with Wright's work, but it seemed like, for the most part up to that point, everybody I saw that was in any way affected by Wright just seemed to imitate him, either literally or very badly. There never did seem to be too many who could understand the principles he was talking about. Goff was an example of somebody that did that. Lautner was another who is a good friend of mine.

SM: Who is that?

BP: John Lautner, in Los Angeles. I would say he is the finest architect ever to come directly out Wright's studio. He is 81 years old. Paolo Soleri and Lautner are the only two real individuals who came out of there. Fay Jones, in a way, is much more literally attached to Frank Lloyd Wright. His work really didn't break away very much, although he does beautiful work in that vein. But of course,

Solari went one direction: he kind of got kicked out. Lautner worked with Wright for six years and yet, when he finally got out and started doing his own work, you'd never associate it with Frank Lloyd Wright except that it's very beautiful, unusual work. I was interested in the work of Mendelson in Germany and and, as I said, Gaudi, Corbusier, and Mies. There is something to learn from all these people if you really study the principles of the work.

SM: That's quite a spread of influences.

BP: There are people like Picasso, Einstein, Debussy, and Stravinsky that were also as important I would say, but they are not as literal: something that you can see in the same way you can looking to another architect. But in terms of the way they think, the sort of creative approach to the work, that's always what's interested me more than just the literal work itself. The creative mind, whether its creating music or literature or art, can apply from one field to another.

SM: Are you a musician?

BP: I play the piano.

SM: Were you trained, did you take lessons when you were young and all that?

BP: Yes, I convinced my mother to buy me a piano. I finally convinced them that I needed a piano. I don't know why that was either, but to me music and architecture always seemed to be directly related. Actually, I can remember early on feeling like it was just the same kind of thing. The same thing with just a different expression.

SM: Is there any methodology or particular approach that you use when you sit down with your clients to talk about what it is they want to do? I

know we kind of touched on that in the beginning of the conversation, but it seemed a fairly loose description. Are there specific things you try to accomplish or things that you always make sure you hit with them as you talk about a building project?

BP: Yes, initially I let them sort of lead the way a little bit and let them tell me whatever it is that they've got in their mind. Seems like on most first meetings there is always a concern on a clients' part that you are not going to listen, or that you're not going to understand. They've got a whole bunch of stuff kind of back logged that they want to get out so I let them. I let that just come on its own, and then I begin to ask them questions about different aspects of it. You know, sometimes it might just be functional questions. It might be something about the house they are in now (if we're doing a house), or something about buildings they like or don't like; just general kinds of things. So its a fairly comfortable, easy going process. Like I said, eventually I ask them to just take their time and sit down together, or even separately, and list things that they think in some way could influence the building. In other words, maybe something about the way they live, you know you get all kinds of things out of that. One person likes to get up at a certain hour and the other wants to sleep. All kinds of things come out that eventually have quite an affect on the design.

SM: How often do you meet with your clients when you are working on a design?

BP: Usually once before I start a design. Sometimes there might be a couple meetings but that's rare. Usually there is one meeting and it usually involves visiting the site together, looking at the site, and talking about things, plus some time just sitting either here or wherever they are. Its usually wherever we're going to be doing the project, discussing it, and then there are some phone conversations and things like that, and they get me this material I asked for. A lot of times I get the list of stuff before we even meet the first time. I'll tell them that that's what I'd like to see and then we augment it later, but normally there is not but one meeting before I show them a design. The amount of time between that meeting and the design varies. Sometimes it depends on the project, it can be just a few weeks or it can be two or three months. It depends on the other work load too.

SM: When you've got a design drawn up and you meet with your client to present the design, how do you handle that?

BP: Well, one is I insist that we do it in person. I don't send the drawing. I put a lot of time into it; its important enough to take the time, do it together. If it involves a couple, I always insist that we have to all be there together on the first showing. In other words, I don't want to show it to the husband and then have him explain it to the wife. I don't want to show it to just her. Sometimes it involves children too. Everybody needs to be there. I often will have a model but I never show that to them until the very end. A lot of times they don't know I've got it. I conceal the fact it even exists. My process for going through the project is pretty well the same. A lot of times I don't label the drawings at all because I don't want them getting ahead of me. It forces them to stay with me when I'm trying to explain the process. I always start with the plan, and I lead them through

the project from the inside: let them fully understand why its planned the way it is. I never show them elevations. Actually, I hardly even show them elevations ever, but at this stage I'm strictly talking plans. If it involves several levels, I might start by showing the site and how you're getting to it, and then show where it is sited, but just strictly from the point of view of location. The next drawing I show them begins with, (depends on the building), the entrance or coming into it. Then how things evolve so that when they eventually see what the building looks like, they understand why it came to be that way. Very rarely do I show them an elevation because an elevation doesn't mean too much with this kind of work. But often it will be a model or maybe a perspective sometimes. That's the very last thing they see, and if its quite an unusual looking thing, it's not as much a surprise by then because they've realized that it grew from this process. Actually, they kind of take delight in showing me, "Oh yeah that's where that is," this is where that is, that kind of thing. I have found that models work the best with most clients. Once I've been through this whole process, described it, shown them the drawings, and discussed how you go through it, at the very end of that process, I'll let them look at a model, then I go through it all again with the model and relate things in the model to the drawing so that they always realize there is an absolute connection: the building itself has grown from this process from the inside out. It wasn't just some kind of a shape or form that I was interested in building and then tried to figure out how to make a house of it. The other thing that's very important, I have found, is that every single thing that they mention in those early discussions, or that was in that list of things, is used in that drawing. Even if its just a silly little thing. It makes all the difference in the world to them. I just presented a project last week and I can still remember them grabbing each other and saying look here's your little magazine rack. Some little thing.

SM: It's like proof of concept.

BP: It really makes a difference because they realize you were listening. Even though it has maybe no effect on the design at all, (something like a magazine rack or a big screen TV), it really makes a difference to them to see that you listened.

SM: Do you find that you generally have a very high rate of success? You'll absorb the information, conceive the design, do the presentation and then have the client say, "let's do it", or do you find that you get feedback like, "lets change this, can we do this, can we do that?"

BP: I never had one that didn't succeed for that reason. I have had some where they had other problems, like their budget changed or they got divorced or something. I've never had one where we didn't go right on ahead as a result of that design. Of the ones that didn't get built, it never was a result of something that came out of that initial meeting. I'd have to go to a specific project, I can think of one where we got clear through working drawings and then it involved a divorce or something like a dramatic change in their finances, a bankruptcy.

SM: You obviously do a fair amount of houses. You also do additional work besides?

BP: I do whatever comes in. I have never gone after a job. So I never know what's going to come

in next. I've done some small office buildings and apartment buildings and additions to houses. Right now I have a $45,000 addition under construction here and a $6,000,000 house under construction in Aspen. Its quite a range of things scale wise. I haven't done work for the university or for the city because I suppose that its the kind of thing where you've to go out and try and get it. I don't know how you get work like that. Everything I've done has all been work that came as a result of somebody seeing other things I did and asking me to do things.

SM: Word of mouth basically.

BP: They see a magazine, they see a building, or somebody tells them. Its almost all out of state too. Next week, I've got to go to Hawaii to do the final inspection on one that's just finishing there and I'm starting one in Mendocino, California and one in Taos, New Mexico for some people that are from California, one in Sante Fe for some people that are from Chicago. I never know what's coming next. Some guy called me last week from New Jersey, all excited. That's how they start. I don't know if I'll ever hear from them again, but if it goes like the other ones, eventually I'll hear from him, we'll set a meeting to see a site, and take it from there.

SM: When you're designing are there any things that you do internally as you're working in imagination to test your process?

BP: When you say internally, what do you mean, are you talking about within myself?

SM: Yes, inside. Because you have the facility to develop solutions without the aid of sketching or models, I just wondered if you sort of mentally run down a particular path in such and such a way, then

do a mental walk through and say, "Yeah, I think this will work".

BP: It is sort of automatic because I know with each design I'm trying to accomplish a certain thing. Sometimes, you're designing two buildings at the same time with absolutely identical programs as far as size goes. It happens that the two I'm talking about now are both three bedrooms and open living areas. The programs are identical practically, but the clients are so different, and the sites are so different, that you would never imagine that the same architect did both of these things. What's different about them is thinking about the process of construction. I'm always thinking about that: The actual process of building. In other words, there is some site where I know I'm now going to be able to use certain materials. I might not be able to get in and out certain size equipment. Before I even started designing, it's like a batch of things that I go through in my mind. I don't see architecture as an "ivory tower" kind of process that is separated from reality, where once you come up with a perfect solution, then let it be somebody else's problem.

SM: Excuse me, I just had the uncontrollable desire to stand up and applaud your statement. I'll digress quickly. From 1984 to 1986, I worked on the Terminal One complex at O'Hare, (the Helmut Jahn Building). There is a well known news weekly published in Chicago called *The Reader*. They interviewed Jahn while this building was under construction. I was involved very much on the technical side and in the field quite a bit. As a matter of fact, I learned a tremendous amount about large

scale construction from that project. But the thing that struck me as particularly hilarious about the interview was the statement something to the affect, and I used to know the quote verbatim, but it was something like; you design the building, or the space, and let the engineers figure out the rest of it. I read that and mentally blew a gasket. I just couldn't understand how someone respected internationally as a great architect could say something like that.

BP: I have seen things that have been done that way. Some are better than others, and I know it can work, but just the idea of an architect thinking that way amazes me. We seem to live in an age where we have forgotten what this really is all about. In the days of building the cathedrals, you couldn't arbitrarily just separate yourself from the actual process. Often times, an idea you had would be tested and then it collapsed. There are many great cathedrals that were built more than once because they didn't make it the first time. But they learned from that, and they started again. That's where the flying buttress came; from when the wall started to angle out and eventually fall over.

BP: Now architects seem to have just lost all connection with that. Its sort of like anything we can think of, somebody will figure out how to do. Even if that was true, why not be the one that's thinking of how to do it and make it make sense? Be tied to some sense of reality, and also make it beautiful.

SM: Indeed. So if you had any advice to give to some young, bright eyed kid that wanted to be an architect, what would it be?

BP: Well, I would say, learn as much about architecture as you can, even just in terms of history.

Study the history of architecture but don't look at these things as objects, as just aesthetic statements, because that's not really what they are. If you understand them in the context of the time they were built, you might appreciate what the people had to go through in order to bring them about, and you'll have a whole different appreciation for what those buildings are. They're not just a whole series of styles since we named them.

SM: They weren't named then, were they?

BP: No they weren't. Now, we're in an age where we name them first and then do it. Deconstructivist and Post Modern and the like. It used to be that the names came about as a result of somebody looking at a body of work that they were trying to describe in some way. Somebody didn't set out to create a Gothic building. It eventually later began to be referred to that way. I think the most important thing for a student would be to try and understand that perspective of history of architecture so they can understand where they are, and understand their own time. Understand the age you are living in so you realize what it is that you're dealing with. Its a whole different set of things, but if you can connect that to the kinds of things that have been faced in the past, you're not going to be creating buildings that are imitations of things that went before us. Not pasting together pieces of facades of old buildings, but creating something that has to do with our time, our age, society and capabilities regarding materials and that involves understanding engineering: at least principles and materials. The other thing they can do is

watch buildings that are being built. Even if you're looking at a horrible building, or something that isn't what you would aspire to, you can learn about why you think it's that way by watching how its being made. Also, the thought about integrating all these other things; the structural systems, the mechanical and electrical systems, these are all things that now an architect leaves up to somebody else and hopes they are going to be as concerned about the building as he is.

SM: Is there anything that occurs to you that I seem to be missing, or need to add or emphasize?

BP: Seems like we touched on most things that would come to mind. I think this thing about exercising and utilizing your imagination and trusting yourself is important. I think we start teaching kids at a pretty early age not to trust themselves, not to trust their own perceptions and not to trust their own ideas. To me that's all wrong, we should be encouraging people to utilize their minds and imaginations and realize that as an architect, that's all we have to offer just our imaginations, our ability.

REFERENCES

Buchsbaum, Ralph and Mildred. 1957. *Basic Ecology.* Pacific Grove: The Boxwood Press.

Busch, Akiko. 1991. *The Art of the Architectural Model.* New York: Design Press.

Ching, Frank. 1979. *Form Space and Order.* New York: Van Nostrand Reinhold.

Cuff, Dana. 1991. *Architecture: The Story of Practice.* Cambridge: MIT Press.

Frantz, Douglas. 1991. *From the Ground Up.* New York: Henry Holt and Company.

Gutman, Robert. 1988. *Architectural Practice: A Critical View.* New York: Princeton Architectural Press.

Horowitz, Lois. 1984. *Knowing Where to Look: The Ultimate Guide to Research.* Cincinnati: Writer's Digest Books.

Hunt, Morton. 1982. *The Universe Within.* New York: Simon and Schuster.

Kaderlan, Norman. 1991. "Influencing without authority." *The American Institute of Architects' Memo.* November/December.

Lawson, Brian. 1990. *How Designers Think: The Design Process Demystified.* 2d ed. London: Butterworth Architecture.

Loken, Steve, Walter Spurling, and Carol Price. 1991. *G.R.E.B.E.: Guide to Resource-Efficient Building Elements.* Missoula: Center for Resourceful Building Technology.

Mead, Christopher. 1991. *Houses by Bart Prince: An American Architecture for the Continuous Present.* Albuquerque: University of New Mexico Press.

Pena, William, Steven Parshall, and Kevin Kelly. 1987. *Problem Seeking-An Architectural Programming Primer.* 3d ed. Washington: AIA Press.

Prince, Bart. 19 June 1992. Interview with author. Indianapolis, Indiana.

Rheingold, Howard. 1991. *Virtual Reality.* New York: Summit Books.

Shoshkes, Ellen. 1989. *Design Process: Case Studies in Project Development.* New York: Whitney Library of Design.

Stockton, James. 1984. *Designer's Guide to Color.* San Francisco: Chronicle Books.

Thiis-Evenson, Thomas. 1987. *Archetypes in Architecture.* Oslo: Norwegian University Press.

Toffler, Alvin. 1990. *Powershift: Knowledge, Wealth, and Violence at the Edge of the 21st Century.* New York: Bantam Books.

INDEX